PEER MEDIATION

A Process for Primary Schools

PEER MEDIATION

A Process for Primary Schools

Jerry Tyrrell

Editor: Marian Liebmann

SOUVENIR PRESS

First published 2002 by
Souvenir Press Ltd,
43 Great Russell Street, London WC1B 3PD

ISBN 0 285 63601 4

Typeset by Dorchester Typesetting Group Ltd
Printed in Great Britain by Creative Print and
Design Group (Wales), Ebbw Vale

Dedication

This book is dedicated to the memory of my Mother,
Marjorie Florence Tyrrell née Winch, 1915–96;
teacher and supporter of the co-operative movement
and the peace movement.

Jerry Tyrrell
November 2001

Publisher's note

Throughout a succession of operations, programmes of treatment and persistent illness during 2001, Jerry continued to work on the book but sadly died in December before he could complete the task. It seems appropriate therefore to dedicate it also to Jerry himself. Its publication is a fitting tribute to him and a lasting memorial to all his engagements in the promotion of peace. With this in mind, Seamus Farrell, Jerry's colleague and dear friend during the period of the EMU Project's engagement in Peer Mediation work in schools, took on the task of offering the finishing touches to the book so as to bring it to publication. Souvenir Press would like to express their great appreciation for his help.

Contents

Acknowledgements

Many people have been involved in providing the experience and research on which this book is based. In particular I would like to thank my colleagues at the EMU Promoting School Project, Brendan Hartop and Seamus Farrell, who embarked on this venture with me until they moved to the School of Education at the University of Ulster in 1999. This book could not have been written without their inspiration and encouragement. Chapter 2 is based very much on Brendan's work as a skilled mentor for teachers in developing and trialling peer mediation. Chapter 8 is based on a case study, one of several significant pieces of research by Seamus Farrell, whose qualities of wisdom and even-handedness are hallmarks of all his dealings with people. My thanks to them also for reading and commenting on my efforts, to my colleague Lucia McGeady whose insights into action-research in particular have been very informative and to Linda Rosenberg, whose comments on Chapter 8 were especially helpful.

This being the first book I have written, I am indebted to Marian Liebmann for convincing me that I could do it. I am grateful to Kjell Andberg and Mark Bitel (Norway) for allowing me to use and adapt their diagrams, to Mark for permission to use his adaptation of Weaver's Diagram and to Alan Wong at Brownlow Integrated College for his cartoons. I take this opportunity to thank Allen Kennedy who, long before this book, has been contributing his photography skills to the Project. E-mail provided me with access to people who were most generous with their thinking, manuscripts and research; I am especially grateful in this regard to Professor Karen Bickmore and to Tricia Jones.

Against the backdrop of their personal journeys of courage and commitment, I have been greatly inspired by the frank and honest opinions of the Northern Ireland politicians whom I interviewed. I have drawn heavily on the deliberations of the 'Future of Peer Mediation' panel at the Mediation UK Conference in Sheffield 1998 and on their responses to my subsequent questionnaire; my thanks to these and to the range of respondents to other question-naires that I sent out.

Particular thanks must go to Kathy Laverty and to her Primary 7 class at Oakgrove Integrated Primary School. Kathy is representative of a host of creative and dedicated teachers who are part of the story of peer mediation in Northern Ireland, all of whom deserve my acknowledge-ment. By the same token the children of her class represent those many children who, through demonstrating capacities and potentials far exceeding our adult assumptions, con-tinue to astound and confound us.

The Northern Ireland Department of Education, core-funders of the EMU Promoting School Project, together with Barrow Cadbury Trust, made it possible for me to spend the time writing this book. My thanks to these and to the Board of the Positive Ethos Trust which has responsibili-ty for the Project. Its Chairperson, Anne Murray, Principal of Oakgrove Integrated Primary School, has played a central role in the on-going development of peer mediation in Northern Ireland. She has been most ably supported by other Board Members, Jim O'Neill, Edwin Kavanagh, Hilary Sidwell, Norman Richardson and Seamus Farrell.

Let me thank, last but emphatically not least, my wife Jo and children Jack and Sophie (does this mean you are an author, Daddy?), for their long-suffering encouragement and for bearing the stresses and strains when the book felt more like an albatross than an eagle. In particular I must acknowledge their accepting my being closeted in a room every morning during our family holiday in August 2000. Which leads me to grateful acknowledgement of our friends Catherine and Sean Greene, who additionally provided me with the seclusion of their beautiful Donegal home in September of that year.   J.T.

Introduction

This book has been written with a degree of passion. That passion is inspired on the one hand by observing the creativity, patience, commitment and integrity that children demonstrate in resolving conflicts through peer mediation. It is also inspired by sadness that schools, as institutions, are generally not sufficiently child-centred to allow, let alone encourage, such endeavours as part of a whole-school approach. This is often despite the best efforts of principals, teachers and ancillary staff, and of the children themselves.

When I set out to write this book I sought to hide my passion for the subject. But as I wrote I realised that the evidence could speak for itself, with or without any 'passionate' input from me. So I stopped worrying about that aspect and just wrote, reported and commented.

Peer mediation is a very matter-of-fact, logical, linear process, whereby children help each other to deal with their conflicts, playground disputes, and so on. It is a structured process, managed by two mediators, who are children. They introduce the process, establish ground rules, listen to the story from the perspective of each of the disputants and offer to each of them a summary of what he or she has said. They then provide opportunity for both sides to voice their feelings, help them identify the problems, brainstorm solutions, and, ideally, agree a solution. Mediation is a voluntary process, so if either of those in dispute decides that he or she doesn't want to go ahead at any stage, he or she doesn't have to. In that instance the conflict is usually dealt with according to the school's standard discipline policy.

That's peer mediation in a nutshell. End of story: a story

that would make fascinating reading in itself. However, getting peer mediation accepted in schools is another story, a story that is both inspiring and depressing. Inspiring because children are more than capable of resolving their own conflicts; but depressing because, as one teacher put it, 'We don't give children enough credit for what they can do, we really don't.' Peer mediation works only if schools are prepared to undergo major changes.

If you ask a child who has experienced peer mediation whether she would prefer her conflict to be dealt with by an adult or by peer mediation – and this is a question I have posed many times – almost invariably she will reply, 'Peer mediation'. And if you ask why, she may say something like, 'Children understand children', 'Adults are too busy', or 'Children take the time to listen'.

There is currently a great deal of talk about citizenship, in the context of changes in the curriculum, and of preparing children to be citizens tomorrow. But there's little point in extolling the virtues of citizenship in the future, if the reality for our children is that they have little impact on the hierarchical, undemocratic institutions that are schools today.

This book is not trying to sell peer mediation as 'the answer'. It is more about raising questions than providing answers. My seven years' experience of developing peer mediation in primary schools in Northern Ireland, and comparative research with programmes in other parts of the world, raises a number of questions. These questions concern the values of education, as practised by schools.

The current obsession, in the UK at least, with league tables of academic results as the main, if not sole, measure of educational achievement, encourages competition between schools. On the other hand there is research, evidenced in Chapter 5, that this obsession has led to a situation in which children see the relevance of education only as a means of passing exams. At the same time industry, and society generally, require individuals who can work well as members of a team, who can think creatively and solve problems co-operatively. This demands, surely, a skills-based approach to education rather than the current subject-based approach.

Thought needs to be given to the kind of environment needed for the skills of teamwork, problem-solving and creative thinking to flourish. The concept of the *democratic classroom* is one that might provide the starting-point for such an environment. In essence, this is about the teacher and the class meeting together and deciding on ground-rules, addressing problems, agreeing on solutions and also devising sanctions if agreements aren't kept. A microcosm of a society, in fact.

As this book demonstrates, the process of peer mediation training transforms relationships within the class. The training takes place in a workshop context, with children and adults sitting together in a circle. On more than one occasion that I have witnessed, when the children return to their normal classroom environment, they have asked the teacher if they could continue to use the workshop ground-rules, such as 'No putdowns'. Already at an early stage, teachers sense the contradiction between the conventional didactic teaching style of the classroom and the interactive methodologies of the workshop approach, and are struck by how much more effective a learning and teaching environment the latter can be.

In trying to establish peer mediation in schools, the focus of a substantial part of this book, I have come to the resounding conclusion that, if schools are to create a culture which can *sustain* peer mediation as part of a whole-school approach, they must be prepared for change and transformation.

I hold strongly to the view that citizenship is not just to do with conformity and compliance. Concern has been expressed about some peer mediation programmes having been set up with the aim of making children better behaved. I see peer mediation as being about the development in children of a sense of responsibility for themselves and for society. This entails their learning to examine critically the exercise of authority at all levels of society and to oppose what is undemocratic. It is arguably no longer appropriate to respect those in authority merely *because* they hold that authority. Evidence of institutionalised child abuse over the past thirty years on both sides of the Irish Sea indicates that we do our children a disservice if we don't encourage them to speak out against injustice of whatever kind. But, more than that, we have to be willing and able to listen to children and, above all, to refrain from trivialising their conflicts.

I find it extraordinary that we adults so consistently dismiss children's conflicts as trivial. Are we not aware that disagreements in our adult lives are sparked off by seemingly trivial incidents? The mislaid car key, the forgotten phone message . . . And that the child's 'trivial' conflict offers him the opportunity to learn to deal with those he will encounter throughout his adult life. Conflict is inevitable; it is how we deal with it that decides whether it will be constructive or destructive. We must also learn to deal with conflicts before they escalate. I remember a school principal once told me that one great advantage of peer mediation is that it nips bullying in the bud; it deals with issues before they spiral out of control.

Peer mediation provides an opportunity for children to play an active part in decision-making about issues which interest and concern them. It prepares them to be responsible citizens of the future. It gives them practical *life skills* that they can put into effect in school, at home, and ultimately in the community.

Northern Ireland, the scene of political conflict, is where we have been engaged in this work. The development of children's conflict-handling skills was very much related, of course, to the situation. Dimensions of the political conflict sometimes featured in the conflicts which children mediated, but they were basically of a kind that are common among children everywhere – name calling, friends falling out, fighting over football, being excluded from games and so on. But, time and again, when adults saw the children give role plays of mediation, they immediately made a connection between the skills the children had, and those needed in the peace process; and they saw how, through learning to deal with their conflicts, the children were skilling themselves for participation as adults in the peace-building process.

Politicians were among those who recognised the

significance of the programme. Monica McWilliams, Leader of the Women's Coalition Party wrote: 'I often think if we as present-day political negotiators had experienced the peer mediation programme, how much more quickly we could have reached an inclusive accommodation.'*[1] The then President of the Irish Republic, Mary Robinson commented: 'If (peer mediation) works in the playground, there's no reason why adults can't learn a lesson from what, after all, isn't just child's play.'[2]

The relevance of their skills is not lost on the children themselves:

> In the context of the the 'Peace Talks' then under-way in Belfast, the peer mediators were very aware of these also being about conflict resolution and expressed pride at *their* engagement in the same process – that they are doing something that belongs also to the adult world and has to do with peace in the community. They also observed that the difficulties being reported in the Stormont negotiations accorded with their own experience. 'It can be difficult, and sometimes mediation doesn't work.'[3]

These themes are explored in Chapter 6 in which I give an account of interviews I've had with a number of Northern Ireland politicians, basing my questions on ones that peer mediators themselves wanted answered. I asked the politicians about the skills they needed in the peace process. Separately they all stressed that a key skill was the ability to see things from the other person's point of view, in a word, empathy.

Several years ago I saw a programme on BBC2 about the work of Dr Samuel P. Oliner and Dr Pearl Oliner at the Altruistic Personality and Pro-social Behavior Institute at the Humbolt State University in the USA. They had published research comparing rescuers and non-rescuers of Jews during the holocaust. They characterised altruistic behaviour as that which is directed towards helping another,

*References are given on p. 293.

involves a high risk on the part of the helper, is done without expectation of reward and is voluntary. In their study they discovered that the key motivation leading to such behaviour during the holocaust was empathy. The same programme showed instances of peer mediation being carried out in schools playgrounds in the USA, and the point was made that one of the benefits of peer mediation is that it encourages empathy.

I hope this book will challenge us to listen to children, to explore ways of creating a society, both within school and outside it, that gives children a voice and listens to what they have to say, while endeavouring to create a happy learning and teaching environment. Essentially this book is about celebrating the achievement of children, and the need for adults to support such ventures on a whole-school basis. Peer mediation is a specialist subject, but it raises universal issues about the nature of education that are of relevance to parents, aunts, uncles, grandparents and children themselves, as well as those directly involved in education.

1. What Is Peer Mediation?

Jane (mediator):
There's to be one person speaking at a time, there's to be no name-calling, and try not to accuse the other person, and there's no interrupting. And we won't take sides and we won't tell you what to do.

Peter (mediator):
Okay Tracy, would you like to tell your side of the story first?

Tracy (disputant):
One day I went into school and I noticed that Brian was staring at me and pointing at me shoes and I went over to him and I said, 'Brian what's so funny?'

Brian (disputant):
See me and my brother we're not the smartest and we have to get special tutoring and she started calling me 'Dumbo'.

Tracy:
I didn't!

Peter:
No interrupting, Tracy.[1]

When a child comes up to us in an emotional state, particularly if it is our child or someone we are responsible for, and pours out a tale of woe, how do we react? As to how we handle the situation, a lot depends on what we already

know. Sometimes how we prejudge a situation is precisely
that – prejudice. For example, if the child in question is
often in conflict, or has a manner that we perceive as caus-
ing conflict, we are likely to ask what he or she did to upset
the other one. Conversely, if someone who is rarely seen to
be in conflict makes a complaint, then we may instantly feel
she has been wronged.

All too often, however, what we see is just the tip of the
iceberg, and there may be an unseen history, hidden depths
below the surface.

Some definitions of mediation

Mediation has been defined as 'helping people have a difficult
conversation'.[2] Peer mediation is about children helping each
other to sort out their conflicts. Susan Stewart, whose book
Conflict Resolution: A Foundation Guide includes an informative account of peer mediation,[3] argues that peer mediation is
a child-centred approach that relies on, and reinforces, children's natural sense of justice: 'Mediation is seen to be fair, and
the children put great value on fairness. Mediation lets people
be friends again, and that is what the children wanted.'[4] In the
USA, Professor Karen Bickmore has done extensive research
on peer mediation; she comments: 'Peer mediation is assisted
interpersonal conflict resolution, in which a neutral third party
(mediator) facilitates a process of problem identification and
resolution. In school-based peer mediation, the mediators of
conflicts among students are literally peers – other students
without special or judicial power.'[5]

The agreements that children come to as a result of mediation stress the restoration of relationships: 'S will make
friends with K if K says sorry to E', 'D will make friends
with J if he makes friends with H.' R. Cohen, whose books
on peer mediation in the USA are based on a wealth of
direct experience, stresses in his *School Peer Mediator's
Field Guide* that interpersonal transformation is one of the
fundamental pillars of mediation, and that ideally 'agreements grow out of parties' increased understanding of themselves and willingness to understand others.'[6]

Susan Stewart also describes the process of peer mediation in terms of communication and finding solutions, and also defines it in terms of what it is not:

> Mediation is about listening, asking questions and getting people to think of new ways to sort out their own conflicts, and to decide what they are going to do. It is not about giving advice or taking sides or blaming people or forcing them to agree. Mediation means staying in the middle. It is about [being] fair and being a good listener.[7]

Listening is a key part of the process, and if it is simply a case of listening, why isn't it easy? Part of the difficulty is that adults, like all human beings, tend to listen only long enough to apportion blame, decide who is right and who is wrong, and 'get it sorted'. As a result, two things happen. First, we model a way of listening that is about taking sides; and second, young people feel that they are not getting heard. A key part of the process of mediation happens when the mediator feeds back what the disputant has said, without taking sides, without judging, and without adding or taking away from what the disputant has said. This is so difficult to achieve at first that it feels counter-intuitive; our gut reaction is to, well, react.

Peer mediation is a process which endeavours to create a safe environment where disputants will be able to tell their stories and be heard by each other in the presence of a third party. Basically it boils down to being able to listen, to hear both sides of the story and not pass judgement. It involves encouraging other people to come up with their own solutions. It can be carried on into all walks of life, and the hope is that children will have gained skills that will last them into adulthood.

The bare bones of the mediation process

At this point it is worth outlining the elements of the process. First, it is a voluntary process in that both disputants have to agree to take part. So let's go back to the start of this chapter and the dispute between Tracy and Brian. The story starts when Tracy reports to the teacher (Mrs Doherty) that Brian has been upsetting her. Mrs Doherty refers her to mediation, and encourages Brian to go as well.

Since Brian may be under a bit of duress, or at least feel some undue pressure from his teacher, he may be in two minds about mediation. Anyway, he goes along with Tracy to the mediators, who are based in a part of the school outside the classroom but within sight of the teacher. It's break time, so they know they have some free time before the class begins. Peter and Jane, the two mediators, greet them and make them feel welcome.

Checking that the disputants really want mediation

The first thing the two mediators have to do is establish that both Tracy and Brian, as the disputants, actually want mediation. They do this by asking each of them in turn. Peter and Jane have enough experience to be aware of body language, so if Brian mumbles 'Okay' while sitting doggedly with his arms crossed, they realise he may be communicating doubts. Nevertheless, they take his answer at face value.

By now the two mediators are seated between the two dis-

Fig. 1.1

putants, and they go through the ground rules. There are two sets of rules, one for the disputants, the other for the mediators.

Basic rules for mediators

- The mediators won't take sides
- They will 'keep good secrets'
- They will not tell the disputants what to do.

In later chapters the issues that can be mediated – and those that can't – will be discussed. 'Keeping good secrets', for example, is understood to mean that the two mediators won't talk about the conflict to other children; however, there may be occasions when the mediators will have to tell a teacher.

Basic rules for disputants

- No swearing
- No name-calling
- No interrupting
- No blaming or accusing one another.

Peter and Jane ask Brian and Tracy to agree to the ground rules. This is essential, and if any of the four of them fail to keep the rules, the others can remind them what they agreed to.

Telling both sides of the story

Peter asks Tracy if she would like to go first – it could be either of them but since Tracy has brought the issue up, it is likely that she is ready to start. Tracy tells her side of the story about Brian pointing at her. Hearing Tracy's story may well prompt Brian to interrupt, and even think 'What's the point? I've heard it all before.' If he does interrupt, Peter or Jane remind him of the ground rules he has agreed to; and reassure him that he will have a chance to be listened to.

When Tracy has finished, Peter repeats back what she

Fig. 1.2

said; and as a result Tracy feels she has been heard for the first time.

Jane then invites Brian to give his side of the story, and he concurs; hopefully, Tracy doesn't interrupt him, and he for his part refrains from blaming her or calling her names. However, if ground rules are broken, either Jane or Peter is quick to step in and remind Tracy of their 'contract'.

Dealing with emotions

Fig. 1.3

Reliving the tale of the conflict sometimes causes emotions to resurface, so the mediators always ask the two disputants how they are feeling. Children may not have a vocabulary of feelings beyond 'upset' or 'sad', or may use the opportunity to repeat what they think about the other person. If that happens, Jane gently reminds them that the question is about how they are feeling. She may also ask them if they are feeling angry, frustrated, and so on.

Now both perspectives have been articulated and fed back, and feelings sought.

Identifying the issues

The next goal is to identify the issues; this means listing the problems that have to be solved. A third mediator, Seamus, is involved as a 'writer'. (In a training video one child, when asked what qualities a mediator needed, listed 'patience, fairness and being a fast writer'!) Seamus divides a flipchart sheet in half with a vertical line, and on one side of the line writes the heading 'Tracy', and on the other 'Brian'. In turn the two disputants are asked to list what their own problems are. For example, one problem is that Tracy called Brian 'Dumbo'. This goes in Brian's column because it is a problem for him. Brian mentions that Tracy doesn't understand that his reading difficulties make him

Fig. 1.4

self-conscious.

Tracy for her part is upset with Brian because he won't let her play football. Gradually a list is drawn up.

Talking separately

At this stage Brian or Tracy may want to talk to the mediators without the other disputant being present. If so, one disputant leaves while the other one shares a concern, or more often owns up to something previously denied.

Talking separately, Tracy may admit that she did call

Fig. 1.5

Fig. 1.6

Brian names, but she was still upset with him because he wouldn't let her play football in the playground. When it is Brian's turn to speak to the mediators separately, he says he

Fig. 1.7

Fig. 1.8

wasn't pointing at her shoes, he was pointing at her feet and he was saying to his friends that she wanted to play football. His friends were laughing at him, but he was going to try and persuade them to let her play – until she started calling him 'Dumbo'.

Brainstorming solutions

When Brian and Tracy have both had an opportunity to talk separately, the mediation continues. Both children are encouraged to *brainstorm* solutions. Brainstorming is a method of generating ideas without initial comment, so that one idea sparks off another. They are all written up no matter how impractical or outlandish – 'Tape up Tracy's mouth', 'Send Brian to another school', for example. As a

Fig. 1.9

result, instead of there being no solutions, or perhaps only one or two, a whole range of possibilities is elicited.

Peter takes Brian and Tracy through the suggestions, and if Brain and/or Tracy reject any of the ideas as a solution it is crossed off the list. There may be ideas that neither wants to reject outright, but which would be conditional on other things being agreed. For example, Brian might suggest that Tracy help him with his maths, which Tracy would consider only if Brian does something in return. These 'unrejected' ideas are retained for the moment.

At the end of the brainstorming, some solutions have emerged – possibly only a few of the original ideas, but the important thing is that both Brian and Tracy have agreed to these few not being rejected.

Bargaining
By this time things have begun to shift between Tracy and Brian. At the start their chairs were looking away from each other. By now the two are facing each other, with eye contact, and beginning to see a way forward. This constitutes the foundations of an agreement, and a process of *bargaining* or *give and take* (or, more accurately, give and get) starts. Tracy agrees to help Brian with his maths if he lets her play football sometimes.

Fig. 1.10

The agreement

As this tally of arrangements grows it is written down as an *agreement*, and when it is completed to the satisfaction of both Tracy and Brian, they – and the mediators – sign it, and are encouraged to shake hands.

Since the mediation process is voluntary, cither disputant can decide that an agreement is not possible, or that the only agreement that is possible is to avoid any contact with cach other. Nevertheless, since the parties have consented to mediate they are more likely to continue the process to the end and come to a mutual agreement.

Fig. 1.11

A copy of the agreement is kept by Peter and Jane, who will follow it up in a few days' time to ensure that it is being kept.

These are the bare bones of the mediation process. The history of peer mediation in a global context will be traced later in this chapter, and Chapter 2 will illustrate how children are trained. Chapter 3 explores how peer mediation services are established. Chapter 4 gives an account of how it has developed in primary schools; and Chapter 5, where the skills fit into the curriculum. The relevance of peer mediation to the Northern Ireland Peace Process will be explored in Chapter 6.

The background: the sort of conflicts peer mediators have to deal with

'The disputes they are familiar with,' says Susan Stewart, 'involve the falling out of friends, exclusion from friendship groups, quarrels about space and equipment in the playground, name calling and bullying, sometimes physical contact, leading to a fight.'[8] Or as one peer mediator put it:

> If your friends are in trouble or if one of them is being bullied, you would like to help them to solve it and make the bullying stop. Mediation can help stop an ordinary situation before it builds up into bullying, because then the teacher would have to deal with it. We try to help sort it out ourselves.[9]

It is hardly surprising that when adults observe children in the process of peer mediation they have made the connection between it and the adult world. A local minister explained how relevant it was to him from the pastoral point of view.[10]

Mediation as an alternative way to resolve disputes

Mediation in the adult world is an alternative to going to court. In the Northern Ireland political situation it can be an alternative to confrontation.

In the school context peer mediation is an alternative means of dealing with conflict. Children can ask for an adult to sort it out, or they can go to mediation. Mediation doesn't replace the discipline policy but complements it, providing an alternative option to the teacher or the principal having to deal with the problem first. It gives children the choice of going to other children or to an adult. If mediation is discovered to be inappropriate, or doesn't work, the problem is dealt with by a teacher. An example of this came from Annette Millar, an MA student on placement with us in 1994; during her research one child told her: 'Once I did a mediation and one of the parties walked out, then when I got that person to come back . . . the other person walked out and we just could not handle it. So we had to take it to the teacher.'[11]

This illustrates the fact that, apart from the obvious reason, the disputants are an essential part of the mediation process and of the solution, in that if they don't co-operate, it won't work. It also underlines another key factor: that mediation is voluntary. These two elements, the voluntary and co-operative nature of mediation, set it apart from the standard discipline procedure of the school, and indeed from that of the criminal justice system.

We tend to have a clear picture in our minds of what going to court entails, if not from personal experience as a witness, observer in the public gallery, jury member, member of the criminal justice system or defendant, then at least from television programmes. Mediation, however, is a much less public event, usually only involving the mediators and the disputants. Conversely, mediation has a high profile in the media, particularly in relation to regional and international conflicts such as those in the Middle East, Kosovo and Northern Ireland. For these reasons it can seem more remote from the everyday experience of the average citizen. This haziness on the subject is exacerbated when, in the media, 'mediation' is used as a generic term to cover other processes such as *arbitration* or *negotiation*.

Negotiation, arbitration and mediation
There are (here) three distinct methods of dispute resolution: negotiation, arbitration and mediation.

- Negotiation is conducted directly between the disputants, without a third party. (The disputants are in control of the process and of the outcome.)

Common examples include pay negotiations between unions and management, and two children negotiating taking turns in a game.

- Arbitration: the arbitrator decides on the solution for the disputants, and his or her decision is binding. (The arbitrator is in control of the process and of the outcome.)

Common examples include the breakdown of pay negotiations, when the parties are sent for arbitration; and a teacher or parent deciding what should happen when children quarrel.

- Mediation has been described as 'a process whereby an outsider is invited by people with a dispute to help them come to a solution which they can agree on. . . . The emphasis is on the disputants to come to an agreement guided by the mediator.'[12] (Here the mediator is in control of the process, the disputants are in control of the outcome.)

Peer mediation is just one example. In community mediation services, common cases involve neighbours falling out over noise, dogs barking, and so forth.

If a peer mediation service is set up, a whole range of people are involved, and so it has to be of benefit to all of them, or at least they need to be able to see its worth.

The school principal's perspective

At the outset, with mediation very much an unknown quantity, school principals in Northern Ireland, for example, did have misgivings. The principal of one of the schools we worked in first said he'd never heard of peer mediation:

No, not children mediating themselves, no: a completely new idea, and scary. My first reaction I suppose was that this is not something that I would really want to take on. If your discipline policy is working well, as ours is, you don't want to tack something on to it that may disrupt what is already working.[13]

By the end of the peer mediation training programme, because of the professional way the children were being trained and from his own observation of them, this particular principal was becoming convinced of the benefits of mediation.

I do think there is a role for [peer mediation] in education ... You are giving children the ability and the understanding and the skills to resolve conflict. Children do what they see. [When adults] get into a conflict with each other, it becomes a row and a shouting match and nobody speaks for a while and eventually it sort of simmers down but quite often the nub of the problem is never addressed.[14]

The children's perspective

The children themselves articulate why they value peer mediation. This one was in no doubt: 'Children have a better understanding of children's disputes than adults. Children have time for each other, teachers and other adults are often too busy or distracted or having a bad day and shout at children, making them feel small.'[15] The experience of many peer mediation projects is indeed that children sometimes find it easier to talk to other children rather than to adults. They know they will be listened to. They will have a say in the solution. Often the main thing that children want is to be friends again. They know if it doesn't work out they can still approach an adult to get the situation sorted out.

One of the issues that arises is, what happens if children who are mediators become involved in a conflict? Can they use the service themselves? To this question one child answered: 'Being a mediator, if you are in a fight yourself, you can just think back to a mediation and the problems you have solved and then just [put that into practice].'[16]

A parent-governor's perspective

As will be explained later in this book, schools are encouraged to have a team of adults involved in the peer mediation training programme. Ideally, such teams include ancillary staff and parents. One parent governor commented thus on the impact that peer mediation had had on her daughter and her classmates: 'I was astounded at how mature [they] could be. They took it all very seriously and co-operated with everything they were asked to do and were quickly grasping concepts, which as far as I was concerned, were new to them.'[17]

The school staff's perspective

Adults generally portray a healthy scepticism to the whole notion of young people being able to resolve each other's conflicts – but one lunchtime supervisor, after seeing mediations in practice, said, 'You'd be surprised, you'd have to be involved to see that it really works.'[18] This experience in a Northern Irish school was reinforced by a school in the West Midlands:

> During peer mediation training with a group of 9–10 year olds, the process was being explained to lunchtime supervisors. They felt quite cynical about it. During playtime, a dispute occurred in the playground and the particular children involved came in hot and bothered. The group suggested using mediation; the disputants agreed to a more public mediation than usual. The lunchtime supervisors were totally won over by seeing it work in practice.[19]

A parent's perspective

Outside school parents have expressed interest in and support for peer mediation. This comment by a peer mediator sums up the general attitude of parents: 'I explained at home what mediation is all about and my Mum thinks it's great.'[20]

The effect on children's confidence

There has been general recognition that peer mediation increases the self-confidence and competence of children.

This may have as much to do with the training process as with the actual delivery of a peer mediation service. One principal articulated a universal experience of adults seeing peer mediation in practice.

A team of four mediators [was] giving a presentation to the midday supervisory assistants. [The mediators] were so confident and capable and skilled. I was in total awe of them ... They put us through our paces, fielded questions intelligently, and did a brainstorming session. They didn't just tell us what the skills were; they demonstrated them, illustrated them and did it wonderfully. At that point I realised that no matter if they never solved a problem in the playground, they had grown so much and learned so much and had acquired so many personal skills that it was worth it. And four other mediators gave a similar presentation to the Parents' Council ... They couldn't believe that four children from Primary 7 could give such a presentation, that they had the confidence to do it. And what parents were saying was that they would have given anything to have been exposed to a similar kind of development programme at that age.[21]

The development of confidence is an acknowledged benefit of the peer mediation programme. This teacher reported: 'They all gained in confidence, particularly in expressing their opinions and working co-operatively. The quiet and more withdrawn pupils showed the greatest progress and the more aggressive pupils learned to listen to and appreciate the views and ideas of others.'[22]

This chapter illustrates the great value of peer mediation for individual children, and for the relationships within a class. However, the book will also question whether schools as institutions are ready for such a radical child-centred approach. While children can, and indeed do, mediate conflicts, there is still often considerable resistance to them doing so. In the current climate of examination-orientated performance indicators, many schools do not feel it is worth while to invest time and energy in the promotion of what are perceived as 'soft skills'. But such investment is needed if peer mediation programmes are to be self-sustaining; and without it, they cannot succeed in the long term.

The last word in this section goes to a representative of a peer mediation agency in Britain. Asked in a survey (see Appendix 2) of 22 such agencies that I carried out in summer 2000, to instance an anecdote that would sum up the value and/or power of peer mediation as a process for children, she replied:

> Having worked with tinies [5–6 year olds] for the first time, we [decided to introduce them to peer mediation]. It was an enjoyable and stretching experience. Next day we were greeted by a teacher who glowed – 'There was a battle yesterday, after you'd gone – before I could get involved this tiny 6-year-old waded in and said they couldn't hear each other if they didn't listen. I was speechless, because she said, "What's your problem? ... Okay, what's your problem? ... Okay. How do you feel? Can you see how they feel? What do you need to make it better?" They all ran away to play together after that. I couldn't believe it. It works ...'

Where has peer mediation come from?

Peer mediation in schools is a recent phenomenon, becoming a significant movement in the mid-1980s. It grew out of peace education and community mediation programmes in the United States, and was copied and adapted in parts of Europe and Australasia. This section explores the motivation behind its development in various countries throughout the world, highlighting differences and similarities. It questions whether peer mediation is a 'Western phenomenon', as there is little evidence of its existence in Africa and Asia. However, there may well be other countries, not mentioned here, with variations of peer mediation in operation.

United States

Peer mediation started in the USA. It grew out of initiatives in the 1960s and 1970s, partially in response to the Vietnam war. It was also part of a peace education movement that was responding to the harsh realities of the Cold War. A growing awareness of the real threat to mankind posed by the proliferation of nuclear weapons led to the establishment of Educators for Social Responsibility (ESR). This became a national teachers' organisation which was keen to develop critical thinking in young people. Rather than just putting across one perspective on nuclear weapons, as one ESR representative, Tom Roderick, put it, 'I became aware of human survival as something that we couldn't just take for granted, but that we needed to secure by conscious choice and conscious action ... we needed to educate a generation of young people so that they could rise to the challenges of the nuclear age.[23]

This urgency, this generational imperative, was echoed by Stephanie Judson, editor of *The Manual on Nonviolence and Children*,[24] in the context of interpersonal conflict. She explained that parents and educationalists were anxious that a generation of young people should learn skills in order to respond to conflict without resorting to violence. She quoted noted peace researcher Elise Boulding as saying that people who are in the peace movement for the 'long haul' have three characteristics: confidence, competence and high self-esteem.

However, there was strong ambivalence, if not antipathy, about using the term 'peace education'. Leading educationalists in the 'peace education' field preferred alternatives. Tom Roderick, a leading educationalist in the 'peace education' field, focused on 'nuclear age education', commenting that 'people thought the word "peace" was too much associated with communism, that the word had been in a sense corrupted and that we represented a new mind, and so we needed a new label.'[25] He also felt it was pretentious to say, 'We're doing peace education', as if distinct from everybody else, because he felt that nobody wants war.

Lantieri,[26] on the other hand, in an article entitled 'Waging peace in our schools: beginning with the children' published in 1995 in the journal *Peace, Environment and Education*, infers that it is important to at least highlight the difference between the values of peace education and those propagated by society at large. The violence in US society – including the fact that 'a gun takes the life of an American child every two hours' – provides the context for her work with the Resolving Conflict Creatively Program in New York. She quotes Deborah Prothrow-Stith, Assistant Dean at Harvard School of Public Health: 'Addressing the question, "Why are our children killing each other?" [Prothrow-Stith replies], "Because we are teaching them to." Our society glamorizes violence. Indeed, the media often portray the hero as one who chooses violence to get what he or she wants and needs.' Elise Boulding prefers the term 'peace learning' to 'peace education', as it 'shifts the emphasis to what goes on inside the learner rather than on something out there'.[27] She is keen to emphasise the need for global education, with people recognising their role in the world community and in their local community.

Priscilla Prutzman of Children's Creative Response to Conflict (CCRC) in Nyack, NY, acknowledges that it was a conscious decision on her part to use 'conflict resolution' as a term rather than 'peace education'. Interviewed in 1993,[28] she said, 'Up until 8 or 9 years ago, peace education in this country was considered not a very good term . . . it was considered as a really radical, "communist" kind of thing.' By 1993 she felt that peace education had been reinstated; the concept was seen as being positive, less of a movement and more about skills, about educating people in how to become peaceable. She felt that the work had grown out of the peace movement and the goal was to establish it in mainstream education.

Whether 'peace education' was an acceptable term or not, a key part of it was conflict-resolution skills. This was the practical application of the theory, in a way that children could use in their daily lives. Communication skills, co-operation skills, affirmation skills and problem-solving skills could be taught, not just to children but to adults too.

The Community Board Center for Policy and Training, in San Francisco was the first agency to train local mediators to deal with neighbourhood conflicts; and this model spread quickly to the criminal justice system. 'By the end of the 1980s, 1,500 volunteers were active in community dispute resolution throughout New York State alone. This San Francisco initiative also gave birth to a curriculum for teaching conflict resolution to grade 4 children in public schools.'[29] In his digest on mediation for the US Education Information and Resources Center (ERIC), David K. Trevaskis reported in 1994 that the study of conflict and conflict management was being given greater urgency by the general concern about violence in schools.[30] There was a recognition that conflict itself was 'a normal, natural part of everyday life . . . unresolved and lingering conflict frequently leads to violence, interfering with productivity and the quality of life in schools and the community'.[31] This was also liable to interfere with the learning environment of students. The statistics speak for themselves – 'Almost 300,000 high school students are attacked physically each month and one in five students in grades 9 through 12 carries a weapon to school.'[32]

However, responses to this situation varied in their effectiveness. The introduction of metal-detectors and the employment of full-time police officers in school grounds dealt only with the symptoms of the problem. Other initiatives were designed to deal with disputes before they spiralled into violence, such as 'referrals to the principal's office, detention, suspension, and expulsion'. These responses were reactive; what was missing was the training of young people themselves in the skills of conflict resolution that they needed for life.

According to D. K. Trevaskis, it was dissatisfaction with the traditional dispute-resolution processes established that led educators and others to try new ways such as mediation. This search for alternatives was mirrored by a move in US society generally, away from a traditional litigational model of problem-solving in courts. The term Alternate Dispute Resolution (ADR) was coined as a generic phrase at about this time. (In 1999,[33] it was being argued that the word 'Appropriate' should replace the word 'Alternate', because it was about time that forms of justice based on restorative principles were recognised as having a major part to play in the mainstream criminal justice system.)

Mediation in itself was not new in the USA, even in schools. In the summer of 1984, sufficient work was being done in the field of peer mediation in schools to merit the formation of the National Association of Mediation in Education (NAME). Its initial membership was 50 educators and community mediators. By 1999, its membership had changed its name to CreNET (Conflict Resolution Education Network), and it had become 'the largest US membership association for educators, conflict resolution professionals and concerned community members'.

This pattern – of a group of educators and community mediators starting out with a small initiative, often unofficial and clamouring to become part of mainstream education, whose merit is only acknowledged several years down the line – is mirrored elsewhere in the world. Although there is a wealth of information about peer mediation in the United States, its development is less well documented elsewhere. Apart from the sections about peer mediation in Great Britain and Northern Ireland, the information for the bulk of the rest of this chapter was gleaned from a questionnaire that I sent out to individuals in different parts of the world (see Appendix 1).

Canada

Writing in the the *Fourth R* in 1994, Ivan Roy,[34] who was then Youth Director for the Canadian Institute for Conflict Resolution in Ottawa, reported that the previous year the 'Ontario Ministry of Education made an unprecedented move by mandating that "students will . . . be willing and able to resolve conflicts in co-operative and non-violent manner" by the end of Grades 3, 6 and 9'. This decision had taken into consideration the growing significance of peer mediation in the state, which had started in 1989 with a number of 'isolated projects in peer mediation'. By 1994 these had multiplied to several hundred peer mediation programmes in Ontario elementary and secondary schools. Having conflict resolution on the curriculum meant that other themes were now included, such as anger management, cultural diversity and bias awareness. There were also imaginative schemes in place that trained high school students and facilitators, and also attempts to develop pupils' one-to-one negotiation skills. I. Roy stresses the need for conflict-resolution education to be part and parcel of initial teacher training.

In 1994, June Maresca worked with a lawyer from Justice for Children and Youth, a Toronto organisation promoting children's rights within the justice system, to develop a school-based peer mediation model. In an article taken from a research paper that she submitted towards her Master of Law degree in Alternative Dispute Resolution, she writes about this innovative programme in Toronto. The objectives were to train students as peer mediators and provide a process for resolving conflicts which might otherwise be the subject of criminal charges. One outcome of this experience was: 'Students with a large following who were perceived to be a negative influence made the greatest impact as mediators.'[35]

Northern Ireland
In the mid-1980s mediation was beginning to feature in the peace and reconciliation field in Northern Ireland; and a number of individuals travelled to San Francisco to be trained by the Community Boards programme. On their return to Northern Ireland, they formed the Northern Ireland Conflict and Mediation Association, later to become the Mediation Network, Northern Ireland (MNNI). From the outset education was seen as a priority, and there were attempts to trial mediation in a school in Dublin and Londonderry. As peer mediation was an unfamiliar concept, the title and aims of these workshops were couched in terms of conflict management. But it was becoming clear that mediation had relevance in education. An education subgroup was formed, and in 1989 it put a proposal[36] to the Department of Education for Northern Ireland, arguing for peer mediation to be trialled in schools.

This proposal was ahead of its time, and although the civil servants responsible were interested, it was still too much of an unknown quantity. Nevertheless, agencies looking to involve Northern Irish schools in conflict-resolution programmes were at an advantage compared with their counterparts in the rest of the UK. Education for Mutual Understanding (EMU), a Department of Education for Northern Ireland initiative, provided a rationale.*

Originally EMU's work was to promote better understanding between pupils in Catholic and Protestant schools and to arrange activities which would allow them to meet. Such programmes were developed by individual teachers or small groups of enthusiasts, on a voluntary basis. The Education Reform (Northern Ireland) order of 1989 then brought in Education for Mutual Understanding and the related theme of Cultural Heritage as part of the statutory curriculum in all state-funded schools.[37]

The overall goals of the programme include enabling pupils 'to learn to respect and value themselves and others; to appreciate the interdependence of people within society; to know about and understand what is shared as well as what is different about their cultural traditions; and to appreciate how conflict may be handled in non-violent ways'.[38]

In 1988 the Ulster Quaker Peace Education Project (QPEP) was set up by the Ulster Quaker Peace Committee as an action-research** project at the Centre for the Study of Conflict at the University of Ulster. Part of its remit was to 'develop untried strategies'.[39] By 1993 QPEP had been running conflict-resolution skills training in primary and secondary schools in Northern Ireland for five years. Keen to develop the work further in a more systematic way, and inspired and informed by the work of the Good Shepherd Neighbourhood House, Philadelphia, QPEP decided to run a conference on peer mediation.

QPEP had built up a reputation for interactive annual conferences for children in Derry, on such subjects as bullying, gender differences and the 'future of our city'. Two

*For a fuller description of what EMU is about see Chapter 5.
**See Chapter 9: 'Action-research is about people explaining to themselves and others why they behave as they do, and enabling them to share this knowledge with others.'

children from every primary school in Derry were invited to attend. Here they had an opportunity to observe and practise peer mediation.

After the conference was over, QPEP wrote to each school and asked if they would like to be involved in a pilot project to introduce peer mediation. Significantly, the only two to respond were schools with which the project had had previous contact, developing conflict-resolution skills training. Neither principal had initially heard of peer mediation, and for both it was the positive feedback they had received from the pupils who had attended the day conference that had convinced them of the value of the process.

Uniquely in the UK, Education for Mutual Understanding (EMU) provided a statutory requirement in Northern Ireland for children to learn about non-violent ways of handling conflict. This aim provided a rationale for peer mediation, which also met the requirements of other areas of the curriculum, as will be explored in Chapter 5.

The Quaker Peace Education Project started its first peer mediation training programme with two schools in autumn 1993. Coincidentally, Yvonne Duncan from New Zealand's 'Cool Schools'[40] peer mediation programme was visiting Ireland at the time. QPEP was surprised and encouraged to discover similarities between our fledgling training programme and that of the longer-established Cool Schools programme, which had been especially developed for New Zealand primary schools.

New Zealand
Yvonne Duncan (at that time a primary school teacher) reports:

> [In 1981 I] began teaching mediation in my primary classroom, inspired by an idea on mediation in *Learning Peaceful Relationships*, a book published by the Peace Foundation and WILPF [Women's International League for Peace and Freedom]. In 1984 the children in my class thought of using mediation in the playground to solve marble disputes. They called themselves 'Marble Mediators' and set up a Mediation Station and were very successful at resolving disputes.[41]

In 1987 peer mediation was introduced into Hagley High School, a secondary school, on the initiative of three volunteer community mediators and a law lecturer. The motivation was to 'change day-to-day behaviour. [They] thought changes in education in New Zealand [known as] Tomorrow's Schools Reforms would cause stress. This programme did not spread to other schools as hoped.'[42]

Four years later, Cool Schools, an enterprise started by education institutions and the Peace Foundation, introduced peer mediation to a dozen primary schools. Peer mediation is seen in New Zealand as a European, or 'pakeha', model, but one which shares with Maori cultures 'methods which respect the dignity of the pupils and are aimed at helping the disputants recognise the effects of their actions and solving the problems in ways that empower pupils'.[43] One such method is family-group conferencing. Duncan[44] makes the point that serious conflicts that cannot be solved by peer mediation may need a family-group-conferencing process. This is a restorative justice process which emanated from New Zealand and is currently gaining support in social services and youth justice in the UK. How peer mediation fits into the mosaic of restorative justice will be explored in Chapter 9.

The Cool Schools programme quickly took root, and is now practised in 1,200 primary and secondary schools throughout New Zealand.

Australia

In Australia an existing mediation agency, the Conflict Resolution Network (a non-governmental organisation (NGO)), has played a leading role in developing peer mediation, starting in 1989 (although some teachers returning from exchange programmes in Canada may have started before this date). Ten years later its peer mediation booklet had been purchased by 3,000 schools.

The initiative for peer mediation in Australia came from individual teachers and principals as well as from external agencies: 'Peer mediation is a grass-roots program – with recent department of education support in some states.'[45] It was not reacting to either specific or general violence, but rather it was 'a proactive initiative for student development, supported by anti-harassment programs and conflict-resolution training. Its aim was/is the empowerment of students and increasing the skills of students to be responsible for their own choices and decisions.'[46] Information came from Canada and also New Zealand – there seemed to be many people deciding to go this way at the same time, and they influenced each other. The continued cross-fertilisation of ideas is indicated by the fact that materials and resources from the Australian Conflict Resolution Network Schools Development are currently being used in South Africa.

South Africa

One leading agency in conflict resolution in education in South Africa is the Centre for Conflict Resolution, in Cape Town. Their approach is this: 'Peer mediation is just one strategy. In our work with the educators (our primary focus) we advocate a whole-school approach which looks at school ethos, integration into curriculum, and classroom management options before thinking of peer mediation, i.e. creating a culture of constructive conflict resolution.'[47]

The first known introduction of peer mediation in South Africa took place in 1995, at Wynberg Girls' Junior School, Cape Town. The pupils involved in the training were 11 to 13-year-olds, while the actual mediators were 12 to 13-year-olds (in their final year of primary education). The driving force for this programme was two committed teachers, who had the support of the principal from the start. The rest of the staff were brought on board with staff workshops. The Centre for Conflict Resolution had provided the training for two teachers, who took part in a training programme for a group of educators. Their approach is to work with representative teachers from a cluster of schools. (In Chapter 3 we will be exploring the different ways in which the peer mediation training of trainers is conducted.)

Significantly in the light of the violence in South African Society, the motivation for the peer mediation programme was proactive rather than reactive, part of 'a general process of instilling a culture promoting peace in the school, [following up] work already done on this'.[48] The methodology

of the Centre for Conflict Resolution is to provide both
training and support, but it is adamant that the application
and implementation must come from the institution concerned. This is echoed by their response to the question I
asked in the questionnaire about how peer mediation got
started in their country. Valerie Dovey stresses that it was a
process:

> What works in one school community is not suitable
> for another. Some schools have introduced the concept
> of mediation at all grade levels and it operates infor-
> mally like this. Others have a structured programme.
> Many of our schools are operating under very difficult
> circumstances and are impacted by community vio-
> lence. Resources in terms of people power are stretched.
> We cannot be prescriptive. Introducing ground rules
> into all classrooms might be a more manageable
> and realistic strategy than getting overwhelmed with
> the idea of introducing peer mediation at an early
> stage.[49]

Nigeria

As elsewhere, the motivation for peer mediation in Nigeria
was an attempt to promote peaceful coexistence rather than
reacting to violence in society as either a specific event, or
something endemic. The initiative for it came from an
NGO.

In most cultures within Nigeria, there is a tendency to use
arbitration as a standard means of dispute resolution. This
is usually done by an elderly person within the family or
society, or by the leader of the tribe, and is more prevalent
in rural areas than in the cities. It is easier to experiment
with alternative approaches such as mediation in schools in
the cities, where tribal influences are not so strong.

The first peer mediation training programme was implemented in a few schools in Lagos in 1996, when three or
four teachers from each school were trained. The schools
were keen to include peer mediation in curriculum development; they wanted to develop an academic programme, with
academic awards, but reinforced by practical application.

The programme itself caters for young people aged 10 to 17.

As an initiative it was unofficial. After the initial training it was left to the individual school to take it up – so from the start there has been an issue of sustainability. Private schools in Nigeria are in a better position to continue than public (state) schools, as they have more resources.

Norway

In Europe, Norway is the country that has most institutionalised peer mediation. This is hardly surprising, as an Act was passed in 1991 that required each Norwegian municipality to appoint a mediation board, the costs of which would be met by the state; established by 1994, the boards focused particularly, though not exclusively, on dealing with young offenders.[50] Given the Norwegian authorities' commitment to comprehensive solutions, peer mediation was a natural progression, aiming at the bettering of the environment of children and youth.

Encouraged by studies of mediation in schools in the USA and the UK, the first programme was initiated and led by the Ministry of Justice, through municipal mediation boards – it was compulsory by Act of law. Between March 1995 and June 1997 it was introduced into 46 elementary and lower-secondary schools. The age range of the young people involved was 10 to 17. The Ministry of Justice was all the time working in co-operation with the Ministry of Education and Research, as well as with the governmental education offices in every country.[51] Norway is unique in that from the outset peer mediation has been promoted and resourced by the state.

Great Britain

In the 1980s, inspired by initiatives taking place in the USA, agencies in Great Britain were developing conflict-resolution programmes in schools. 'Peace education', as in the USA, was a political hot potato, and was criticised for perceived political partiality by a Conservative government and vilified by a Tory press. 'Conflict management' was considered a more acceptable term in education.

Marigold Bentley, who worked for several years in

London as education adviser for Quaker Peace and Service, argues:

> Peace education in schools in Britain is still recovering from the damage that the Cold War caused. A great deal of fascinating and useful work was done in peace education during the late 1970s and early 1980s, which has now fed into education in schools here under other labels such as global studies, world studies, human rights, anti-bullying, prejudice reduction and conflict resolution, among others. At the time, peace education was rejected as being biased and political.[52]

One body that has had a major impact on peace education in Britain is the Kingston Friends Workshop Group (now Kingston Friends Mediation) in Surrey. It was formed in response to work undertaken by the Quaker Peace Action Caravan – a group of people who toured the country raising consciousness about peace issues by a variety of means, including street demonstrations and work in schools. Part of their programme in Kingston included a sixth-form conference, the venue being Kingston Quaker Meeting House.

The local Quaker peace committee asked themselves how they would follow up this work. As Sue Bowers, co-founder of Kingston Friends Workshop Group,[53] explained, there was a feeling of reticence about street protests, and so they decided instead to hold a sixth-form workshop called 'Can We Make Peace?' Twenty-four sixth-formers from three schools attended – it was interactive and drew on the trainers' youth work experience. After this Sue Bowers attended a mediation workshop, which had a profound influence on her.

They didn't set out to form a group. They were influenced by what was happening in the USA; the resources they used were *A Manual of Nonviolence and Children*, produced by the Children and Nonviolence Program in Philadelphia,[54] and *The Friendly Classroom for a Small Planet* by the Children's Creative Response to Conflict, Nyack, New York.[55] However, both manuals were written within and for a US context, and Sue Bowers and her colleagues, in drawing their materials from them, were aware of constraints such as 'the different way they talk to kids [in the USA]'.[56] They realised that although the manuals acted as their 'bibles', they needed to adapt the activities they contained. They were also beginning to create their own, and so began to record them for each other.

They wrote up activities in a card-index file, each exercise detailed under headings such as 'Aim', 'Equipment', and so on. Eventually this became a loose-leaf file, someone offered to produce 50 copies of it, and *Ways and Means: An Approach to Problem-Solving*[57] was born. It was the first attempt to write a manual for interactive peace education workshops for schools in Britain – although it wasn't called that.

Bowers echoed the opinions of US peace educationalists when she said, 'We didn't dare, well, we chose not to use [the term] "Peace Education" because it was seen (with, I think, some justification) as sort of left-wing antinuclear propaganda at the time. We called it "Problem Solving and Personal Relationships".'[58] The work of Kingston Friends Workshop Group gained a foothold in schools through the support of a local authority education inspector. Close liaison with the local polytechnic also helped.

Ways and Means is a practical guide to a workshop approach, with sections on interactive exercises, designed to build confidence and self-esteem. The methodology is built around the concept of an iceberg, an image first used in this context in this manual. The idea is that the obvious conflict above the surface hides the fact that 90 per cent of the conflict is below the surface. Various activities in these manuals provide a mediation structure for the workshops, and one particular exercise – 'Goal Wish Problem Solving' – places a strong focus on helping an individual to deal with a conflict by encouraging him or her to choose from a variety of alternative suggestions from his or her peers on how to respond to any given demanding situation.

The workshop approach, with its emphasis on affirmation, communication, co-operation and problem-solving, was to provide the context for subsequent peer mediation initiatives. Projects like the West Midlands Quaker Peace

Education Project, Bristol Mediation and Mediation UK began actively to promote peer mediation. Initially at least, the first steps in establishing peer mediation came from a peace education context, outside mainstream education.

The European Network for Conflict Resolution in Education (ENCORE)

In 1989 the Council of Europe published a report entitled *Violence and Conflict Resolution in Schools*.[59] It had been researched and written by Jamie Walker, a conflict resolution practitioner living and working in Berlin. Inspired by this report, the Quaker Council for European Affairs organised a seminar in Brussels in 1990 to discuss the setting up of a European network on conflict resolution. This seminar brought together practitioners predominantly from England, but also from Northern Ireland, Germany and Belgium. As a result of the seminar the European Network of Conflict Resolution in Education (ENCORE) was born, which meets annually and provides opportunities for practitioners involved in conflict resolution in education to meet and to share developments in training and practice. Peer mediation is one strategy that is common to a number of agencies within ENCORE.

Recently established peer mediation programmes in Britain

In the 1990s there was a significant increase in the number of community mediation projects working in schools, a strategy that was to be boosted by funding from the National Lottery Charities Board. In summer 2000 I sent a questionnaire to 22 UK agencies that promote peer mediation (see Appendix 2). Twelve agencies responded, all but one (set up in 1984) having been established in the previous five years. There was a variety of funding sources: trusts and foundations were major contributors, and three programmes were being funded by the National Lottery. Local council or Local Education Authority was cited by two agencies, and individual agencies gathered support from diverse other sources. These included a housing association, a Quaker meeting, a police authority and European Community funding.

What was the inspiration behind these initiatives? For some it was a response to societal problems: 'The community mediation service wanted to respond to the long-term and major issue of homelessness and crime in the local area. Having the opportunity to share peer mediation skills with young people is our aspiration – to influence the future of this locality.' One agency, itself a school, was motivated by 'the level of violence outside school being brought into school'. A concern about 'the level of violence young people were encountering' led to a desire to 'offer [them] the opportunity to develop skills in resolving conflicts non-violently'.

Others instanced factors such as these:

- a rise in the number of young people involved in community mediation cases, either as catalysts to a dispute *or* as witnesses to the mediation
- their existing links with schools or with concerned individual teachers
- a request from one local school for conflict/peer support training.

The influence of a number of individual teachers with mediation experience was significant, as well. One respondent said that his past personal experience as a teacher in mediation led him to want to 'explore the link between interpersonal violence and wider world conflict – to link peer mediation, peace education and development education'. The agency that was established in 1984 said that its involvement had grown out of 'a programme of taking peace films into schools . . . and wanting to do more'.

By the turn of the century community mediation programmes had grown in confidence and stature, and were looking outward: 'Once we had established a professional competent mediation service we wanted to develop peer mediation in schools. We feel it is important to impart conflict management skills to young people as early as possible.' The individual experience of a young person galvanised one agency into action. The motivation was 'a schoolgirl being bullied and wanting to have some sort of response at school, that is, peer mediation. An introduction course in listening skills resulted in a pilot peer mediation course.'

Who or what was the inspiration behind the peer mediation programme?

Most of the respondents said it was an individual who motivated everybody else; or, in the case of a group, it was 'spearheaded by an individual'; or, more specifically, 'a group of mediators with backgrounds in education who had the vision and drive to push this on'. Sometimes it was a synthesis between concerned individuals at a school and a mediation agency with whom they had an existing link.

From this small survey a picture emerges of agencies having become established in community mediation, practising skills that have a clear value in the community. At the same time, being aware of the abrasive nature of society and its bruising effect on young people, these agencies wanted to assist schools in giving them the skills for handling conflict. While existing links with schools often provide the context, and the individual involvement of teachers helps to provide support, the question remains as to the degree with which a whole-school approach is possible without substantial school staff involvement.

This chapter has selected instances from different parts of the world where peer mediation has become established. In some countries it has been achieved with state support and intervention; in most cases, however, it has been an individual school, or cluster of schools, that has taken the initiative.

2. How Are Children Trained in Peer Mediation?

In this chapter I shall explain the methodology behind the interactive training approach required for peer mediation training. I shall take the reader through the training process from start to finish, and explain how and why certain strategies have been developed. The chapter is based on the peer mediation manual of the Education for Mutual Understanding (EMU) Promoting School Project (EMUpsp),[1] and draws on the manuals of Bristol Mediation[2] and peer mediation trainers Hilary Stacey and Patricia Robinson[3] as well.

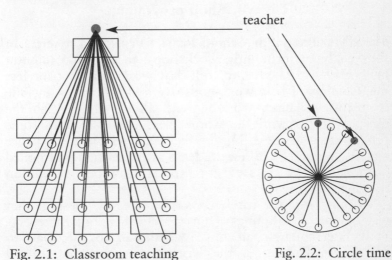

Fig. 2.1: Classroom teaching   Fig. 2.2: Circle time

Figure 2.1 represents a traditional format for classroom teaching, with all desks facing the front and the children speaking only to the teacher. Alternatively, children may sit in groups. In some primary schools in Northern Ireland where the 11+ transfer test is taken in the autumn term of the final year, the children sit in rows during that term, reverting to sitting in groups after the exams.

A prerequisite for training children in peer mediation is to move from the scenario in Figure 2.1 to that of Figure 2.2.

The transition to the circle (Figure 2.2) for peer mediation training is made much easier if the children and teacher already have experience of *circle time*, as described in Chapter 4. Children as young as four can learn and put into practice a rule such as 'one person speaking at a time', particularly if it is reinforced by passing a cuddly toy around the circle and establishing that only the person who has the toy is able to speak. If the class (and the teacher) have got into the habit of using circle time on a weekly basis – and for dealing with particular issues as they arise – peer mediation training later on will have a solid foundation to build on.

The workshop programme

The EMU Promoting School Project developed a series of six weekly, or fortnightly, workshops, each of 105 minutes in length, with a seventh, full-day, workshop to complete the training. These workshops were designed to include co-operative games, working with all the children in the class. Working with the whole class contrasts with some programmes in the USA, for example, which use a cadre approach whereby 'a few students are identified and pulled out of regular classes for special conflict resolution training.'[4]

Working with the whole class reinforces the message that peer mediation training is not for an elite, but for everybody; later, children can choose whether or not they want to become mediators. So the workshops consist of 25–30 children in one large group, who then split into small groups, with six or seven children in each group. These children are often chosen with some thought given to established friendship groups within the class. It is often in these small groups that the most significant learning is done – which depends a lot on the facilitation skills of the adult involved. It is important that the whole group, including the adult(s), adhere to the ground rules (see p. 54).

A feature of all of these workshops is that the adult team (recommended minimum: three people) meet beforehand to plan the workshop and decide who is going to do what, and to ensure that the necessary preparation with the class is done. Each workshop focuses on a particular stage in the mediation process and concentrates on identifying the necessary skills, enabling the children to role-play the stage in the mediation process that requires those skills and reinforcing previously learned skills. The workshops proceed as follows:

Workshop 1: ground rules, an introduction to mediation
Workshop 2: using children's own conflict stories
Workshop 3: everybody having a go
Workshop 4: generating solutions
Workshop 5: thoughts on a peer mediation service in our school
Workshop 6: real mediation – a live conflict!
Workshop 7: the final day of training

As will be described later, during the first workshop the children see a mediation from start to finish, through every stage. The workshop programme seeks to give children the skills to go through the entire mediation process by themselves.

The mediation process

Introduction	Setting the scene. The adults ensure that both disputants are there by choice; the stages of mediation are described and the ground rules are agreed upon.
Story-telling	Each disputant tells his side of the story without being interrupted;

immediately afterwards his story is
fed back to him by one of the mediators. When both disputants have been
through this process, they are each
asked how they are feeling.

Identifying issues   With the help of a writer, each disputant's problems or issues are written
up on a flipchart sheet.

Speaking separately   Each disputant is given the opportunity of speaking with the mediators pri-
vately, without the other disputant
being present.

Brainstorming   At this stage the emphasis shifts from
trying to find out what happened to
looking at possible solutions. These
are written up, and any that neither
agrees to are crossed off, while any
that both agree to are kept.

Give and take   As far as the remaining brainstormed
solutions are concerned, the dis-
putants see if they can 'trade' solutions in as much as one will do one
thing if the other will do something
else.

The agreement   In the final part of the process, solutions that the two disputants have
both agreed to are written up on an
agreement form, and signed by them
and by the two mediators.

Workshop 1: ground rules: an introduction to mediation

Circle time and peer mediation training both require the
establishment of ground rules. In fact, establishing ground
rules is such a key element of the process that the class
teacher is encouraged to negotiate them in advance of the
first workshop. This idea may be introduced to the class
with a statement such as 'So that nobody will feel nervous

and everyone will feel comfortable and able to enjoy the workshop and learn things, it would be good to have an agreement with each other about how we will treat each other.'[5]

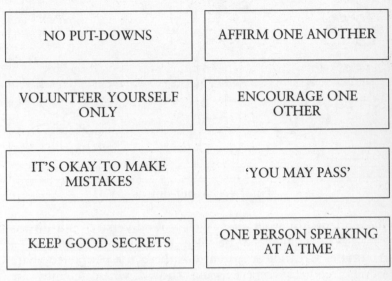

NO PUT-DOWNS	AFFIRM ONE ANOTHER
VOLUNTEER YOURSELF ONLY	ENCOURAGE ONE OTHER
IT'S OKAY TO MAKE MISTAKES	'YOU MAY PASS'
KEEP GOOD SECRETS	ONE PERSON SPEAKING AT A TIME

Fig. 2.3: Ground rules for mediation

Certain ground rules have evolved over several years of interactive workshops, and are worth exploring in order to explain the rationale behind them.

No put-downs
This ground rule is linked to issues of self-esteem. Mediators require self-confidence and a sense of their own self-worth – as do the disputants if they are going to believe that they can help to solve their own problems. We live in a 'put-down culture', where 'slagging off' and the ability to give and take jokes at each other's expense are often seen as a measure of friendship.

However, put-downs tend to make people wary of expressing themselves, of being different from the 'norm' or even just different from their friends. If we are to model listening to disparate and contradictory views, encourage

Fig. 2.4: No put-downs

independent thinking and welcome diversity, put-downs
need to be challenged because they usually reinforce a
stereotype. Creating a safe atmosphere for people to share
feelings requires respect being shown when feelings are
expressed.

One objection that is sometimes raised – particularly by
adults – to the 'no put-down' rule is along the lines of 'Does
this mean there won't be any craic [fun]?' Actually the
reverse is true: knowing that they are not going to be made
a fool of makes people more likely to relax and enjoy themselves, and there is usually a lot of laughter and fun – there
has to be, to make the activities enjoyable. It is important to
establish a balance between the seriousness of conflict issues
and the lightness and creativity which conflict resolution
requires.

Affirm one another
'No put-downs' is one of the hardest ground rules to keep.
Another objection often voiced is 'Does that mean that we
have to be nice to each other all the time?' Well, yes – except
that 'nice' is a lukewarm word. Being affirming rather than
putting people down is very creative; thinking well of other

Fig. 2.5:
Affirm one another

people, and affirming them and ourselves, energises and empowers. There is considerable emphasis on affirmation activities in all peer mediation training, creating opportunities and new ways of thinking. The ground rule 'Affirm one another' helps to create a positive environment.

Volunteer yourself only
This is one ground rule which teachers find as difficult to keep as children do. Part of classroom management is organising a division of labour so that tasks are shared out equally – and waiting for volunteers, or relying on those who always volunteer, may be impractical. A child who is reluctant to take part in a particular activity may camouflage his or her own reticence by urging another child to do that activity instead. Peer mediation is very much about encouraging people to be responsible for their own actions, and not to be over-influenced by peer pressure. Children

Fig. 2.6: Volunteer yourself only

generally understand the rationale behind this, but one Primary 7 class, when reviewing the ground rules three weeks into a six-week programme, suggested the following additional rule:

Encourage one another

Fig. 2.7: Encourage one another

In classes where the teacher stresses and demonstrates that all children have different skills, a climate is created where everybody has a role to play. If this is coupled with an ethos in which children are used to affirming each other they will naturally encourage each other to use their different skills. It was for this reason that the Primary 7 class wanted to add the new ground rule 'Encourage one another'. The children explained that sometimes they knew that a classmate would be particularly good at doing something. So although they were generally happy with the 'volunteer yourself only' rule, they thought there were exceptions and times when this rule was in conflict with the 'affirm each other' rule. Since that time we at EMUpsp have included it in our standard list of ground rules.

It's okay to make mistakes

Fig. 2.8: It's okay to make mistakes

This statement contradicts the experience of many adults recounting their own schooldays. Tales of teachers hitting children for each mistake they made in a spelling test, or for each sum that was incorrect, are all too frequent in the memories of adults. Current educational thinking, with its emphasis on positive reinforcement, values praising what children do well and encouraging them to do better. As one principal said to his Primary 7 class in response to this ground rule, 'The person who never made a mistake never made anything.' The methodology of mediation – particularly when it comes to brainstorming solutions – emphasises that out of a whole series of answers a solution will emerge. Often there is no single 'right' answer, and no single 'wrong' answer. Problem-solving sometimes requires lateral thinking. There is the well known example of two girls fighting over an orange. The teacher took it off them and divided it in half. This apparent 'right' solution didn't actually take into account their needs. When both had had a chance to tell their story, it transpired that one girl wanted the orange in order to drink its juice, while the other wanted the rind to make marmalade.

In this instance it isn't clear who made the mistake; what is clear is that once everybody had been heard and their needs identified, it was easier to come to a solution. Teachers have given examples of admitting and apologising for mistakes; and this is the other part of the equation – that if it's okay to make mistakes, it's also important to take responsibility for them. If making a mistake isn't such a big deal, it encourages honesty and discourages covering up.

'You may pass'

In schools where pupils are encouraged to participate actively in all subjects, 'passing' is sometimes judged in terms of the individual 'not playing their part'. During circle time activities teachers have voiced concerns regarding this, along the lines of 'Billy always passes. . . . surely we should encourage him.' But the pressure to participate shouldn't come from the teacher – the ground rules are agreed by the group, and if they aren't working, it's something that has to be discussed with the class. The benefits of circle time (and by extension, peer mediation) have been described thus: 'circle time isn't about children learning about themselves, it's about children learning about themselves in a group, how they operate in a group and how the group functions.'[6]

Usually children are prepared at least to take part in an

Fig. 2.9: 'You may pass'

opening circle, which requires them to say their name and mention something they like, for example. As children grow in confidence they take a more active part. They are then responding to the interaction of the group rather than to the directives of the teacher.

Keep good secrets

Fig. 2.10: Keep good secrets

Roughly translated, this refers to confidentiality – but the wording is deliberate. 'Keep secrets' turned out to be a contentious ground rule, as it didn't deal adequately with child-protection issues. It is important to differentiate between 'good secrets' and 'bad secrets'. Bad secrets are those which children have no choice in keeping, which are kept because of emotional blackmail or physical threat, for example. Good secrets, on the other hand, are simply the content of the mediation processes; but if the mediators are in any doubt about keeping them, they are encouraged to tell a teacher. It is important in workshops, as in actual mediations, that adults are made aware of issues when children disclose information. The 'keep good secrets' ground rule is designed to ensure that what is said in the workshop remains in the workshop – and children are usually very clear, when asked by other adults what happened in a particular workshop, that it isn't to be repeated outside. This shows the need to trust children to be able to keep good secrets – as with most things, children live up or down to our expectations. The higher the expectations, the better – within reason.

One person speaking at a time

Fig. 2.11: One person speaking at a time

If children have experience of doing circle time, then this ground rule will already have become a habit. Passing a 'talking-stick' or a cuddly toy and ensuring that you only speak when you have it, reinforces the 'one person speaking at a time' rule. As with all these rules, the integrity of the process by which everybody agrees to it is the measure of the degree of everyone's ownership of it, of everyone's willingness to take full responsibility for it, and for implementing it. If there really has been a consensus in agreeing to the rules, then it is in everybody's interests that they are kept, and everybody's responsibility to do so. One of the strengths of the circle in reinforcing rights and responsibilities is that it is up to everybody – not just the teacher – to ensure that the rules are fair and are adhered to.

The 'Quiet Please' sign

Fig. 2.12

Fig. 2.13

Education for Mutual Understanding started life as a cross-community contact scheme – to encourage social interaction between children from different denominations. As one teacher wryly commented, observing a workshop in Strabane involving children from the Primary 7 classes of three schools, 'Social interaction is noisy!' The 'Quiet Please' sign[7] came into its own in that kind of environment, obviating the need for facilitators or teachers having to shout.

Likewise in peer mediation training workshops, the simple expedient of showing a 'lollipop' sign and encouraging the children to let each other know it is being displayed can achieve a quick and quiet response at the end of the busiest activity. It can also be used as a game: the children are encouraged to make as much noise as possible, the 'lollipop' is turned round to display the 'Quiet Please' sign so as to hush them, and then the reverse side is exhibited, which says 'Thank you'.

The ground rules need to be constantly reinforced, and reviewed. An effective way of doing this is to start each workshop by asking the children to try and remember them, and to state the reasons for having them. Each week they can be asked how they are doing as far as keeping them is concerned, and which are the most difficult to keep. If some are proving difficult for everybody, then special attention can be given to them, and indeed a game can be designed for reinforcing them.

For example, if 'no put-downs' is proving to be a struggle, it can be worth referring to a commonly used put-down (so that no single individual is 'shamed') – in Northern Ireland the use of a traveller's family surname, for example – and to explain *why* it is a put-down. It may be worth while using part of a workshop to explore this issue, and motivate children to reflect on their experience of put-downs. Although most mediation training programmes have a timetabled structure, it is usually more effective to address conflicts as they arise. Several exercises have been devised to deal with issues of put-downs in an easy way, such as 'Dummy Bump'[8] and 'IALAC: I am lovable and capable'.[9]

Since these ground rules reinforce the essential rules of circle time (one person speaking at a time, 'you may pass', and not criticising people by name), they demonstrate how valuable it is to have circle time established throughout the school prior to peer mediation training.

After being identified and discussed, the workshop ground rules can be displayed on the wall during the workshop. Teachers and children have been known to try to integrate them into the classroom. The practice of continually reviewing the ground rules leads to them becoming second nature, while the children's behaviour illustrates that they are being consistently kept. As the rules become redundant they are amended or improved – unlike some school rules that are so archaic that nobody remembers the rationale for them in the first place. (One school had an open quadrangle and a school rule that nobody was allowed to walk straight across it, you had to go around it – nobody could remember why.)

Rules, along with collective and individual responsibility, are part of citizenship. Ed Sellman of West Midlands Quaker Peace Education Project, maintains that 'citizenship involves acknowledging that children are already citizens, [and] have a contribution to make to society, which will increase with age',[10] then the process of questioning, agreeing to, abiding by and reviewing ground rules such as these can make a major contribution towards developing citizenship.

Introducing the mediation process

If mediation is well established in a school, then children will be aware of it because older brothers and sisters will have been through it, and indeed they themselves may have been 'mediated' or know of a friend or classmate who has. Sometimes children's grasp of the concept is a little shaky: one Primary 5 child asked a Primary 7 child, 'Are you a medion?'[11]

The word 'mediation' is regularly in the news, often inaccurately applied to an arbitrator (who decides the outcome of a process) or to a negotiator (who acts on behalf of disputants). There is a need to simplify the idea of mediation to make it accessible to children. Notwithstanding the confusion caused by being unable to distinguish between the roles just given above, a useful description is 'someone who is in the middle' or 'someone who helps people have a difficult conversation' – someone who tries to hear both sides.

Story-writing

Between Workshops 1 and 2 comes story-writing time. The use of fables, nursery rhymes and fairy-tales has proved invaluable in this regard. Usually such stories are based on stereotypes – 'the Wicked Witch', 'the Ugly Duckling', 'the Beauty and the Beast'. Typically, the perspective of the 'baddy' is ignored – the wolf in 'Red Riding Hood', Goldilocks, the wolf in 'The Three Little Pigs', and so on. Typically also, these tales rely on only one side of the story, and because we have heard them so often, that side is assumed to be right. (The fact that wolves don't eat little children is left out of the equation.) One of the first attempts to rectify this situation was the rewriting of the story of Little Red Riding Hood from the maligned wolf's point of view.[12] Tom Leimdorfer,[13] a co-founder of the European Network for Conflict Resolution in Education (ENCORE), has produced a book of such stories, *Once Upon a Conflict: A Fairytale Manual of Conflict Resolution for All Ages*, from which we have adapted the story of the Ugly Duckling, scripted for a mediation. The format usually consists of a teacher and one of the facilitators being either the Ugly Duckling or the Pretty Duckling, and another facilitator and a child being the mediators. There is usually no shortage of volunteers for the latter role, and the child mediator is chosen from them in consultation with the teacher.

The sight of their teacher playing the role of a duckling is guaranteed to maintain the interest of the class, particularly if this is done in costume! Since a subsequent part of the workshop involves them discussing this role-play, their concentration during the course of the mediation is vital.

Fig. 2.14: Dressing up as Ducklings

The mediation is conducted in front of the whole class, with the script encouraging the two ducklings to admit any faults they have as the mediation unfolds, and to include 'some "anger", some "hurt feelings" and a little "interrupting", "name-calling" and "blaming" so that the mediators have an opportunity to enforce their rules'.[14] The role-play provides the first opportunity for the children to observe the feedback process. They see that when the ducklings are telling their stories, the mediators have to listen and then summarise – not pass judgement or propose solutions. This feedback skill is one of the most difficult for children (and adults) to put into practice.

Afterwards the class is split up into small groups and the children have an opportunity to discuss the role-play, and respond to questions about whether the ducklings obeyed the rules and whether the group took sides. On this latter point the children invariably admit that they found it difficult not to take sides, and also recognise that it is important for the mediators not to take sides.

The discussion is followed by a listening activity, in pairs, which demonstrates the difference between being talked at, being ignored and being listened to. This activity helps to strengthen the importance of communication and begins the process of buttressing children's listening skills.

The format for Workshop 1 sets the trend. A combination of large-group, small-group and pairs work secures a variety of experience, and allows children who feel somewhat intimidated when speaking in a large group to build up their confidence by talking to one other person, or just a few people.

Workshop 1 thus focuses on the ground rules, and introduces the basics of peer mediation through the story of the Ugly Duckling. The learning from the workshop is sustained afterwards when the teacher reviews the programme with the class and asks them what they learned from each activity. This, coupled with an evaluation form that every child is expected to complete, ensures that the subsequent workshops are pitched at the right level for the class, and take on board specific areas – for example, ground rules – that need attention.

Workshop 2: using children's own conflict stories

Having started with a fairy-story, the setting of the mediation needs to become rooted in the experience of the children's own daily lives. They are asked to write the story of a conflict they have direct experience of, before Workshop 2. These stories have often formed the basis of demonstration role-plays for interested adults; for example, concerning games that have been a cause of playground conflict – such as 'Pogs'* in 1996 and 'Pokemon'** in 2000.

---

*'Pogs was a game involving circular discs that a child flipped, and according to which side they landed on their owner won or lost.
**The Pokemon cards would have different values and would be swapped in the playground. Since some cards were rarer than others, they would be worth more than one 'ordinary' card. This led to conflict when the children got home, because their parents, who had bought the cards for their son or daughter, would question why they had fewer cards than when they went to school.

There is a tendency for adults to be dismissive of children's conflicts, at least until they reach a dimension that can be identified as being of major concern, such as bullying. But it is a common phenomenon, after the lunch break in the average primary school, for a teacher to be faced with a number of children vying for his or her attention to deal with the results of conflict in the playground. Such conflicts invariably have an emotional content – and often a physical one – and whatever the combination, the net outcome is that very little learning can be achieved in the lesson until the wronged individual(s) has at least been calmed down.

Asking children to identify and write about the conflicts that are important to them acknowledges the need to take such incidents seriously and to deal with the children's agenda, rather than just superimposing our own.

For adults, too, a relatively small issue can have huge repercussions (the top left off the toothpaste, again; the shirt in the laundry basket that still has its buttons done up; the car being left low on petrol when your partner has a long trip the next morning – all these little details can become the 'last straw'). It is worth remembering that, just as adults sometimes feel that children's playground conflicts are trivial, children also wonder 'what the fuss is about' when adults get upset with each other, and indeed with the children themselves, apparently out of all proportion to the question in hand. One person's mountain is another person's molehill – such is the nature of conflict.

If conflicts are ignored, or not handled properly, they tend to escalate. Even the process of writing down a conflict in preparation for a workshop can help to resolve it, since the instructions will include: 'Your story will have two characters (like the Ugly Duckling and the Pretty Duckling). Tell the story from each side.'[15]

The main focus of Workshop 2, then, is on the children's own conflicts. The specific conflict and the children to play the two disputants are preselected from the stories the children have written between the workshops. Some preparation is needed in advance of the workshop to rehearse the conflict. Then, during the workshop the two children role-play the conflict, and at an appropriate point the role-play is frozen. The full group is now involved in a discussion and responds to questions about what the issues were and what the feelings of each party were – and 'Whose side were you on?' This is a useful learning process for the class, and for the two disputants.

The disputants are now offered mediation, which is carried out by two children who take the mediation through the first stages – hearing both sides' stories, feeding back and then asking each side how he or she is feeling. The mediation is then stopped, and the class breaks up into small groups. A discussion ensues, encouraging group members to reflect on the conflict and on the mediation, and to identify what people were feeling, what the argument was really about; things that the two parties agree on, even if they don't realise it; and finally to think of 'four different ways that the conflict might get sorted out'.[16] The outcomes of the small groups' discussions are fed back by the children to the large group, when they have all reassembled.

Even at this stage – it is, after all, only the second workshop – a process and a structure are beginning to evolve that address conflict in a constructive way. One of the concerns that adults have about children doing peer mediation is that it is placing an adult burden on their shoulders. But as long as children have the necessary skills, clear guidelines about what is and isn't mediable, and the support and encouragement of a teacher, the question of burden doesn't arise. A more relevant question, in terms of burden, is the effects of unresolved conflict that spirals into bullying, and the effects of such situations not just on the disputants but on the class and on the school itself. It is our experience at EMUpsp, having talked to peer mediators, that children get a tremendous sense of satisfaction, of a job well done, from being involved in a successful mediation. Far from being a debilitating or stressful role, being a peer mediator can be both energising and empowering – but to achieve this, the training and service have to be undertaken in a supportive environment.

In addition to the role-play of the conflict and of the mediation, the workshop includes a number of co-operation games.

Workshop 3: everybody having a go

Having worked through just one example of a conflict in the previous workshop, now each of the small groups has the opportunity of being involved in the mediation of a conflict from the start to the identification of feelings. Rather than the conflict being role-played, all the children in each small group are invited to read out their stories, and one is picked to be mediated. This provides the opportunity for an individual child to observe how others might play his or her role, and how the other disputant might react. (The child whose conflict it is doesn't participate in the role-play.) In each small group there are four active participants – the two disputants and the two mediators – and the rest have a 'check it out' sheet which they use to assess how the mediators do. During this workshop children who are regularly in conflict sometimes volunteer to be a mediator, and relish the change in role and perception that they thereby gain (and that others gain of them).

The emphasis in the games during this workshop is on affirmation, with the children being encouraged to think of a positive word to describe a quality that 'my friend has', and also a couple of co-operation games are played.

When the children revert from the small groups to the large group, they listen to the fictional story of Michael and Laura.[17] Michael is running along the school corridor and bumps into Laura, knocking her books and artwork from her grasp. The ensuing row and its outcome form the story of a conflict. The purpose of this is for the children to begin to identify feelings, and to identify problems. Afterwards they are invited to list the feelings of the two disputants, and to indicate the problems that each of them has. In doing so the children also learn how to separate feelings from issues.

Each workshop ends with a *closing circle* – in this workshop the closing has as a theme 'something I have learned'. It is helpful to start with a child who is able to articulate an answer to this question, as he or she will act as a model for others. Sometimes it is necessary for children to share their answer with their neighbour, before they find the confidence to address the circle.

Workshop 4: generating solutions

This workshop represents the halfway mark of the training, and so there is a review of (1) what has been learned so far with reference to mediation, and (2) the ground rules. Also, for the first time the mediation moves beyond the problem-identifying stage, and the children use a couple of problem-*solving* approaches. One of these approaches is 'brainstorming' (see p. 25) and, as a practice exercise, the class is asked to brainstorm the uses of a coat-hanger. The facilitator might say, 'Brainstorming means allowing your brain to work quickly, without worrying too much about what the ideas sound like. I wonder how many ideas our class can come up with in three minutes.'[18]

To inject a bit of energy into this we might sometimes quote a spurious world record of 40 different uses for a coat-hanger having been achieved in one of the other local schools. 'It doesn't matter if your ideas sound crazy. Don't worry that someone will say your ideas are stupid – remember our ground rules. Don't think too much about an idea, just say it.'[19] This inspires children to think beyond the single use – to hang coats on. And after a short time there is no need for persuasion; once they realise they aren't going to be made fun of if they come up with ludicrous solutions, they happily make weird and wonderful suggestions. For example: a fishing hook, earrings, to open a car door with when you've lost the key, a mobile, a TV aerial, a coat hook, a car radio aerial, a picture frame, a baton, a nose-pick, a musical triangle, a weapon, a hanging basket, a Christmas decoration.

The list goes on, and the net result is that one answer inspires another, and rather than its originator being penalised or mocked for coming up with a 'silly suggestion', each idea is treated equally, without adverse comment. By releasing the children from the rigour of finding 'one right answer', more possibilities than could be imagined by one person evolve. The relevance to a conflict situation where often the parties are unable to see even one way out is stressed – the more ideas the disputants have about solutions, the better. This process can generate a range of alternative solutions when previously only one, or none at all, could be discerned. The brainstorming process can help quiet children to share an idea; conversely, an extrovert child who says something outlandish (such as 'nose-pick') has her contribution written up without comment while the next one is quickly moved on to.

The main part of this workshop programme is a role-play about a school quiz, with one person being held responsible by the rest of the team for giving the wrong answer and letting the side down. The children who will be involved in the role-play, including the mediators, are chosen beforehand and the two disputants are given scripts. After the role-play the children remain in the large group and brainstorm a list of problems that the two disputants have mentioned.

The second part of the brainstorming process is then put into action – the children who role-play the disputants go through the list of problems that the class have come up with, and tick for themselves the ones they identify with. Again it is stressed that all the answers are valid, but that it is up to the disputants to decide which are relevant to them.

The adult facilitators from each small group make a copy of the issues and take them back with them to their own small groups. Sometimes children confuse listing the problems with solving them. For example, instead of the problem being identified as 'Paul's football keeps getting taken', it is listed as a solution – 'Sam should give Paul his football back.' There is thus a tendency to move straight from the stories to the solutions, without identifying the problems.

Having spent the first half of the workshop working on the problems, the small groups explore three ways of responding to them. *Talking separately* provides a space for the disputants to be able to give the mediators information that they would rather the other disputant didn't hear, initially at least. Talking separately also provides an opportunity for a disputant to acknowledge his or her role in the conflict, by admitting to having called the other child names, for example. Furthermore, talking separately creates an opening for solutions to start to be suggested.

Brainstorming helps to generate a variety of solutions; when the list of possibles has been exhausted, the two disputants are invited to say which solutions are out of the question, which they particularly like, and which are conditional on something else happening. The facilitator crosses out any which either disputant thinks are out of the question (while reassuring the class that their solutions, even though not appropriate today, have played a vital role in helping to create an environment in which other solutions have been forthcoming). Any solutions that both participants particularly like are ringed, and the others are left.

Throughout the process it is the disputants who have the final say in what makes a good solution, and the facilitator's or mediator's role is not to act as judge, but to help them come to a solution.

When the brainstorming is complete, and the relative merits of the solutions processed, the next stage of problem-solving, *give and take*, can get under way. At this point the list of problems is revisited, and bearing in mind the solutions that have now been identified, the disputants are invited to say what they might be prepared to do in exchange for some specified action by the other party. The 'quid pro quo' nature of this exercise prevents a loss of face, as each move by one party is matched by a move by the other.

Each of these three processes – talking separately, brainstorming, and give and take – requires skills that need to be reinforced. They illustrate, as with other stages in the mediation process, that distinct life skills are embodied in the training – sometimes we adults limit the capabilities of children by our low expectations, by assuming either that mediation doesn't require much of children, or that it requires too much of them!

There is a difficulty, though, in reinforcing these three processes: 'The first part of the mediation process is understood well (it's repeated in every workshop, which is great). However, brainstorming, give and take, and the agreement are not as fully communicated through the workshops.'[20] In developing the training programme we had to recognise that the later in the workshop sequence a particular skill was introduced, the less time there was remaining for the children to practise it. It was important to simplify the problem-solving skills of brainstorming and give and take, and allow plenty of time for the children to integrate them into their practice. The fact that children do require specific skills to be mediators obviously influences the progression of the training programme; equally, it underlines the need for continuing support and supervision when they are delivering a peer mediation service. With such guidance, children do adapt these approaches and make them their own.

Between Workshop 4 and Workshop 5 there is a review of Workshop 4 by the children, which helps to inform their evaluation of it. To standard questions such as 'What did you enjoy most in the workshop?' and 'What did you least enjoy in the workshop?' is added a mini-brainstorm (for instance, 'Give four uses for a waste paper bin'). Then the adult asks whether the respondents would use mediation if they were in a conflict; and how they think brainstorming, talking separately and give and take might help people to resolve their conflicts. For the adults, the team meeting before each workshop enables them to decide who will lead each exercise, and to query whether any activities need to be rehearsed.

Workshop 5: thoughts on a peer mediation service in our school

Each workshop begins with a round of labels, and in previous workshops each child will have written on his or her label:

- My favourite food [Workshop 1]
- Something I like about my school [Workshop 2]
- A quality my friend has [Workshop 3]
- A quality I have that has the same initial as my first name [Workshop 4]

Workshop 5 begins with each child writing, for instance, a sentence on 'Where in the world I would like to be with and with whom'. This generates contrasting responses. One Primary 7 boy in Workshop 5 started the ball rolling with '*Baywatch* with Pamela Anderson', and the theme was repeated by others. But usually this exercise generates responses concerning holiday places visited with members of the family or friends.

There is a progression even in the activities that seem to be repetitive. This workshop includes a discussion about the ground rules. The children might be asked for examples of ground rules that:

- help us play
- keep us friends
- help us learn
- would help the canteen to be a happier place.

Before the mediation is role-played, the two disputants act out a scripted conflict. The mediation role-play is unscripted, to give it more spontaneity. This is done in front of the large group up to, but not including, the *agreement* stage. The children then split into small groups and continue the same role-play (with four children in each group now playing the roles) in an attempt to bring it to a successful conclusion. The role-play in the small groups simply picks up from the point where the issues or problems are identified. The small groups then take the process forward through talking separately, brainstorming and give and take, until an agreement is reached, which is then signed by both parties and the mediators.

At this point in the training programme the children have gained a clear picture of the peer mediation process, and some idea of what's involved in terms of time and commitment. Between each workshop the relevance of the process is reinforced in the classroom, and on other school occasions.

With little prompting, the children will have started to visualise what peer mediation might look like in their school. The facilitators lead a discussion in the small groups. Questions about the advantages all those involved see in having mediation in their school, problems the mediators might have to deal with and the kind of difficulties they might expect to meet in doing their work, can begin to be addressed. The questions raised by the small-group members will be addressed in workshop 6.

It is important that the children begin to visualise the existence of the peer mediation programme in their school – of course, others will be making the decisions about whether it happens, but the children are well placed to raise the pros and cons of having it at all. They are well aware of the likely everyday conflicts and where they happen; and they always come up with thoughtful and imaginative ways of running a peer mediation service. The role of the supportive teacher in eliciting this information and helping to put it into practice is crucial.

Workshop 6: real mediation – a live conflict!

This workshop is the last in the series before the full-day workshop, which is better held at a venue outside the school. The class teacher and the other school adults are spurred on to discover whether an existing conflict can provide the basis for a mediation, to be used in this workshop. This – it goes without saying – gives an edge to the mediation process, and certainly does away with the need for a script. It also requires considerable confidence on the part of the disputants and the mediators.

Case study
At one school, a lunchtime supervisor had participated in all the previous five workshops. The class teacher was aware of an ongoing conflict between her and one of the children in his class. It had come to a head with a particular incident early in Workshop 6 week, when the boy had been rude to the supervisor, who had complained about the boy's behaviour to the class teacher. The teacher approached the lunchtime supervisor and asked if she would be willing to have the conflict mediated – after some thought she agreed, so the teacher then approached the boy, who also agreed.

On the day of the workshop the two disputants took part in the mediation, with an adult and a child acting as mediators. It was unambiguous from the outset that both parties were upset and that it was a very real conflict. Both were able to give their side of the story, and the mediators duly fed a summary back to them. Their feelings were elicited and the issues identified.

At that point the two disputants were asked if they would like to talk separately. The supervisor left while the lad remained. When prompted, he admitted (for the first time) to the mediators that he had been rude to her. When she came back into the room, he apologised to her. From her response it was noticeable that she was impressed by this gesture. It seemed to mark a turning-point, for as they continued with the mediation, the solutions became more visible and led to a give and take and an agreement. The teacher monitored the situation afterwards: the relationship between the lunchtime supervisor and the boy became more positive, and they were often seen talking together good-humouredly.

The supervisor later remarked that one of the factors that had made her decide to take part in the mediation was that she had been involved in the training programme with the class and she trusted them.

On that particular occasion the children who observed the mediators, as well as the disputants and the mediators themselves, were able to perceive that something did change. The advantage of having a real conflict to deal with – as long as it is handled sensitively – is that it is easier to visualise what mediation looks like in practice. Another example of a successful real mediation during the Workshop 6 was of a real and ongoing conflict between two boys who had been friends. Heart felt emotions and a lot of hurt were expressed and dealt with during the mediation, and the young mediators performed outstandingly well.[21]

It is the last day for the small-group format that has been in use since the first workshop. As explained earlier, the children in each small group will have been picked so as to divide up the friendship groups in the class, and so initially they might not know each other that well. By the time Workshop 6 comes around, they have worked together a great deal and built up a team spirit. The last activity of the small group is 'affirmation hands',[22] where each person draws around her hand on a sheet of paper, writes on it a quality she has, then other members of the group write other qualities on her hand.

The final activity in the large group is the 'chair game', in which people sit in a circle with one more chair than there are people. If the chair on your right is empty, you have to ask someone to fill it. The only way this can happen is by your expressing something genuinely appreciative about that person.

Workshop 7: the final day of training

When the first training of primary school peer mediators was undertaken in 1992–4, the whole Primary 7 class from two primary schools conducted the first six workshops separately, and then children were chosen from both classes to participate in the final day together. The mediators were chosen before the final day's training. When this procedure was evaluated, it was agreed that it made more sense for the whole class to undergo the whole training, even if at the end of the day not everybody was ready to become a mediator. This conclusion was reinforced subsequently by a growing awareness of the value of the training, irrespective of whether a service was later established.

The last day's training is designed to give the children both a sense of occasion and a sense of achievement. Like Workshop 6, it takes place away from the school – leisure centres and conference centres make suitable venues. Having this extended time together on the last day ensures that every child has the opportunity of playing a role in a full mediation.

With the focus on the establishment of a peer mediation service, in small groups the children are encouraged to brainstorm potential pitfalls and challenges under the heading of 'What if?s' – as in 'What if my best friend is in a conflict and I am one of the mediators?' 'What if?s' that have come up in the past include:

- What would you do if the children wanted to mediate their problems but the adults wanted to do the mediating?
- How would you decide when *not* to mediate, or to stop a mediation?

- What would you do if the parties were behaving awkwardly and not keeping the rules?
- What would you do if not many people were coming for mediation?
- What would you do if the same people were always needing mediation?
- What would you do if one or both parties weren't happy at first to use mediation?
- What would you do if it became difficult to come to an agreed solution?
- What would you do if there was an agreement but afterwards it was broken?[23]

After eliciting 'what if?s' *and* getting the children to come up with effective responses, a list can be drawn up that will be of value to the school in terms of the necessary planning and management that a peer mediation service will require. It is particularly valuable if lunchtime supervisors can be involved in the whole training programme with the children, or at least be present on the final day's training.

How not to mediate
The programme has its light-hearted moments, such as when two adults role-play a mediation and keep getting it wrong – by taking sides, say, or by making judgements when feeding back. The children are invited to interrupt the process when the adults make a mistake.

The role-play scenario used to demonstrate how not to mediate concerns neighbours who are in conflict over the behaviour of the dog that belongs to one of them. (This role-play sets the scene for a role-play involving the neighbours' respective children later in the day.) There is much hilarity during the role-play as the adults make glaring mistakes – much to the delight of the children. The exercise also illustrates how much the children have learned.

Invariably the 'how not to mediate' role-play collapses under the strain of inadequate mediating, and it is necessary to recap each side's story.

Now divided into their small groups, the children list the problems. One person is designated the writer – as mentioned earlier, this is a key role in real mediations as well. Although two children are mediating, often a third child is needed to record on a flipchart or large sheet of paper the problems of each disputant, then later the results of the brainstorm, the give and take and the agreement, if any, that is reached. It is a task that requires skill and that often suits a quieter child – although in a workshop setting the scribe is often also the reporter and has to convey the small group's findings to the large group.

Brainstorming and bargaining, again in the small groups, follow the process through to agreement.

The mediation

The children will have been sorted into groups of five or six individuals prior to the full-day workshop, the disputants will have been given the scenario for the role-play, and the mediators and the writers will have been coached in their respective roles. The next part of the programme of the full-day workshop is especially significant. For a full 30 minutes, each of the small groups role-play a mediation from start to finish, from introduction to agreement, with no adult intervention.

If ever adults doubt the capability or the sense of responsibility of the children, this exercise manages to convince the most doubting onlooker of their commitment and stamina; each small group becomes fully engaged in the task. (If the class doesn't divide easily into groups of five or six, any extra children can be given the role of observers and handed a 'check it out' list that they can use for assessing the mediators. It is difficult for the adults to stand back and allow it all to happen, but their detachment pays off, although they can still be on hand to give advice if needed.

After half an hour the circle is re-formed, and each mediation group is invited to tell the rest about their agreement, if any. The conclusion of the long day is the closing circle, when comments can be made, say, about 'something I noticed that someone else did well', and questions asked about what the children particularly enjoyed during the workshop. At the end of such a workshop, that had called for concentration, listening, writing and oral skills, one lad said that what he particularly enjoyed was 'not having to do any work'. He had been so engrossed in the day's activities that he simply hadn't experienced what he was doing as work.

This chapter has taken you through a particular training programme. It was designed for Northern Ireland primary schools, but, as you may have noticed, its content is not specific to the conflictual situation of Northern Ireland. Equally, this training programme does not differ radically from others. What I am trying to demonstrate here is that the process of mediation requires specific discrete skills that can be taught. One of the things about the training process is that it 'clicks' at different times for different children. Although the mediation process can be broken down into distinct stages – the introduction, the storytelling, the feedback, the checking of feelings, the talking separately and so on, it takes a while for children to get the whole picture, as each stage is explored and practised. Indeed, it may only be in the last-day workshop (or subsequently) that the whole jigsaw falls into place. This may give rise to some anxiety: 'At one stage I expressed the concern that the children weren't "getting it", that the skills were coming at them from all directions and they weren't understanding them. However, from the reaction of the teachers and the subsequent role-plays it was clear that they did get it.'[24]

Once children feel comfortable with the process they stop having to rely on the 'menu' – the mediation process (see Chapter 1) – each stage described on red cards, which each mediator is expected to go through. In one instance two mediators, having become exasperated with the two disputants who seemed to be hell-bent on breaking all the rules of mediation, excused themselves from the room, saying they would be back in ten minutes and asking the disputants to sort out the problem for themselves. This unusual tactic worked – the disputants realised that they would do better to channel their energies constructively.

The EMU-Promoting School Project peer mediation training programme, with its emphasis on agreed ground rules, its 'circle time' format, and its emphasis on the idea that the disputants are responsible for signing up (or not) to an agreement, relies on values that might not be evident elsewhere in the school. Other programmes such, as 'Let's Mediate',[25] also take on board this issue, by stressing the need to build an environment of positive relationships, trust, mutual respect, tolerance, support, co-operation and open communication, and a readiness to work through problems. 'Let's Mediate' concentrates on progressing through valuable exercises that reinforce these skills and values, before peer mediation training is embarked on. The authors conclude: 'If a class has worked through the skills and some of the activities in this book, then peer mediation will be the icing on the cake, and will provide genuine practice of the skills they will have acquired.'[26] Likewise, Bristol Mediation's manual *Peer Mediation Scheme*[27] is divided into two parts, the first developing the necessary skills and the second concentrating on the process of mediation. Both *Let's Mediate* and *Peer Mediation Scheme* reiterate the importance of children and teachers being conversant with circle time.

Whilst it is possible to train children successfully in isolation, as it were, from the curriculum, hidden or otherwise, of the school, it is vital that the values of the training programme are not challenged by those of the school. What this means in practice will be explored in future chapters.

3. Can Children Mediate Conflicts? Yes!

'If [peer mediation] works in the playground, there's no reason why adults can't learn a lesson from what, after all, isn't just child's play.' (Mary Robinson)

'Peace education involves connecting the interpersonal to the cross-cultural and international, in order to develop transferable (usable) understandings regarding the management of conflict.' (Karen Bickmore)[1]

I start this chapter with the selection of peer mediators and an account of the experience of the delivery of peer mediation services. I shall show that the selection process in itself can provide an opportunity to empower young people, and yet it can also reinforce existing divisions within the culture of the school rather than bridge them. I do acknowledge the need to include in the training programme people with a history of conflict, even to the extent of training bullies as mediators. Extracting findings from the EMU-Promoting School Project's own research, I will illustrate that a peer mediation service, whilst a bonus, is not essential as a measure of an EMU programme's success. I also put the view that training without practice is of limited value.

I shall also demonstrate that the skills children learn in the process of peer mediation training are not just relevant to the playground, but relevant throughout their lives. I shall describe presentations given by groups of peer mediators, including role-plays of mediations and their answers to questions about their experiences; and report on the almost universal response of the adults present, amazed by these children's confidence and competence, and connection made by adults and children alike between the peer mediators' skills and those needed by the politicians involved in the Northern Ireland peace process.

Children as mediators

Professor Karen Bickmore,[2] whose research was mentioned in Chapter 1, points out that most North American schools use a 'cadre approach' to peer mediation training. What this means is that a small group of children is chosen for peer mediation training. In the UK, however, at primary school level at least, training a whole class tends to be the norm. In Northern Ireland we started out by training whole classes for six weeks, and then children were selected to go forward for further training. This caused a great deal of concern at the time. Judith Ferrara, in her book *Peer Mediation: Finding a Way to Care*, states, 'Any selection process affects *and rejects* students.'[3] The Project team was searching for ways of being inclusive rather than exclusive:

> Team members ... would have preferred that all trainees be formally recognised as mediators and that all those who wished to function as such be enabled to do so, [in the hope that] by giving everyone a chance to practise, those children with particular ability as mediators would emerge in the process, and that children with conflicts to resolve would choose these.[4]

Since that time, in each primary class the Project worked with, all the children undertook the full training. The practice evolved of all children being given a certificate (denoting that they had completed the training course) at a special assembly held when the peer mediation service was launched. The certificates were distributed to pupils irrespective of whether or not they subsequently became mediators.

Northern Irish primary schools usually have a one- or two-class intake each year. As one of the two schools involved in the pilot project had two Primary 7 classes, there was also concern that the other Primary 7 class would feel left out, both of the excitement of the training sessions and, subsequently, of the selection and the delivery of the peer mediation service. As a result, future engagements with schools involved the whole year being trained.

In the USA, even at elementary school level, the tendency is for the selection to take place before training. It is interesting to note some of the different approaches to selection, in itself arguably the most difficult part of the whole process of setting up a programme.[5] James Gihooley and Nannette S. Scheuch have written a step-by-step guide to introducing peer mediation, based on their experience in the USA. On the one hand they maintain that 'a core group of faculty, counsellors and staff who know the students well are best suited to make the selection of those to be trained as mediators'.[6] On the other, Ferrara, in her book *Peer Mediation: Finding a Way to Care*,[7] agonises over the most effective way of selecting, being aware of the need for the process of selection to be as empowering for young people as the rest of the peer mediation programme. She comes up with a five-part selection process involving *student nominations; teacher nominations; interviews with volunteers; a selection meeting (involving staff) and finally a check-list.*

The latter is a means of creating 'a group that is representative of the school's ethnic, gender, and age mix'.[8] Needless to say, the whole process is lengthy, but one advantage is that it does engage the different constituencies in the school community who deserve to be consulted. J. M. Ferrara also advocates a sensitive and constructive way of handling the selection process that will ensure that students don't feel rejected. Richard Cohen, who also talks about the selection of trainees, cites five main criteria – diversity; personal skills and abilities; commitment; grade level and availability. He makes the point that 'excellent mediators can spring from unlikely places so that you should be open-minded in this regard'.[9] All the same, he also advocates caution in the first year of any programme.

The benefits of selection after training
There are four major advantages in a whole-class approach to training, rather than a cadre approach:

1. It is inclusive. It demonstrates that these skills are for everybody. Hilary Cremin (née Stacey), who is a leading exponent of peer mediation in the UK, in her doctorate research found: 'Pupils with emotional and behavioural difficulties appeared to gain a great deal from this approach, with all pupils benefiting from a general reduction in disaffection and aggressive behaviour.'[10] There is evidence that it transforms relationships within the class, and between the class and its teacher.

2. In the course of training, children demonstrate new skills and new aspects of their personality Feedback from parents and teachers indicates that children grow in confidence and competence during the training. If selection takes place before the training, these factors may not be evident.

3. Within the research literature there is an awareness that troublemakers can become problem-solvers. The 'poacher turned gamekeeper' syndrome is a common phenomenon. The relish with which youngsters known for their ability to start conflicts get into the mind set of a mediator in a role-play, is a wonder to behold. Later in this chapter the qualities of mediator are explored, and one of these is 'clout', or street-credibility, along with leadership. The potential for the transformation of previously negative role models is a universal outcome of peer mediation. Again, these positive qualities often only emerge during the training process.

4. Because of the experiential nature of the training, it is through practice that the children become aware of the skills and qualities needed in being a mediator. They are then in a position to gauge whether they and their classmates have such qualities. They can be effective consultants in the selection process.

Later in this book we shall explore the question, 'For whose benefit is peer mediation?' Is it for the benefit of the school in terms of better-behaved children, or is it about empowering children, or is it both? Peer mediation provides an excellent opportunity to counter the tendency to choose the children who get chosen for everything. Encouraging children to volunteer themselves and nominate each other is a good strategy. However, our findings in the pilot project were that children's choices of peers tended to reinforce the teacher's choice. To rectify this, teachers would deliberately choose some children who might be considered confrontational:

> Somewhat paradoxically, the decision by the teacher at the Model [primary school] *not* to intervene [in the selection process] produced a result which indicated that the children themselves operated from the assumption that academic ability and suitability of character were important criteria for selection.

> 'This year the children elected their own – and they voted for all the "nicest" and "best" children. And, yes, they were the children who exhibited the best mediation qualities, but it did have a divisive effect.' (Hartop, Brendan, 1994).

> At Oakgrove, where half of the mediators were selected by their peers and the other half by the principal and vice-principal: 'We did put some in who were sort of confrontational children, and I am glad we did. I think it has really done them a lot of good' (Laverty).[11]

A good question to ask when it comes to the selection of children is 'Who will benefit most from *being* a mediator?' There is a constant need to renew the commitment to a child-centred approach and, if necessary, to think afresh in terms of structures so that it remains that way.

Hall reports advice against choosing children who see themselves as law enforcers – which is one reason why the role of peer mediator is separate from that of prefect. Hall talks of one peer mediation scheme where the mediators take a proactive role 'patrolling the playground', looking for fights.

What qualities are needed?

'An effective mediator is someone who feels good about himself or herself and likes to help others.'[12] One learns a lot about school values from the descriptions of effective mediators. Gihooley and Scheuch, for example, report: 'An effective mediator cares about his or her school and wants to make it a more peaceful and orderly place . . . is a conscientious student who keeps up to date with his or her work. It is not a requirement to be an honours student.'[13] They go on to talk about the ability to keep confidences and being willing to participate in training. Ferrara also stresses that academic standing has not been a criterion for selection, and Robin Hall, who has written an excellent review of the literature, concurs by saying there is a consensus 'not to pick the intellectually best and brightest'[14] but to select a cross-sectional representation of the student body.

The qualities of peer mediators include 'a willingness to learn, good verbal skills, and the respect of peers . . . a confident and strong character, a good understanding of the process, the ability to write agreements clearly and to be directive, responsible and caring.'[15] These qualities can, arguably, be identified as easily by children as by adults.

How many mediators?

One of the main reasons why it is not possible to select everybody who wants to be a mediator is that often there isn't enough work to go round. Different researchers have suggested various ratios, such as one mediator for every 30 students. In their book *Let's Mediate* Hilary Stacey and Patricia Robinson suggest that an ideal team of mediators should consist of 12–16 pupils.[16]

Setting up the peer mediation service

This requires a significant amount of planning and thought, as the logistics have to be tailored to fit the individual school. As with the initiating of the overall programme, time invested at this stage pays dividends in the future.

Stacey and Robinson[17] encourage the involvement of the peer mediators in the design of the service, after – all, it is their programme. They also stress the need for team-building. Later in this chapter the outcomes of four peer mediation services will be analysed.

Location and timing

In our pilot project one school had made available a room where a teacher (on the other side of a glass door) was always accessible. The other school used part of the play-ground, and so the mediators had a higher public profile. One school preferred playground mediations, at lunch and break, with opportunities to continue into class time. The other school slotted the mediations in first thing in the morning. Again, the location and timing are things that each school can decide on, to suit its own needs.

The mediator's profile

In 1988 when peer mediation was first being discussed in Northern Ireland, teachers had the opportunity of watching a video of a US peer mediation service. Commenting on the fact that the mediators were identified by baseball caps, one teacher said that it wouldn't work here because it was 'too American'. Six years later in Northern Ireland, when several teachers were discussing how best to distinguish the peer mediators, one of them suggested baseball caps, and the idea was immediately taken up. The point of the story is that it is important to achieve a balance between being prescriptive and being elicitive, even if the final answer is the same.

Some schools have photos of all the peer mediators dis-played in the entrance hall, with a sign indicating who is on duty on a particular day.

Referring for mediation

There are a variety of ways in which disputants are referred for mediation. It has to be made clear that if either of the parties in the dispute doesn't want mediation, it can't go ahead, because it is a voluntary process. The teacher responsible for co-ordinating the service is usually the contact point for referrals from other staff. Ancillary staff have a vital role to play here, because they often have to deal with a great deal of conflict, particularly in the playground. It is also important to include self-referral, as this means that if Johnny and Siobhan get into a fight they can keep a sense of responsibility for it by taking their conflict straight to their peers.

What is and isn't mediable
Stacey and Robinson stress the need for regular adult support and supervision: 'All will need a weekly team meeting to debrief, to share experiences and to keep up a regular programme of review and development.'[18] In Chapter 7 a principal describes issues that involved 'teeth, skin and hair'[19] as not being mediable.

Kjell Andberg, reflecting on the experience of peer mediation in Norway, is categorical that 'mediation is not a credible method in cases of bullying'.[20]

However, not everyone agrees. Peer mediation has the capacity to deal with issues before they would otherwise reach the attention of adults. By the time an issue reaches a teacher it has often escalated, and it has been known for conflicts that could easily become 'bullying' to be nipped in the bud by being dealt with promptly by peer mediation. If complaints about bullies are ignored by teachers or do not come to their notice, the problem will escalate. A peer mediation programme provides a win–win scenario. Precisely because it outlaws blame and punishment it offers a non-threatening process whereby both potential victim and potential bully may find ways of meeting their needs without it having to be at the expense of the other. Dr Colin Webster of the University of Teesside has published an evaluation of the influence of peer mediation on school bullying. He recognises the difficulties of an external agency implementing a controversial programme within a school. Nevertheless, he concludes: 'Peer friendships can and do have both negative and positive influences on bullying, as sources of rejection and stereotyping and as sources of support and security. As such they offer an untapped source of entry into influencing bullying behaviour for the better.'[21] Hall outlines an argument in favour of training bullies to be mediators:

> Bullying stems from pressures such as the need for power/recognition, anger expression, self-protection against fear or low self-esteem, venting frustration and exercising leadership. These pressures might be absorbed by learning a new set of skills like assertiveness, anger management, problem-solving, teamwork and negotiation, which are also the skills required to be a mediator. Training bullies in mediation skills and assigning them mediation roles might cause a reduction in bullying behaviour.'[22]

This theory would make an interesting research project.

Publicising the service

Stacey and Robinson make a couple of key points here: 'The level of publicity and support from staff can determine whether a mediation service will stand or fail.[23] . . . Pupils are in the best position to know how to market and advertise their service amongst their peers, but will benefit from a partnership with IT, media studies, etc.'[24] A useful way of publicising the service is through an assembly for the whole school. Examples of successful assemblies include Primary 7 children doing a role-play of a conflict followed by a role-play of a mediation, and then having a panel answering previously agreed questions. Another school made up a 'rap' about peer mediation. Bristol Mediation stress the idea that 'the school might like to issue their own certificates for successful completion of the training, whether or not the children choose to become mediators'.[25]

While researching for her book *Conflict Resolution: A Foundation Guide*, Susan Stewart visited schools that our project had worked at. She reported on one such assembly:

> Once the mediators were appointed the team presented their service to the whole school assembly . . . [They] performed a demonstration dispute, then the mediation] . . . The children clearly felt ownership of the

process and took it very seriously. The whole school
assembly down to the very smallest children watched
and listened with rapt attention ... and [the trained
mediators] were presented with certificates.[26]

The impact of an assembly at School C (see p. 94) was similarly appreciated:

An assembly for the whole school to launch the peer
mediation service was presented by the Primary 6 class.
They returned to their class to find that the Primary 7
children, on their own initiative, had put a message on
their blackboard: 'That was terrific! From your friends
in Primary 7'. Staff and parents also affirmed their
teacher and the children.[27]

The launch of the service can also be a good opportunity
to renew the school's commitment, with an in-service
training (INSET), particularly if the children are involved
and the participants include ancillary staff. In addition, letters to parents and invitations to them and the governors to
attend the assembly are effective ways of spreading the
word.

Taking into account the need to involve children who
have been unsuccessful when applying to be mediators,
there are a number of key roles to be filled – making
posters, for example. And a very effective way of publicising
the service and making it accessible is for groups of children
to go round the classes and do role-plays and answer
questions.

Evaluating the service

Chapter 9 contains a more detailed exploration of the role
of evaluation in peer mediation. This chapter concentrates
on the statistics from the EMU-Promoting School Project.
From January to June 1998 the Project followed up the peer
mediation programme in six of the schools it had been
operating in until the previous term. A detailed summary of

the evaluation of one of these schools is included in Chapter 8. In four of the schools a peer mediation service was set up by the school, and the following statistics from the agreement forms were collected and analysed by Seamus Farrell.[28]

School A

By and large the disputants only featured in one dispute each. However, one girl and one boy featured on the same three occasions, and another girl and another boy featured twice. In a Primary 6 class two girls featured in four disputes – all with each other.

The agreement forms from this school contain quite specific details as regards what each disputant has agreed to on a quid pro quo basis. These details indicate that some of the issues are quite serious, and with a potential for escalation that the mediations may have defused; there is bullying, name-calling involving family background, and threatening to get a gang or brothers to deal with the other person. A very frequent issue, especially with girls, is that of one person having taken away the other's friend(s); for both boys and girls there is also exclusion from a group and from game teams. At the same time, beyond the give-and-take details of the agreement, there is equal emphasis on 'making friends, saying sorry etc.' – though sometimes the agreement is about staying away from each other.

School B

The information from School B included the fact that three Primary 5 children feature in two conflicts each and seven were involved in one mediation each.

School C

Notably, one Primary 5 boy features in five disputes; three girls and one boy in Primary 6 feature in two disputes each. All but one of the agreement forms relating to Primary 5 mediations have no written agreement. There is *some* detail in the Primary 6 forms but the emphasis is on *both* parties 'being friends, being fair, stopping fighting, trying to get along, playing together'.

School D

Many of the agreement forms do not carry the dates of the mediations. However, it is clear that, following an initial flurry in December 1997 and January 1998, though they were somewhat less frequent from then on, they none-the-less continued till the end of June '98. In this school there was no significant pattern of the same children featuring in many disputes – perhaps no more than two or three. The disputants were girls and boys in about equal number. In the one dispute involving two Primary 5 children there was no immediate settlement, but rather an agreement to 'try to think of solutions for Friday [two days away] and return to mediation'. A note on the form says the disputants returned to say they had made friends.

All years in the school are double-entry. The majority of same-year disputants in any conflict were from the same class. In one dispute between a girl and a boy in Primary 6, the girl agreed to stop kissing the boy and looking at him while the boy agreed to stop giving the girl nasty looks!

While a number of the agreement forms from this school contain quite specific details about what each disputant has agreed to on a quid pro quo basis, in several cases the emphasis is simply on 'saying sorry', 'making friends' and so on.

Besides agreement statements (detailed or simple), these agreement forms very frequently also contain the notes taken by the mediators in the course of the disputants telling their stories and identifying the issues. These indicate that the issues/problems were, more often than not, quite 'heavy', and that the mediators carefully and competently helped the parties identify the problems they wanted addressed before proceeding to search for solutions.

Of particular significance are the notes which feature on the agreement forms from the 'brainstorming for solutions' process. A pattern seems to have developed in this school in which the mediators used this component of the process to enable the disputants to vent their emotions. The disputants proposed solution and counter-solution after solution and counter-solution, which, apart from the reasonable ones, included 'proposals' for sentencing each other to the worst of fates! The mediators duly recorded these also –

perhaps with some enjoyment and certainly without censoring!

Not all such 'heavy' disputes ended in friendship restored, of course; there were more realistic agreements such as a one-week trial period of not hurting or being mean to each other, or staying away from each other, or being friendly sometimes or trying to be nicer to each other. Issues of rumour-mongering, talking behind the other's back, stealing or alienating friends through telling lies, exclusion from groups and so on were dealt with very responsibly.

Here is a good example: A promises to be more loyal to B and not try to boss her about. B admits that she had been giving in to pressure from C to have nothing to do with A, and is sorry, especially because she knows now that A wants to be her real friends. But she still wants also to be a friend of C even though A and C just can't get on.

What is clear from all of this is that in this particular school the emotional dimension of conflict was given the attention it deserves; and its competent facilitation by the mediators is quite remarkable. In some cases it seemed to be sufficient for the disputants to vent their emotions and have them acknowledged; they did not need to formalise an agreement. More often, however, it led to very realistic agreements – initially to do what they knew was *feasible*, given the feelings that persisted and the need to cool off.

A *process approach* to conflict resolution was adopted. With their emotions dealt with, the disputants are able to be more rational. This is probably a key reason for the fact that the language used in the terms of agreement is remarkably frank. Disputants agree to 'be sensible and think before acting', to 'stop taking things so seriously', to 'stop complaining'. Disputant A agrees to 'stop acting foolishly' while *both* agree to 'wise up'.

Where mediations in other schools did not deal with feelings to the same extent, one wonders whether quick-fix agreements about 'being friends' may have proved precarious. It is significant that in this school there were no repeat mediations (involving the same disputants), and individuals did not often appear as parties in different disputes.

Findings

In each of the four schools the children worked in pairs –
same sex or mixed. While the same mediator teams featured
frequently, there was nothing rigid about this: new pairings
were established as the need arose – e.g., where the regular
partner was not available or where it was not appropriate
because of the relationship (positive or negative) of a mediator with one or both of the disputants. In boy–girl disputes
there was often a boy–girl team of mediators. In all-boy disputes it was not unusual to find an all-girl mediation team –
and vice versa. But certain teams seem to have established a
reputation and got most 'business'. With these especially, one
notices that, as they gained in experience, the quality of the
agreements, as reflected in the agreement forms, improved.

Mediators themselves featured occasionally as disputants
in all the schools.

Agreement forms

The agreement forms shown in Fig 3.1 indicate a total of 78
formal mediations (42 of these in one of the four schools),
which proceeded to agreement between the disputants.
There is no record of those which did not reach agreement
but, from the observations of teachers, most of the formal
mediations had a successful outcome. The numbers of less
formal dispute resolutions throughout the six schools are
not quantifiable, but it can be assumed that these were not
substantial. There is evidence, however, that the *training
programme* in all six schools contributed significantly to
better peer relationships and to the competence of children
to deal with their disputes without the need for third-party
intervention. All schools noted a reduction in the levels of
conflict in the class involved; as role-models for junior classes, the quality of the interactions of the children who had
done the training often had a noticeable influence on children's interactions throughout the school; and the services
did prevent specific conflicts escalating to the point of needing adult intervention.

Obviously the number of mediations that took place, formal or otherwise, is not by itself an adequate measure of the
programme. This book deals elsewhere with the broad but

Statistics from agreement forms			
School	A	B	C	D
Duration of	6 months	3 months	3 months	10 months
Mediators				
Year	P7	P7	P6	P7
Gender	7 boys 2 girls	3 boys 7 girls	2 boys 4 girls	9 boys 2 girls
Total mediations	18	7	11	42
Between P5s	6	4	5	1
Between P5s and P6s	0	0	0	2
Between P6s	8	2	6	21
Between P6s and P7s	1	0	0	2
Between P7s	3	1	0	16
Disputes				
Between boys	3	not recorded	6	20
Between girls	10	not recorded	3	17
Between boys and girls	5	not recorded	2	5

Fig. 3.1: Analysis of agreement form of mediations at
schools A, B, C and D

less quantifiable benefits of the programme in terms of improved teaching and learning, better teacher–pupil and peer relationships, the acquisition of basic conflict-resolution skills and, centrally, the enhancement of self-esteem and confidence in both children and teachers.

One issue that arises from the peer mediation schemes analysed here, and that is reflected in experience elsewhere, is that there is a dip in the number of mediations after an initial enthusiastic take-up. Research has shown that there can be positive reasons for this. Children can be using the skills they have learned with each other, without recourse to third-party intervention. Another reason is that after the novelty has worn off, the peer mediation service, being conducted in private, is no longer in the public perception. Either way, creative channels are needed for using the pool of mediators – for example, in promoting positive play or even training other children. In this context it is worth noting that Stacey and Robinson cite the example of seven-year-olds being trained to mediate with – or at least support – children who have fallen out, to get them to listen to each other. They outline the skills needed, simplifying the steps using pictures to show what you do next (a heart sign means 'State feelings', a parrot means 'Repeat back what has been said').[29]

However, one contentious conclusion drawn from the relatively small number of mediations that occur – that these may not merit a mediation service – is reported by Hall:

> Johnson, Johnson, Cotten *et al*[30] note that a very small number of students accounted for a substantial proportion of the mediated conflicts and suggest that providing that small group with special training would reduce the incidence of aggression and violence. The question is whether it is mediation which is the appropriate form of training and whether a mediation role is the most appropriate role.[31]

In general the US experience of peer mediation takes place in the context of violence prevention, whereas the experience of the EMU-Promoting School Project and other programmes in the UK indicate that elementary school conflicts are more about name-calling, teasing, threats, and the like.

Informal mediation practice

The EMU-Promoting School Project is concerned to develop training programmes with a structured approach that will lead to the provision of a peer mediation service. In the process it has discovered that children are putting their skills into practice informally as well: 'C tried mediation at home between his brothers but he was disappointed; they were too small really to understand ... Children have told of incidents when they have tried to sort out conflicts with younger brothers and sisters.'[32] Parents themselves reported the benefits that their children had gained from the training:

> School B   Quite a number of parents are very support-
> ive and are very pleased to see it in operation. A num-
> ber of parents told me during parent interviews that
> their child had really enjoyed the training. It has been
> explained in more detail in both the School Prospectus
> and the Happy School Book, thus making more parents
> aware of the programme. At the parents' meeting with
> the Inspectorate, a number of parents raised the subject
> of peer mediation and their comments were very
> favourable and positive.[33]

Public demonstrations of peer mediation

In June 1994 the then Ulster Quaker Peace Education Project organised a group of four children to give a demonstration of peer mediation at a House of Commons committee room in London. The children role-played a mediation and answered questions from a group of interested adults and children from schools and mediation agencies. The success of this presentation led to other opportunities, and a growing awareness that children, with their candour, humour, understanding and expertise, make the best ambassadors for peer mediation. 'This workshop was a live experience of citizenship and democracy in schools and of what children can do. The children's parents participated fully in the proceedings – responding to our questions and clearly confirming that the peer mediation programme has helped their children acquire life skills and awareness of their own worth and abilities.'[34] There was one memorable occasion when a group of children from five schools in Northern Ireland gave a demonstration of peer mediation to the then President of Ireland, Mary Robinson:

With all the children sitting in a circle she engaged them in discussion. She asked them to tell her some of the difficult times they had mediated, without breaking confidence. Michelle said it was difficult if there were a lot of interruptions. Rory said if the parties didn't agree, you kept on trying, but if all else failed you told a teacher. Stephen said sometimes it was difficult if your best friend was in conflict, and then it usually made sense to get someone else to mediate.

The active interest that President Robinson took in the role-play, the naturalness of her questions, and the ease with which she struck up a rapport with the children, soon made them feel at home. She summed up her response to the children's input by saying that it had been a 'very good experience. I must say peer mediation doesn't only occur in schools as you are well aware, or even in the community or cities, but at every level of things.'

She went on to say: 'I've talked to some very good people who try to mediate internationally and in Africa, especially Burundi and Rwanda. They are actively mediating at the moment trying to prevent conflict, and make it work, and it's very much the same kind of approach. They have to listen a lot and get the parties to clarify and work it out. I am particularly impressed that this project has brought the work into schools [in Northern Ireland] ... if peer mediation works in the playground, there's no reason why adults can't learn a lesson from what, after all, isn't just child's play.'[35]

Meeting a group of mediators *in situ* led to this report by John Feerick, Dean of Fordham Law School, New York:

There are moments in life for each of us which are different from all others. I speak here of moments that are uplifting and inspiring. One such moment occurred for me on a recent visit to Northern Ireland. I visited a school to learn more about its peer mediation programme. We inquired of the students about the qualities that they felt were necessary to be good mediators.

Without any hesitation they emphasised the importance of patience and good listening. A mediator who lacks such qualities, they indicated, can hardly hope to smooth the waters among disputing angry parties.

When we asked the students to describe some of the disputes they had mediated, they declined to provide such information, stressing in their response the confidential nature of mediation in which the mediator is expected to keep the confidences of the parties who participate. (They did provide general information about the type of disputes.)

As we left the school that day, each member of our group felt that we had been exposed to an incredible group of young people. The world cannot help but be a better place with people such as the children we met. Their mastery of difficult concepts and their understanding of the essentials of conflict resolution were truly remarkable, and need to be exported to people of all ages and in all corners of the globe.[36]

4. How Did Peer Mediation Get into Primary Schools?

In Chapter 1 we saw why peer mediation has developed as it has, with the inspiration for it coming from educationalists, peace activists and community mediation programmes, in different parts of the world. This chapter will use a 'training the trainer' course as a case study to illustrate one way of involving teachers experienced in peer mediation, and other adults within the school community, to pass on their skills and expertise to individuals who are new to peer mediation. It will also draw on the perspectives of different agencies in the UK who have been promoting peer mediation.

A number of references are made in the chapter to 'circle time'. This process has been extensively developed in the UK by Jenny Mosley,[1] and separately by Lucky Duck Publishing.[2] Circle time provides a democratic forum through which participants – a whole class or a smaller group – offer each other mutual support, build up a team sense, develop social skills and, above all, enhance each other's self-esteem.

The participants sit in a circle and take equal responsibility for expressing feelings, sharing concerns and solving problems of direct relevance to their lives and experiences. The teacher encourages the group, agrees ground rules with them to make the group work smoothly, and introduces a range of strategies to encourage co-operation, honesty, warmth and empathy. The circle is the ideal device for these processes, in its symbolism and in its reality: it is about sharing, unity, interdependence, equality and inclusion. It lends itself to endless adaptation for use with children of all ages and to suit particular circumstances, constrained in its use only by the teacher's level of confidence and creativity. It provides a strong foundation for peer mediation work.

The Northern Ireland experience – year 1

In Northern Ireland peer mediation in primary schools started in the city of Derry/Londonderry. Schools whose pupils had participated in a day conference on peer mediation organised by the Ulster Quaker Peace Education Project (QPEP) in April 1993 were invited to take part in a pilot project. Two schools responded positively to the invitation. The principals of both schools had previously had experience of the Project and had a good relationship with it.

Two things in particular convinced the principals that the pilot project would be worth the necessary investment of time and energy. First, the response of the children: 'They got a lot from it and [both principals] wanted a follow-up . . . so this is where the interest came from.'[3] The fact that the principal put such an emphasis on the children's feedback was in itself an indication of the child-centred ethos of the school. The other critical factor was that both the principals had the opportunity of meeting Mary de Largy, a Belfast secondary school teacher who had introduced mediation into her school:

> It was good to hear someone who had been through it. We had an opportunity to ask her lots of very straight-forward questions that you can't ask a book. We had the awkward questions and just the nitty-gritty questions that sometimes get skated over in a report. . . . I found her very open and honest; she didn't paint a picture of this being the most wonderful thing in the world. She was very realistic about the context of it. But she was very enthusiastic about it and that partly helped sell it to me because she was a practitioner as well – a professional teacher and realistic and sensible.[4]

The principals consulted with their staff and then chose the Primary 7 teachers who would become directly involved. Like the principals, neither teacher had heard of peer mediation. They had no training in advance of the children, apart from a short introductory session attended by the QPEP team and the director of the Mediation Network, Northern Ireland (MNNI).

It was decided to train the two classes, one from each of the participating schools, separately, because the principals anticipated the conflict issues at the two schools being different. The training took the form of six one-and-three-quarter-hour weekly sessions. At each school four members of the QPEP team, alongside the class teacher, led the workshops; two of these QPEP team members attended workshops at both schools. The QPEP team also met one morning a week to debrief, to evaluate the previous week's workshops, and to practise the exercises they were to carry out at the schools later in the week.

There was no 'manual'; the programme was being written by one of the QPEP team who was responsible for training. (The pilot project at these two schools has been written up in great detail, and the report[5] includes significant quotes from children, teachers, principals, ancillary staff and QPEP members.)

The advantages of the timing of the training programme was that the same workshop was being delivered at each school on consecutive days in the same week. Thus the workshop experiences could be compared; and it was fascinating to hear how identical workshops had elicited radically different responses. For example, at one of the schools most children were reticent to speak in a whole-class situation. The following week the programme was amended to provide an exercise for them to 'find their voice'.

The evaluation forms that all the children filled in each week provided information about their degree of comprehension of the concepts that we were trying to get across.

There was one major disadvantage – the lack of time between workshops. Class teachers were having to learn 'on the hoof', and at best had only a short time before the workshop to go through the programme, and afterwards to evaluate it – and, at worst, no time at all for either briefing or debriefing. As well as this, as far as the rest of the school was concerned the programme was 'being done for the Primary 7 class', and there wasn't adequate time provided for the other staff to become aware of what it was all about.

Attempts were made through in-service training (INSET)

and through presentations by the children to rectify this situation. Nevertheless, it quickly became apparent that more work was needed to ensure that there was a genuine opportunity for a whole-school approach. A key issue to emerge in one school was that it hadn't been possible to keep the ancillary staff informed, including lunchtime supervisors who played a key role in responding to conflict.

It also became clear as the programme progressed that it was vital for the school staff who were to be directly involved in the implementation of the programme to have specialised training in advance. The resulting six-week programme, described in detail in Chapter 2, led to the organisation of a joint day workshop for all the mediators selected from both classes. Subsequently a peer mediation service was established in each school.

The Northern Ireland experience – year 2
The following school year the two schools repeated the process with the same teachers but with different classes. By this time the two class teachers felt more confident and were able to take more of a leading role in the proceedings, and ancillary staff were involved as well. The project recruited additional teachers from the Teachers' Centre substitute cover list.

Because the class teachers had had the benefit of full involvement in the training the previous year, they grew in confidence and competence. They were thus able to be even more actively involved in the delivery of the second year's workshops, a development to which the children responded positively.

The Northern Ireland experience – years 3 to 5
During the period June 1996 – September 1997, the EMU-Promoting School Project developed a 'training the trainer' programme. It was designed to provide an intensive introduction to peer mediation training for teams of adults from primary schools. After an initial taster session for the whole staff at one school, and an agreement to go ahead with a peer mediation programme, the 'training the trainer' programme brought together a team of three adults from each of three or four schools.

By 1997 the Project and its predecessor Project had been

developing peer mediation in Northern Ireland for three and a half years. We had demonstrated that peer mediation worked, but the programme as we had designed it, and had been delivering it, was dependent on our continued availability year after year. The workshops needed three adults – which in practice had meant the class teacher and at least two project staff. We were trying to encourage schools to find other adults (such as playground supervisors, parents, classroom assistants) who would 'journey' with the teacher and ourselves through the programme. In June 1997 the Project decided that its level of commitment to its seven current partner schools (schools A–G) would end in December that year. It did not envisage being directly engaged, in the provision of peer mediation training workshops for children, after that. Partner schools wishing to continue the peer mediation programme by themselves in future years would need their own team with the confidence and competence to do so independently, and this would include being able to adapt the basic model to suit their particular circumstances and expectations.

The autumn 1997 'training the trainer' course was special in a number of ways. It was geared to the Project *disengaging* from schools in order that they could be self-supporting. It was written up as a piece of detailed action-research. Its particular value as a case study is that as well as describing the content of the course it includes reflection on it, as well as the participants' own reflections on its value.

Its design had to take account of considerable diversity as regards both schools and individuals participating.

A case study: the 'training the trainer' course (year 5)*

The participants

1. *The schools*
There is a variety of different levels of experience:

- Teacher transfer has meant the loss of a key person

*The use of the present tense in the original report has been retained.

- Two schools are sending individuals with considerable previous peer mediation experience
- Two schools have individuals previously trained in peer mediation, but who haven't been involved in delivering workshops.

Two schools won't be participating. Both were involved in the original training programme. One has developed its own training programme and is self-sufficient. The other has taken peer mediation as far as it can go at this time.*

2. *The individual participants*

- Key Stage 1 (KS1) teachers, classroom assistants and playground supervisors who may or may not be involved in training Primary 6 or Primary 7 children to be mediators, but who may be participating with a view to engagement in circle time activities with younger children
- Project 'associates' who have already worked with the Project, facilitating its peer mediation programme, or who are planning to do so
- An Education Board officer with particular responsibilities in the field of pastoral care and the performance enhancement programme of his Education and Library Board
- A worker in the field of community mediation whose current project is exploring engagement in peer mediation in schools.

Their skills

- Some need enhancement of their confidence and skills.
- Some with little more than an awareness of the existence in their school of a peer mediation programme are now to be involved in the training-provision team.

Aims
1. To enable participants who have been involved in the delivery of peer mediation to reflect on their experience.

*Two years later this school would be adopting a whole-school approach to circle time, on its own initiative.

2. To introduce participants who are new to peer mediation to the workshop process.
3. To support participants to take a leading role in the subsequent delivery of training to children in their school.

(These aims were displayed in large print on A3 sheets around the venue.)

Objectives
1. To support the establishment of a peer mediation service this term, involving the children who trained last year when in Primary 6.
2. To build the confidence of adult teams to train Primary 6 and Primary 7 children with minimum support from EMUpsp.
3. To help schools to start thinking of a timetable for the training of peer mediators.
4. To share the experience of teachers who have been involved in the programme already.
5. To begin networking between schools, teachers and pupils; the Project to offer a hotline to school teams.
6. To get schools to commit themselves either to establishing a peer mediation service or to do circle time activities for building confidence.
7. To encourage schools to identify strategies in order to customise the programme in 1998/9.
8. To explore circle time especially in Key Stage 1 (if appropriate).

The course: day 1

After their arrival, an introduction and some ice-breaker activities, the participants were invited to share their personal goals for the two days.

Goals
Each person received a sheet with space to complete the sentence 'My goal for the two days is . . .'. A representative sample of goals:

- to gain a sense of direction about how peer mediation can be initiated in our school
- to get information to enable me to share peer mediation in schools as part of pastoral care and discipline policies
- to refresh my memory about mediation
- to learn more about peer mediation and how it can be put into practice in school – with particular reference to Key Stage 1/P1-4
- to get an injection of enthusiasm and maybe become more confident with the running of workshops (in case the support is withdrawn!)
- to learn and develop the skills needed for taking it on in school
- to gain more experience of the concept; to be convinced that it works in practice.

Our agreement

As an integral part of the workshop the participants worked together to create an agreement, or set of ground rules, which was truly theirs and not just a collection of standard ground rules. The result was an agreement written in positive, creative and sensitive language to do the following:

- Treat all questions and comments with respect
- Listen while people are talking
- Recognise that everyone here has equally important things to contribute
- If you're not comfortable you may pass
- Treat everybody with respect
- Preserve confidentiality
- Recognise that nothing's agreed until everything's agreed
- Encourage each other
- Value our own contributions
- Take risks
- Be sensitive to other people's feelings

Communication exercise

This involved one facilitator giving directions to another to draw a picture, which he couldn't see. The exercise was all the more worth while for the fact that giving the directions proved a struggle. (It is sometimes more encouraging for children to see adults struggling than to witness a flawless performance.) Having seen the demonstration, everybody split into pairs and did the exercise.

Conflict freeze

The Project had *pre-selected* the membership of each small group for this exercise. The idea was for each group of four to come up with a scenario of a conflict that an individual member of the group had been involved in. It had to have two distinct sides, and to refer to a particular incident. This particular incident was 'frozen' at a certain point – for example, a householder questioning the validity of an invoice with a builder; a teacher asking a pupil why homework had not been completed. The group members then formed a tableau depicting the conflict and discussed it with the larger group. The 'freeze' became the conflict situation that would subsequently be mediated.

Mediation briefing

Each small group had a lead mediator, who was experienced in peer mediation training. He or she would brief the co-mediator about the role, and divide up the duties. The 'disputants' familiarised themselves with their respective roles, and were briefed about the need to be in role whilst not being rigidly intransigent. (It is not within the scope of this book to explore the merits of role-play in detail. Its appearance in workshop programmes brings mixed responses. It is common for ground rules to include a request for 'no role plays'. All the same, however artificial they may appear, they do stimulate real emotions. It is for this reason that thought needs to go into briefing, and more importantly debriefing, the participants. Role-plays are a very useful tool in demonstrating succinctly what mediation is about.)

Mediation

Before the mediations began, the facilitator spoke a few words about the importance of putting a positive perspective on conflict. He also laid to rest any notion that peer mediation eliminates all conflicts in schools! Significantly, some 'veteran' teachers remarked that for the first time, as a result of this activity, they now clearly understood the difference between *framing issues* and searching for solutions through *brainstorming* and *bargaining*.

Debriefing
Each participant was given a sheet with two questions on it. The written comments handed in are summarised below.

What went well?
The mediators did a good job. They calmed the disputants and gave each a chance to be heard. They stayed neutral. A final agreement was reached. The red card (an *aide-mémoire* for the mediators) helped a lot.

The mediators were familiar with the process, and that made it run more smoothly. They listened well and respected each other and the disputants. There was a willingness to communicate. We reached an agreement and saw both sides. The relationship between the disputants was re-established. Everyone stayed calm. There was an atmosphere of trust in which you could share your feelings.

After an initial stand-off, a bit of 'give' developed. The disputants began to focus on a solution instead of point-scoring.

What were the difficulties?
The mediators had not had time to co-ordinate their functions. This indicated how new is the notion of children being involved in finding solutions to their conflicts. It was a struggle to get the problems or issues set out before moving on to trying for solutions. Summing up the problems – finding the quickest way of recording them without having to write too much – was also hard.

Other difficulties: establishing and putting into practice the difference between framing the issues and brainstorming; expressing feelings – difficult in a role-play situation; and as a disputant it is hard to stay quiet and listen.

Sessional evaluation

This featured in the middle and at the end of each day's programme and consistently proved to be an excellent opportunity for the participants to communicate with facilitators.

Day one: session one – evaluation

The rolling evaluation consisted of a flip-chart sheet divided into three columns. The feedback in the last column could be used by the facilitators to fine-tune the planning of the subsequent programme.

	☹	
What was good	**What was not so good**	**Ideas/things to bear in mind**
• the atmosphere • the labels ready for each person • the ice-breaker exercise – it got people mixing, making decisions and discussing • how well everybody worked at developing 'our agreement' • the skill with which the agreement was developed • the mediation – it was a powerful experience, doing it ourselves for the first time	• misspelling of the names of two participants • beginning to tire of 'affirmation adjectives' exercises – done too often?	• the mediation – the 25 minutes flew and there was no time wasting • the children need sufficient time • having structured pairs is easier than finding a partner yourself • doing it ourselves gives it credibility

Ice-breaker exercise

Workshop 1 (of the peer mediation training programme for children)

(In Chapter 2 the workshops of the children's peer mediation training programme were described in detail. An

integral part of this 'training the trainer' programme was that the adults had the opportunity of experiencing for themselves what the children would later be experiencing. Whilst the project facilitators led the exercise, the rest of the adults became a class of Primary 7 children.)

Almost all the participants – and some in particular – gleefully seized the opportunity to 'be children' when invited; for some, the opportunity to be 'teacher's worst nightmare' was just too good to pass up. On all such occasions, it is probably inevitable that this will happen. It's worth bearing in mind when planning that all activities involving participants in 'children mode' will take longer than one would expect.

All the facilitators used the situation *powerfully* to model a positive approach to dealing with 'the disruptive child' – acknowledging her need for attention, seeking to give her roles or tasks that would help her feel valued and involved, and appealing to her best instincts when it came to respecting *everyone's* need to be heard and to be happy and for the work in hand to be done.

There is a need to 'de-role' thoroughly after each activity. Perhaps built-in commentary points between activities would put a brake on what seems to be a dynamic of steady regression towards infancy! At these commentary points participants are, of course, required to return to being their adult selves.

The Project had pre-arranged the composition of the small groups – an excellent decision. But the time they were given wasn't long enough. When the groups are all in the same room it's best for them to be 'facilitated' centrally – unless experienced participants are available in each small group and adequately briefed.

Ice-breaker

Debriefing
This activity was introduced by describing Workshop 1 as the participants had just experienced it as 'The EMU-Promoting Schools Project's (EMUpsp) way of training children in

mediation'. He introduced the topic of 'customising' the programme for the circumstances and needs of each school situation, in the context of the objectives of the course. The
participants, in pairs and then in the large group, were invited
to consider two questions. Their responses are listed below:

1. What would you do differently with *your* class?

- I'd spend a little more time discussing the importance of
  the rules of peer mediation
- introduce an additional rule catering for excessively difficult behaviour
- explain the use of first names and get everyone to feel
  OK about it
- explain more thoroughly to the children why they are
  doing the course
- secure the services of more adults so that small groups
  can be even smaller
- bring in trained child mediators to tell the new group
  what peer mediation is all about
- use a real situation because it would be better for the
  role-play of mediation
- have an outsider to the class taking the leading role (to
  avoid bias)
- make small-group time must be longer – to allow quieter children to voice their thoughts
- incorporate some of the games into PE; otherwise, I'd
  follow the EMUpsp outline

2. How would you prepare your class for Workshop 1 so as to reinforce and integrate it into your scheme of work?

- I'd give them practice in talking, listening and writing
  – in skills of constructive criticism, reasoning,
  summarising, concluding etc. And I'd introduce EMU.
- introduce the idea of ground rules and work on formulating them.
- prepare the ground rules carefully.
- reinforce the ground rules in normal (non-workshop)
  situations.

- introduce additional exercises on talking and listening.
- establish 'circle time' and get the children used to it.
- have 'circle time' ongoing in the infant end of the school.
- set aside a suitable room for mediation.
- explain what mediation means.
- establish the peer mediation rules as rules for life – not just for the school context.
- introduce ice-breaker activities so that the children can be comfortable with the format and with one another.
- should a real-life conflict arise note the details and use them in a forthcoming workshop.
- encourage speaking out.

Day one: session two evaluation

What was good	What was not so good	Ideas/things to bear in mind
• the listening exercise – will be very useful in the classroom • the conversation between facilitator and teacher about the parents issue • the Ugly Duckling and Pretty Duckling role-play* • the pace was good	(nil)	• okay to make mistakes in front of children (here, to do with direction–following) • children to be given a synopsis of Ugly Duckling story in advance

*(see Chapter 2, workshop 1)

The course: day two

(The morning contained a presentation about 'circle time')

Briefing for three mini-workshops
(The 'mini-workshops' were shortened versions of the workshops 2–4 of the project's peer mediation training

programme (described in greater detail in Chapter 2). Each mini-workshop was prepared by a team of two or three adults, who then shared the facilitating of the workshop.)

Three teachers were each assigned to lead each team. They took on the challenge, but did need initial support from EMUpsp staff, after which the latter were able to leave the room. The process of teachers briefing their teams helped clarify *their own* understanding of mediation.

At this point it became observable that one participant, a Key Stage 1 classroom assistant, was feeling uncomfortable. Her team leader on the mini-workshop was quick to notice and worked very impressively to help her. Whether the participant *brought* her uneasiness to the course on that day (she had seemed fine on the previous day), or whether it developed during this preparation for the mini-workshops, it is impossible to know.

The mini-workshops

Before the workshops began the facilitator, very appropriately, asked those role-playing the children of the class, for the purposes of these mini-workshops, to be a 'a good average class'. 'Winding up the Project people is one thing, but . . .' he remarked. But for all that, his request was ignored. In fact, some of those on the 'adult team' sometimes resorted to being 'children' when they should have been in adult mode. There is a need to achieve much more clarity concerning roles and functions, and to mark clearly the point of changing from one role to another or to being oneself. Consideration might be given to the use of badges, to be worn when 'in role' and removed when leaving the role. This was a major factor in programme times going completely haywire at this point. There was no time available for the third mini-workshop (Workshop 4) nor for the planned post-mini-workshops debriefing. But even if this had not been a factor, the original time allocations to each mini-workshop were probably quite inadequate.

Our emphasis on the writing role in mediation led initially to *everything* being written down – the main points of each disputant's story, his or her feeling and so on. It was salutary when someone queried the stage when writing was actually needed, observing that it didn't need to begin until the point of 'framing the issues' and that phrases rather than sentences would do fine.

There was a decided reluctance among participants to volunteer as *mediators*. Facilitators had to take on the role of mediators in Workshop 3. The role is more intimidating than we who are now familiar with it probably realise.

There is a need to reinforce the *stages* of the mediation process.

The closing circle of Workshop 3 invited 'children' to say what they were planning to do at the weekend. For 'little Henry', who had been constantly seeking attention, the response was consistent with his behaviour and revealing: he was not looking forward to anything, least of all his uncle being about, and would gladly be at school if that were possible. It pointed to the reality that for many children, school was the best thing in their lives.

Day two: session one evaluation

What was good	**What was not so good**	**Ideas/things to bear in mind**
• circle time • briefing and the encouragement that was given • the enjoyment (but the learning too) • the participation in the mini-workshops • the ice-breakers • the playing of the leadership roles in mediation – leaders' eagerness is encouraging • the ability to be children!	• not enough time – one group did not get to lead a workshop	• the need to be clear about what the issues were for each disputant • more variation in the ice-breakers – more games? produce a *booklet* • moving around

The ice-breaker

Video of peer mediation
It was just right – including pauses for teaching points to be made. But it may not have been particularly useful for those who had seen it before. It may be worth considering an alternative activity for these.

Panel
This consisted of three teachers and facilitator. (They were posed good questions and they gave good answers (the video informed the questions). For future reference – it's important that we facilitators button our lips and save our wisdom for the other ten hours, when we can share it!) The activity reinforced the importance of a teacher within EMUpsp. A facilitator asked, 'How can the Project help?' The response was:

- through substantial direct engagement in the first year
- by organising 'training the trainer' refresher courses like this one
- by supporting the school's efforts to disseminate the ideas throughout the adult community of the school, especially those involved with Key Stage 1.

One teacher's concluding remark bears repeating: 'My involvement in this programme has changed the total way I teach.'

Day two – final session evaluation

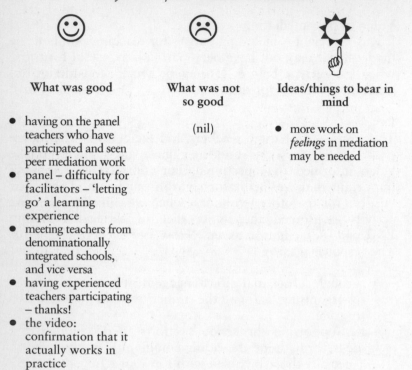

What was good	What was not so good	Ideas/things to bear in mind
• having on the panel teachers who have participated and seen peer mediation work • panel – difficulty for facilitators – 'letting go' a learning experience • meeting teachers from denominationally integrated schools, and vice versa • having experienced teachers participating – thanks! • the video: confirmation that it actually works in practice	(nil)	• more work on *feelings* in mediation may be needed

At this point the participants were invited to revisit their goals, write comments alongside them, and indicate how near to the target they had got. (A number of participants had indicated more than one goal.)

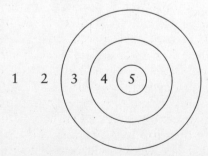

1   2   3   4   5

Fig. 4.1: The target: participants were asked to mark how near they had reached it

Twelve people indicated that they reached their target of 5; four scored 4; three scored 3, and one each scored 1 and 2.

Comments
'I've put my dart where it is 'because I think I can only fully assess the realisation of the goal when the programme is initiated and up and running.'
'Never has learning been such fun!'
'The dot is just off centre because I need to do a little more work, so that I clearly understand the sequence – 'framing the issues', 'brainstorming' etc. – for peer mediation. Many thanks for a very useful two days.'
'The two days have refreshed me and have been enlightening. It makes me feel enthusiastic about EMU as a whole, and I will give it support in any way I can. I would like to see peer mediation develop throughout a school; maybe to see 'feelings' becoming more of an issue – 'If someone did that to me, how would I feel?' should I do it to someone else? And so on.

The closing circle
The highlights were impressively varied.

The logistics of working in primary schools

It is often the logistics of organising the training that indicates the type of obstacles that the school has to overcome, and also its commitment to overcoming them. In one school on a June afternoon during their mediation training programme, eight boys and the principal were not available because of a cricket match. This type of situation is steeped in the reality of school; so the hallmark of external involvement in schools has to be *flexibility*.

In UK primary schools the norm is for each class to have a single teacher, who teaches all subjects. It is possible to run a two-hour workshop in a primary school at the same time each week for six weeks without disrupting the timetable unduly. Indeed, there is evidence that peer mediation training enhances the learning and teaching environment in general and the English curriculum in particular. This will be explored further in Chapter 5.

In the survey of agencies promoting peer mediation in Great Britain, eleven of the twelve respondents were working in primary schools, and ten in secondary schools. There was a variety of responses to the question, 'Why did you choose to work in the particular age range?'

Two agencies said they chose to work with all school-age children, because peer mediation 'is suitable for all ages from 5 to 16 . . . within our team of project workers we have people with experience in different age groups'. One agency didn't choose, the implication being that it was decided for them by the schools that approached them. There were several who were keen to build links between primary and secondary:

- 'We wanted to work from primary to secondary, trying to develop conflict-resolution skills as young as possible.'
- 'We now choose to work in primary schools' (although they have worked in secondary schools in the past).
- A secondary school head has asked us to go into their feeder primary schools.'
- '[The] project was written on these lines. The aim was to have a primary feeder school to secondary school. [This] age range [was chosen] to give the school benefit of service/exam times.'
- For one agency it evolved as their work in the secondary sector grew, as 'it supports our peer tutoring/transitional model'.

There was an alternative approach *from* primary *to* secondary: '[We were involved] mainly [with] Primary 6 and 7 for the full peer mediation programme – [we were] able to cascade [the] training down the school and take valuable transferable skills to secondary.' However, there was an acknowledgement of the 'difficulties in delivering full peer mediation in secondary, due to national curriculum timetable constraints'.

A number of agencies had decided on the particular age range of Year 5 (9–10 year olds) and Year 6 (10–11 year olds) after consultation with teachers, after reading informed research, or on the strength of past experience. The agency that worked only in the secondary sector did so because their contact was a secondary school teacher.

Skills training in resolving conflict, and circle time

Programmes such as those of Kingston Friends Mediation, Bristol Mediation and the West Midlands Quaker Peace Education Project see their initial focus as being on skills training in resolving conflict in schools, with peer mediation as an option at a later stage.

Highfield Junior School in Devon was one school which developed peer mediation within a 'programme of consultation and power-sharing aimed at preventing and resolving conflict in the school'.[6] This was part of a successful attempt by a new headmistress to turn the school around; and circle time was an integral factor in the strategy.

Bristol Mediation in their peer mediation manual[7] stress the need for children to have experience of 'circle time', since most peer mediation activities are conducted in a circle and all are based on the skills and values of that process.

Chapter 2 illustrated exactly how peer mediation training differs from the usual classroom experience of children and teachers. Key elements, as well as operating in a circle, include the degree of interaction between children and the need for non-verbal ways of achieving silence, such as a 'Quiet Please' sign. Experience of role-playing is also necessary.

Because of the crucial role that circle time plays in the peer mediation training process, a number of teachers have seen it as a useful preparation for, and a way into, peer mediation. The peer mediation training process that the Project is most familiar with focuses on the Key Stage 2 age range (9–11). Inevitably this has meant that at the end of an after-school INSET session, the Key Stage 1 staff have tended to respond along the lines of 'Yes, I can see the value, but how is it relevant to Key Stage One?'

Starting with the youngest

The publication of *Playground Peacemakers*[8] in 1998 marked the first co-ordinated attempt to provide a resource that supported a vertical (i.e., from first years to Primary 7) whole-school approach to peer mediation. Its aim was to enable children to incorporate the skills and values of conflict resolution into the 'daily school life from age 5 to 18.[9] Whilst recognising that the activities can be followed 'rigidly, diligently or selectively',[10] it also made it clear that if the eventual aim is to set up a peer mediation service, then this will have to be flagged up throughout the Playground Peacemakers programme; Circle time can provide the framework, but 'it will be up to staff and pupils to adjust the framework to meet the needs of the individual school'.[11]

The Playground Peacemakers programme started out as a peer mediation programme, but because it has proved so globally relevant to schools the publishers maintain that it has 'become a child management tool . . . a major time saver . . . a means of introducing pupil democracy . . . a booster for the use of circle time . . . and invaluable in the development of emotional literacy', as well as helping to tackle bullying, raise self-esteem and improve school ethos.

A lesson learnt in the process of initiating the programme is that it 'should ideally be introduced simultaneously across at least a cluster of schools, if not a whole LEA. Individual school efforts tend to be hard work for the staff involved, whereas a cluster or LEA approach spreads the workload and brings into play a multiplicity of ideas and efforts.' This aspect of collaboration between schools and Education Authorities deserves to be emphasised; according to the book's publishers, 'thirty-two Local Education Authorities are either actively using, planning or studying the possible benefits of Playground Peacemakers . . . Almost 700 schools are actively introducing the programme.'

Conclusion

The importance of taking the necessary time to get peer mediation into primary schools cannot be overemphasised. Peer mediation training is interactive, informal, experiential and democratic – in contrast to other more formal, didactic parts of the school day. It often requires a change of school ethos, and the ingredients of a successful programme are as much about managing change and nurturing relationships as about introducing a new way of handling conflict.

It should be stressed that by the end of the first year of the pilot peer mediation programme of the then Ulster Quaker Peace Education Project, thirty young people in the two relevant schools had acquired a wealth of experience in mediating – *more, indeed, than the majority of the Project staff and volunteer team.* As has already been stated, the Project team was learning about peer mediation training 'on the hoof'.

Part of the rationale for the 'Training the Trainer' workshops was to allow teachers and other adults the opportunity to experience for themselves, at least in role-play, what mediation itself was about; and, ideally, to acknowledge that it could transform conflict.

It is important that adults as much as children have the opportunity of experiencing for themselves the benefit of mediation; the idea of staff – pupil mediation begins to make sense in this context.

The answer to the question, 'How did peer mediation get into primary schools?' involves teachers having to gain new skills. It is this issue which requires the most creative response from external agencies. As described in Chapter 2, children react very positively to the stimulus of a workshop approach. They see it as fun and games; an attitude summed up by one boy who, asked to say what he enjoyed about a day workshop spent talking and listening, acting and working co-operatively in a small group, replied, 'It was great, spending a whole day without having to do any work.'[12] It was obviously fun and games to him, despite the hard work he had been doing; and at first glance and first hearing – because workshops are inevitably noisier than usual classroom experiences – it can appear to be just fun and games to the teacher too.

This initial impression often leads to a feeling of uncertainty in teachers. Schools are hierarchical institutions, and to a certain degree everything works as long as people know which rung they are on. Workshops attempt to flatten that

hierarchy, giving everybody an equal place, an equal voice
and equal value – and equal respect. To some teachers this
seems to imply a loss of control and, coupled with an unfa-
miliarity with the skills of facilitating, the prospect of being
involved even in a modest way in such activities can be
daunting.

The net result has sometimes been – if the teachers have a
choice – for them to sit outside the circle, to mark books at
their desk while the workshop is going on, or even to make
their excuses and remove themselves altogether. It is all too
easy for the external agency to take over, to run the workshop without the teachers' involvement. This is a mistake,
since one of the key relationships is that between the teacher
and his or her class, and teachers have consistently reported
that the experience has had a profound and positive effect
on that relationship.

In Chapter 7 ways of dealing with resistance will be
explored, and it will be demonstrated that introducing peer
mediation in a sustainable way requires confronting change
and managing it.

For these reasons it is important that all the views of the
staff are taken into consideration, that scepticism is
acknowledged, and that a consensus is sought before going
ahead with 'getting peer mediation into primary schools'.
Work with the children has to come *after* working with the
adults.

5. Children's Needs and the Learning Process

One of the major concerns expressed by employers is that the curriculum focuses on cognitive learning without the need to apply it to real-life contexts. A four-year longitudinal study of the views of nearly 3,000 Key Stage 3 pupils reveals that young people have difficulty in seeing relevance in much of what they are required to learn in school, except in the sense of acquiring qualifications which will allow them to progress to higher education or employment. Findings of recent brain research suggest that long-term effective learning takes place when the learner is motivated by relevance and by emotional engagement with the subject matter.[1]

'I've learned you have to do something for each other if you want to sort out a conflict.' (Primary 7 child)[2]

'I'm learning to make new friends.' (Primary 7 child)[3]

The Encyclopaedia of Conflict Resolution states that peer mediation is used to 'help teach students conflict resolution skills, enabling them to handle their own conflicts without the intervention of teachers or principals[4], and that it 'teaches skills in conflict resolution and problem solving that will last a lifetime'.[5]

Chapter 2 described the programme of workshops and the procedures employed in them. This chapter will concentrate on the relevance of peer mediation skills to the children's learning process, and on where such skills training fits into the curriculum. The chapter also reflects the current educational debate in Northern Ireland, which has been sparked off by at least two significant factors:

1. the major review of the curriculum being undertaken by the Northern Ireland Curriculum Council for Examinations and Assessment (CCEA).
2. the fact that 'Northern Ireland is entering a momentous and historic phase in its political and social evolution, and the restoration of democracy poses a tremendous challenge for education in Northern Ireland.'[6]

At first glance, focusing almost exclusively on educational developments in one small area may seem a parochial approach with limited value for a wider audience. However, CCEA's review has been far-reaching, with a series of conferences that has drawn on the latest research and experience from different parts of the world.

Examining where peer mediation fits into the curriculum now and in the future in Northern Ireland constitutes a useful case study. If peer mediation skills training can be taken as a metaphor for any experiential approach to education that explores issues of citizenship and democracy, its relevance can be extended. It is a cliché, but true, that you can gauge a great deal about a school by spending ten minutes in it; equally, a more extensive intervention by an external agency with a programme like peer mediation throws up all sorts of issues about management, ethos, discipline policies, staff relationships *and the curriculum.*

This book is not trying to 'sell' peer mediation as *the* answer, or even as *an* answer. Rather, it is arguing for schools to take on board the need to enhance the learning and teaching environment by giving weight within the curriculum to the skills and values that underpin mediation.

The US psychologist Abraham Maslow, noted for his creation of the 'hierarchy of needs' model, describes the basic human needs as physiological safety, belonging, esteem, self-actualisation, the desire to know and aesthetic needs. While it's unrealistic and unnecessary for schools to 'spend all their time dealing with the emotional needs and concerns of their students, they have to be attended to before more complex learning needs are attended to'.[7] Schools are in the business of creating effective learning and teaching environments, and some would contend that 'it takes an entire community to create safe, caring and productive learning environments'.[8]

In exploring how the curriculum might assist in the creation of such environments, this chapter will put forward the argument that training in life skills such as peer mediation should have as high a priority in the curriculum as traditional subjects, if not higher. It has been argued that employers are impressed by a potential employee who relates well to other people, is a dab hand at resolving conflict, and works effectively as a member of a team. Asked what she felt should be a key message of this book, a representative of one peer mediation agency said: 'Having just heard [on the radio that morning] about employers' concerns with respect to university graduates' lack of communication and interpersonal skills, I would say that youngsters who are taught mediation skills will grow up with an advantage. Another lack [in graduates] was the skills of working in a team – again part of basic peer mediation skills.[9]

Education for mutual understanding (EMU)

As indicated in Chapter 1, peer mediation in Northern Ireland is rooted in the progression of Education for Mutual Understanding (EMU), a cross-curricular theme that became a statutory requirement in 1992. CCEA is responsible for producing curriculum materials, as well as for advising the Minister for Education on curriculum, assessment and examination matters. In 1996 CCEA produced guidance materials for the themes of Education for Mutual Understanding and Cultural Heritage, stressing that the rationale for both 'emerged, first and foremost, from a desire within education to address issues of conflict, mistrust and division within Northern Ireland society.'[10]

The aim of these guidelines was to 'provide ideas, case studies and exemplars of good practice for schools wishing to enhance provision for EMU and Cultural Heritage'.[11] Included amongst the case studies were two accounts of peer mediation, one from the perspective of a teacher, the other from the perspective of a pupil. These case studies helped to offset a criticism of EMU, namely that it was so abstract that it was difficult to translate it into 'concrete educational practice'.[12] Thus the value of peer mediation training as an example of good EMU practice was being recognised officially by CCEA.

Education for Mutual Understanding, or EMU, is unique to Northern Ireland. The National Curriculum in England and Wales does not have a comparable mandate to deliver the EMU objectives, which are:

1. fostering respect for self and others and building relationships
2. understanding conflict
3. appreciating interdependence
4. Fostering cultural understanding.

The first two objectives are specifically addressed by peer mediation training and delivery:

Fostering respect for self and others and building relationships
Pupils should have opportunities to develop knowledge and understanding of themselves, and to learn how to handle a range of personal and social situations and react appropriately to them.

Understanding conflict
Pupils should have opportunities to develop knowledge and understanding of conflict in a variety of contexts and of how to respond to it positively and creatively.[13]

The CCEA EMU guidelines encourage teachers to use interactive methods; the peer mediation workshop format and processes could have been a model for them:

The teaching styles associated with EMU and Cultural Heritage are more likely to be experiential and active, with the learning emerging from the experience of being involved and valued. The teacher, as a facilitator, encourages:

- a climate of caring and mutual respect involving listening and contributing constructively;
- increased group and individual responsibility; and
- a sense of achievement and value for each pupil.[14]

As the opening quotation to this chapter illustrates, the Curriculum Review in Northern Ireland (as elsewhere in the world) is beginning to recognise that school league tables, assessment and examinations that merely attempt to measure the amount of knowledge obtained, are inadequate indicators of educational achievement.

EMU as a cross-curricular theme was already providing a context in which to pioneer innovative teaching and learning approaches. The guidance notes acknowledged that subjects like English and religious education 'will be able to deliver the themes, in terms of specific knowledge, quite explicitly. For other subjects the contribution may rest largely within interpersonal relationships and the style of teaching rather than the content.'[15] Or to put it another way, such skills and values as more likely to be 'caught rather than taught'.

In Chapter 6, Northern Irish politicians reflect on their own experiences of conflict resolution; Sean Neeson, leader of the Alliance Party (who has a teaching background himself) is of the opinion that the only way of passing on such skills is by modelling them.[16]

The *process* of establishing peer mediation in any given school, then, emerges as something of a metaphor for the changes that are necessary in education generally. Peer mediation training involves very real skills, life skills that employers value, and yet these precious skills are undervalued precisely because they do not fall neatly into conventional measurement criteria. Nevertheless on a number of occasions Department of Education inspectors have commented on the effectiveness of peer mediation training: 'The range of extra-curricular activities provides a worthwhile extension to the children's learning. In particular, the Peer Mediation programme for the children in year 7 encourages them to settle their disputes rationally, and is contributing much to their confidence and maturity.'[17]

'Dr Hunter enjoyed the Peer Mediation session he saw in Primary 6/7 . . . it shows – co-operation, building self-esteem, children are able to talk about themselves, character building.'[18] On the one hand, teachers are being exhorted to 'take greater advantage of opportunities arising from, for example: . . . points of pupil interest including open and empathetic reaction in class and at school.'[19] On the other, CCEA's own research threw up a finding that 'reveals that primary school pupils have an alarmingly narrow view of "important learning". For 10-year-olds, this was almost entirely confined to the three areas of the curriculum which feature in assessment.'[20]

As far as junior school children were concerned, if it wasn't English, maths or science, it didn't count. 'Focusing too strongly on assessment runs the risk of measuring only that which is measurable and therefore teaching only what is to be assessed.'[21] The reality is that in the final two years in the primary school, any notion of a broad curriculum that cherishes inquiry and discovery and an interactive learning process is rudely assaulted by the blunt instrument of the 11+ transfer test.

Peer mediation and the 11+ transfer test

Northern Ireland is exceptional within the United Kingdom, and indeed within Western Europe, in that it retains the 11+ transfer test[22] – a selection process implemented for the benefit of grammar schools. It involves two tests taken a fortnight apart in the autumn term of the P7 year, the final year of primary schooling.

The test used to have a simple pass or fail grade; now it has a grading system of A, B1, B2, C1, C2 and D. In the 1999/2000 academic year, according to CCEA,[23] 30.86 per cent of children were graded at D (for many children this is still perceived as 'failure'). The inequities of this selection process in terms of class division, human rights, its psychological effect and issues to do with equity are part of this debate. In September 2000 the results of two years' research into the 11+ transfer test selection were published by Queen's University Belfast and the University of Ulster at the request of the Department of Education.[24] It recommended five options, only one of which is a fully comprehensive education system. The Minister of Education, Martin McGuinness, set up a review to consider future arrangements for secondary education in Northern Ireland.

It is the author's fervent hope that by the time this book is published the new Northern Ireland Assembly will have seized the opportunity to do away with the invidious 11+ transfer test. The Good Friday agreement is based on concepts of equity and parity of esteem, but as journalist Eamon McCann argues, 'Any equality agenda that doesn't include abolishing the 11+ is a fraud.'[25]

However, if it is simply to be replaced by another form of selection, the danger is that the curriculum will continue to be exam-driven rather than cherishing children's disposition to learn. The 11+ transfer test *distorts* the curriculum during the final two years of primary school education. This is relevant to schools that take on peer mediation because it is precisely during these two years that children are trained to become mediators.

When the peer mediation training programme was first introduced into Northern Ireland in autumn 1993, the principal of one of the two schools involved was anxious that the start of the training be delayed until after the children had sat the first 11+ transfer test.[26] The reason for this decision was that the class would be concentrating on practice tests for the forthcoming exam – to the exclusion of almost everything else. For example, one class missed several Physical Education lessons because of this emphasis. So it was hardly surprising that there wasn't time to do peer mediation training. Significantly, the following year, the Project was asked to start the programme early in the term. This was because Wednesday afternoons (when the training took place) were a rare time in the week when the children could relax and enjoy themselves, and have a sense of their own self-worth, irrespective of how they were getting on in the practice tests. The curriculum is meant to be broad-based, but the transfer tests focus exclusively on maths, English, and science and technology, so that, for example, music, art and environmental education are not included and therefore tend to be sidelined. In the two terms leading up to the exam, what isn't tested is often neglected. The test itself is a multiple-choice test reinforcing the concept of learning as assimilating knowledge and coming up with one right answer.

The learning that the 11+ transfer test represents is based on a convergent, cognitive, competitive, elitist approach measuring a single intelligence quotient (IQ). Peer mediation training is the opposite: it represents divergent, affective, co-operative learning, acknowledging the existence of multiple intelligences:

1. Instead of teaching children that there is a right and a wrong solution to a given problem, it encourages them to generate a variety of possible solutions (*brainstorming*) and negotiate an agreed solution (*bargaining*). In this way it supports divergent thinking rather than just convergent thinking.

2. Peer mediation training is a participatory, experiential process. The mediation process itself, it has been argued, teaches children logic, so it does have a cognitive element to it. But the training acknowledges the importance of feelings and encourages empathy, and is very much part of an affective approach to education.

3. Throughout the training the emphasis is on co-operation; from the games that are played through to the mediation process itself, which requires co-operation, mutual respect and reliance. The disputants have to co-operate with each other and the mediators, if there is to be an agreement.

4. The selection of mediators was explored in Chapter 3, Farrell and Tyrrell recommending that 'in addition to considerations of competence, selection criteria ought to

be weighted in favour of the inclusion, as mediators, of children with a history of conflict.'[27] Less than a month into the first training programme in Northern Ireland, Farrell was proposing that 'all the children who have participated in the initial training be encouraged to use the skills they have learned, mediating at an informal level where the opportunity presents itself, so that mediator will be seen as the role of everybody who wishes to claim it. The distinction between those selected for further training and the rest will not then be so marked.'[28] One practical way of demonstrating the egalitarian nature of peer mediation training was suggested by Hartop: 'I would give all the children who were involved in training a certificate, "qualified as mediator".'[29]

In Farrell and Tyrrell's report *Peer Mediation in Primary Schools*, comments about the value of peer mediation are peppered with references to the 11+. A lunchtime supervisor at one school made the following observation:

> Mediation isn't a thing about brains; anybody can do it if they are shown how to do it. [When those who get picked are] the ones who do the 11+ and who can do quizzes, the others just sit back and say, 'Well, I must be useless; I can do nothing.' Mediation is something those children can get involved in – and feel important.[30]

A teacher commented:

> I would like to see [the children] recognised from the moment they get into P7, [by saying to them]. 'This has got nothing to do with the 11+ or anything else. The fact is that you have been selected for mediation and there's a note going home to your parents congratulating you.' We would be telling their parents that we place value on their child and that his/her peers place value on their child. 'That's what I would like to see.'[31]

However, perhaps the biggest indictment of the 11+ and the subject-based, academic, league-tables approach that tends to drive education, is that the 11+ transfer test is based on a concept of intelligence that is outdated. 'The intelligence which forms the main focus in education [because it is most easily measured] is only one aspect of intelligence, which relates to academic success in schools, and not necessarily to success in life.[32] At least seven intelligences have been identified:[33] linguistic, logical/mathematical, kinesthetic, visual/spatial, musical, personal and intrapersonal. Howard Gardner, who is best known in educational circles for his theory of multiple intelligences, believes that the educational system places too much emphasis on memorising and standardised tests. He argues that students should be taught how to apply knowledge and problem-solving techniques to new situations.'[34]

In a chapter entitled 'Multiple Intelligences', Pruett gives 'samples of activities that students would encounter in each intelligence'.[35] For example, logical/mathematical intelligence involves deductive reasoning and problem-solving; kinesthetic includes 'dramatising events' [*role-play*]. Perhaps most significant of all, interpersonal intelligence encompasses 'develop[ing] cooperative learning skills as [students] solve problems, answer questions ... brainstorm ideas'. Intrapersonal intelligence involves developing thinking skills through reflection – another aspect of peer mediation training, which encourages children to reflect on each session during the following week.

This chapter argues that peer mediation training, along with other experiential processes that encourage children to participate in and evaluate their own learning, identifies and develops skills that should have a higher priority within the curriculum. The issue is not so much 'Where does interactive learning fit into the curriculum?' as 'How does the current curriculum prepare young people to become citizens and members of a work force that requires new skills of problem-solving and team-building?' Put bluntly, the greatest challenge to schools in embracing a whole-school approach to peer mediation is not the management of the necessary change in the school ethos but the fact that the 'burden on teachers to regulate their day by "literacy hour", "numeracy hour", "stand-up hour", "sit-down hour", "do the hokey-cokey hour", etc. – stifles innovation'.[36]

Jenny Mosley, who is a key player in developing circle time, says, 'It is ironic that business and industry send their managers on team-building courses, and programmes to build their self-esteem. Does this mean that insufficient attention is being paid to such skills in formal education?'[37]

Figure 5.1 indicates how peer mediation fits into the current curriculum. As well as the more obvious links with religious education and English, teachers have also made links with subjects like science. One reported:

> In science we were investigating wheels. It was a very open-ended type of investigation, in small groups. Some of the groups were much more successful than others and it became clear to me that the more successful groups were the the co-operating groups. I decided at the end to ask them to evaluate their working together. With no input from me they came up with the idea that the rules that we had used in the mediation workshops were the rules that would be good for a maths or a science workshop. I was delighted; that is a direct area of application.[38]

Some would argue that conflict-resolution skills training should become the 'Fourth R;[39], others would advocate relationships education as deserving that recognition.[40] 'Conflict literacy' is a term that has been coined to sum up the skills of affirmation, co-operation, communication and problem-solving that transform the underlying causes of conflict.[41]

Throughout the years of peer mediation training, the EMU-Promoting School Project received feedback indicating that the process was reinforcing the traditional 3Rs. For example, a principal noted that the children's 'reading, writing and oral skills had improved demonstrably'. Talking and listening skills were constantly reinforced in the pair, small-group and large-group settings that constituted peer mediation training. 'I'm learning to talk in a group,' Stephen, Primary 7, Donemana Controlled Primary School commented in answer to the question, 'What have you been learning?' 'There is a noticeable increase in confidence in Primary 7 about speaking out in large groups . . . the quality of speaking and listening has improved, e.g. in English language classes.'[42]

Just as the 'You may pass' ground rule provides children with the choice *not* to participate if they don't want to, it also provides an opportunity for participating when they are ready. There were several occasions when a small group needed someone to report back and a shy child would volunteer, safe in the knowledge that he or she would be given support and treated with respect. When a group of children did a role-play in front of Mary Robinson when she was President of the Irish Republic, the children were chosen because of their confidence rather than their academic ability. This high profile of children who were not previously known for their confidence became a hallmark of such presentations. 'Mediators demonstrated their skills to several conferences of educators, who were invariably impressed by their skills and by the self-confidence that was evident in their responses to questions about their experiences.'[43] The principal of the school commented:

> The Primary 7s have had a great year this year and the [peer mediation] training was a big factor in this. Since their training the mediators have met with a whole range of visitors – Korean and Japanese students and teachers, alumni from Fordham Law School in the USA, a group of journalists, and several other groups. All of these have been quite amazed at their confidence, their understanding of mediation and their articulateness in responding to questions about their experiences as mediators.

It is easy to see how peer mediation skills relate to a subject like English. It is clearly relevant to religious education as well. As one teacher reported, 'As part of class RE we were looking at keeping rules. It was agreed that having our own class rules [carried over from the peer mediation training] makes our class a happier place to be.'[44]

As Figure 5.1 shows, there is no end to the possibilities of fitting peer mediation training into the curriculum in primary schools. Bickmore refers to the generally underused

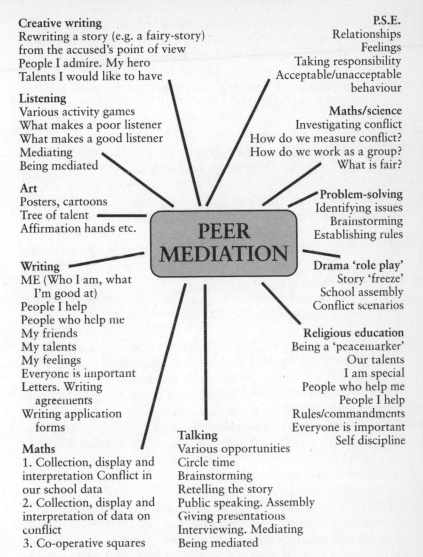

Creative writing
Rewriting a story (e.g. a fairy-story)
from the accused's point of view
People I admire. My hero
Talents I would like to have

Listening
Various activity games
What makes a poor listener
What makes a good listener
Mediating
Being mediated

Art
Posters, cartoons
Tree of talent
Affirmation hands etc.

Writing
ME (Who I am, what
  I'm good at)
People I help
People who help me
My friends
My talents
My feelings
Everyone is important
Letters. Writing
  agreements
Writing application
  forms

Maths
1. Collection, display and
interpretation Conflict in
our school data
2. Collection, display and
interpretation of data on
conflict
3. Co-operative squares

P.S.E.
Relationships
Feelings
Taking responsibility
Acceptable/unacceptable
behaviour

Maths/science
Investigating conflict
How do we measure conflict?
How do we work as a group?
What is fair?

Problem-solving
Identifying issues
Brainstorming
Establishing rules

Drama 'role play'
Story 'freeze'
School assembly
Conflict scenarios

Religious education
Being a 'peacemarker'
Our talents
I am special
People who help me
People I help
Rules/commandments
Everyone is important
Self discipline

Talking
Various opportunities
Circle time
Brainstorming
Retelling the story
Public speaking. Assembly
Giving presentations
Interviewing. Mediating
Being mediated

PEER MEDIATION

Fig. 5.1: Peer mediation as a cross-curricular project

Brendan Hartop 1999 (Reproduced from HARTOP, B.,
FARRELL, S., and TYRRELL, J. (1999). *The EMU Promoting
School Project Peer Mediation Manual,* University of Ulster:
Centre for the Study of Conflict.

links between conflict resolution and the curriculum: 'conflict is an important theme in virtually all literature, science, arts, and social sciences: thus the academic curriculum seemed an untapped resource for conflict mediation, and conflict mediation seemed a nearly untapped resource for the academic curriculum.'[45]

Peer mediation and the current curriculum review in Northern Ireland

At the time of writing, the current aims of the Northern Ireland curriculum are:

1. to promote the spiritual, moral, cultural, intellectual and physical development of pupils at the school and thereby of society; and
2. to prepare pupils for the opportunities, responsibilities and experiences of adult life.[46]

It is proposed to change this to: 'to enable young people to achieve their potential and to make informed and responsible choices and decisions throughout their lives'.[47]

In the CCEA's notes accompanying these suggestions, it is acknowledged that the emphasis in the outcomes will be on 'how young people will *make use of* the skills, values, attitudes and knowledge gained in making life decisions'. (*original emphasis*).

The rationale for the change in aims has arisen from the growing awareness of teachers and others, of the need to cater for the emotional development of young people. It is also acknowledged that it is not sufficient to prepare children for the future – that is, adulthood – the curriculum has to be relevant to the issues and decisions children already have to face. In addition, as well as 'competence in literacy and numeracy, modern conceptions of preparedness for work stress qualities such as interpersonal competence and confidence, thinking skills, responsibility, creativity and the ability to work in a team'.[48] In the context of ICT (information communication technology), 'schools' contribution to the learning revolution should focus on helping pupils to . . . develop teamwork and communication skills'.[49] What this might look like in practice is a 'process' curriculum in which the teacher adopts the workplace practice of coaching mixed-ability, mixed-age teams to handle open-ended problems.[50]

Early-years education

Currently the introduction of structured peer mediation, particularly with a service, tends to be at Key Stage 2 level (8–11 years old). As this book has stressed, it is vital that children in Key Stage 1 are prepared for this training. The proposals for changing the Northern Ireland curriculum highlight research by Katz, Pascal, Laevers and others. 'This research stresses the importance of the social and emotional development of the child and the crucial need to develop, through an enjoyable, creative and failure-free experience, children's dispositions to learn.'[51]

The idea of a failure-free environment is particularly attractive. It is arguably what a peer mediation workshop is trying to provide, with its emphasis on it being 'okay to make mistakes', and ensuring no one is put down. Moreover, the CCEA report reflects on the need for social skills to be emphasised much earlier in a child's school life.

> The single best childhood predictor of adult adaptation is not IQ, not school grades and not classroom behaviour. Rather it is the adequacy with which the child gets along with other children. Children who are generally disliked, who are aggressive and disruptive, who are unable to sustain close relationships with other children and who cannot establish a place for themselves in the peer culture are seriously 'at risk'.[52]

In the CCEA Curriculum Review, early-years education is seen as needing to nurture children's disposition to learn, through the mastery of basic concepts through play. It stresses the need for young children to be socially competent, that is, to be able to interact effectively with their peers.

In May and June 2000, CCEA spent several weeks consulting on proposals for a new curriculum framework. It was an extensive consultation, with 37 meetings and talks with a wide variety of groups, in addition to 20 regional seminars for teachers. Within a month of the Northern Ireland Assembly being reconvened in May 2000, CCEA had presented its initial findings to the Assembly Education Committee: 'There has been a broad welcome for the idea of moving from a subject-led curriculum to one based on skills, relevance and enjoyment, emphasising personal development, citizenship, employability and ICT skills.'[53]

Conclusion

The peer mediation programme was developed as one approach to the delivery of Education for Mutual Understanding (EMU) at the senior end of primary schools in Northern Ireland. The findings from our research are that, given an amenable school ethos, it can be an excellent way to do so. It also helps prepare children for citizenship. 'Peer mediation . . . creates active roles for young people in order to help them develop capacities for democratic citizenship [such as critical reasoning and shared decision-making].'[54] Currently, in Northern Ireland at least, citizenship education is relevant to only Key Stage 3 – secondary school pupils. Bickmore, writing about a US context, argues that schools have to be proactive and energetic in this area: 'It would be difficult for any school to overcome the typical hidden curriculum of passive citizenship, unless it built conflict management activity, and critical reflection about conflict, into the timetable, into the core curriculum, and into the lives of the whole range of students.'[55]

As a programme focusing on basic relationship skills for children in the 9–11 age group, peer mediation offers a good foundation programme for secondary-level skills in exploring controversial issues in the social, civic and political field. The core values and skills needed for interpersonal relationships are precisely those on which social harmony is predicated. Without such preliminary programmes it is difficult to envisage citizenship education at secondary level proving viable or effective. Several schools have therefore begun to address the need for a series of social-engagement skills programmes to precede peer mediation in the earlier years of primary schooling, each one serving as a foundation for the next. It seems appropriate to encourage schools to think in terms of programmes that permeate the curriculum, supported by a scheduled circle time slot in the weekly timetable throughout the year. When confined to a series of workshops in a single term, the effects tend to become dispersed when the series of programmes is completed.

6. Peer Mediation Skills and the Northern Ireland Peace Process

Throughout the introduction of peer mediation in Northern Ireland in 1993/4 and its subsequent development, children and adults alike made connections between the skills of peer mediation and the skills required in the ongoing peace process. Politicians themselves have alluded to the relevance of peer mediation skills, and between May and September 2000 the author interviewed individuals from six of the parties involved in the negotiations leading up to the Good Friday Agreement.

Background[1]

In 1996 Senator George Mitchell was appointed chair of the Peace Process. On 30 May of that year elections to the all-party negotiations and proposed Northern Ireland forum were held, and multi-party negotiations began on 10 June. 'All 18 parliamentary constituencies elected five delegates to the talks/forum, but voters simply chose a party list of candidates. The ten parties which had gained the most votes across Northern Ireland were then awarded two top-up delegates. The total number of potential delegates/forum members was thus 110.'[2]

In addition to established political parties like the Democratic Unionist Party, (DUP), Social Democratic and Labour Party (SDLP), Ulster Unionist Party (UUP) and Alliance Party of Northern Ireland (APNI), smaller parties were represented, some for the first time: the United Kingdom Unionist Party (UKUP), the Northern Ireland Women's Coalition (NIWC), the Progressive Unionist Party (PUP), the Ulster Democratic Party (UDP) and Labour.[3] The latter four small parties, who had just two seats each, combined to become an informal 'group of four' so that, as Kate Fearon, political adviser to the Women's Coalition, commented: 'we punched above our weight, not on every issue . . . but on issues like process because we all stood the risk of being excluded, or being kept outside, or being kept away from negotiations'.[4]

Sinn Fein (SF), although achieving 15.5 per cent of the vote, was excluded from the negotiations until after the IRA ceasefire in September 1997. Eight days after Sinn Fein joined the negotiations, the UKUP and the DUP left in protest at their presence, and did not return.

The PUP and UDP were both closely linked to Loyalist paramilitary organisations, the Ulster Volunteer Force and the Ulster Defence Association/Ulster Freedom Fighters, respectively; Sinn Fein and the IRA were also closely linked with each other.

On 10 April 1998 the parties signed the Good Friday Agreement. On 22 May 1998 a referendum was held as to whether or not the Agreement should be accepted. The referendum took place simultaneously in the Irish Republic and in Northern Ireland. The results in Northern Ireland were: Yes, 71.12 per cent – No, 28.88 per cent (turnout 81.10 per cent); Republic of Ireland – Yes, 94.39 per cent – No, 5.61 per cent (turnout 56.26 per cent).

On 25 June 1998, elections for the 108 seats in the Northern Ireland Assembly took place. Of the small parties who had been involved in the Good Friday Agreement, the UDP and Labour failed to get a sufficient mandate to have seats in the Assembly. On 1 July the Assembly met for the first time, but it was to take a further 17 months before the Executive came into being on 2 December 1999. On 11 February 2000, barely two months later, both the Executive and the Assembly were suspended. The issue that caused the delay was the one that also led to the suspension: disagreement over the decommissioning of weapons.

After the IRA agreed to allow some of its arms dumps to be inspected, the Executive and the Assembly were reinstated, on 29 May 2000.

The interviews

The author interviewed the following representatives from the six parties:

Kate Fearon, political adviser to the Women's Coalition (15 May 2000)

David Ervine, leader of the Progressive Unionist Party (30 May 2000)

Sean Neeson, leader of the Alliance Party (13 June 2000)

Sean Farren, negotiator for the SDLP, Minister for Higher and Further Education, Training and Employment (26 June 2000)

Alan McFarland, negotiator for the UUP (17 July 2000)

Martin McGuinness, negotiator for Sinn Fein, Minister of Education (6 September 2000)

Each was interviewed separately. The interviews were open-ended, and included some of the following questions suggested by children from Oakgrove Integrated Primary School:

- Do you find it hard to listen to the other side and to appreciate what they are feeling?
- Do you ever listen to both sides separately? We do that in mediation and it is sometimes helpful.
- Has brainstorming ever worked when you are negotiating?
- In mediation we learn to give and take and to bargain. Can you use these tools in your discussions?
- Why was it so difficult to come to an agreement? Why did it take such a long time?
- Is it hard to put your own feelings and background to one side when you are trying to find mutual agreement?

These questions proved to be invaluable, and helped to focus the interviews.

'Why was it so difficult to come to an agreement? Why did it take such a long time?'

Sean Farren (SDLP) responded on two levels. He explained that once Sinn Fein joined the negotiations in September 1997, it then took only seven months to reach agreement. However, the 30 years of the troubles it took to get to a point where peace could be agreed was an inordinate amount of time, and 'the longer the conflict exists the more elaborate becomes the final set of arrangements because more angles have to be covered'.

The peace process had to be seen in the context of the previous violence, stated David Ervine: 'There are two processes prior to conflict resolution. One is management of the conflict, and the other is transformation of the conflict from one of violence to politics, and then subsequently conflict resolution is a serious option.'

Martin McGuinness said that the Sinn Fein leadership had recognised in the early 1990s (prior, for example, to the first IRA cessation in 1994) that:

> there needed to be a peace process, a conflict resolution process which addressed the issues which we believed lay at the heart of the conflict. [We recognised] that we on our own, in Sinn Fein, couldn't [bring about a peace process]. It had to be a collective approach, and if there was to be a collective approach then Sinn Fein would have to make a connection with people who were our political opponents, and indeed with people whom we considered to be our political enemies.

What is the value of 'process'?

Implicit in the question is the length of time it took from the signing of the agreement to the setting up of the Executive. Interviewed in May 2000, during the suspension of the Executive and Assembly, Kate Fearon said, 'The situation we are in at the moment is because the process hasn't been managed since July 1998'.

Ervine maintained, 'We should have had the systems in place after we left Castle Buildings [when the Belfast

Agreement was signed].' The Women's Coalition tried to establish a process, without success. McFarland said that at the time, his party (the UUP) thought that there was no need for one, because 'all the boxes had been ticked ... But in retrospect it would have been helpful to have some system of implementation, where you could say, "Hang on a minute, there's something wrong here, what are you doing?" ' McGuinness made the point that 'it is easy to say that things would have been okay, if only we had kept the process going'. However, he maintained that that analysis needed to take into consideration 'fall-out from the Agreement itself coming to fruition on Good Friday – and the fact that different forces came into play ... to work *against* the Agreement'.

Talking to the different politicians, it appeared that there was a tacit need for a process to deal with different interpretations of what was agreed, if only to resolve the inevitable conflicts when the reality of any agreement has to be put into practice. McGuinness maintained that:

> The difficulty then is that people will say that the Agreement was left open to interpretation, and I don't believe it was. I think that the agreed interpretation that we had with the British Government and the Irish Government fell apart because the British Government succumbed to pressure from within the Unionist political leadership.

Moving from fixed positions to agreement

Peer mediation starts with the parties taking up positions and then, through becoming involved in a process, working together towards finding a solution. In the context of the negotiations towards the Good Friday Agreement, the traditional positions were either Nationalist/Republican (in favour of a United Ireland) or Unionist/Loyalist (in favour of remaining part of the United Kingdom). The Women's Coalition was, Kate Fearon said, 'careful not to tie ourselves down to a fixed position, being either of those positions or another one. What we were interested in was going in to try and reach an accommodation, something that took other politicians a long time to get to grips with, and something that we were criticised for a lot, certainly at the outset.'

Nevertheless, there was a general recognition that it was time for new processes and new structures. These took time to establish. For example, the concept of 'sufficient consensus', first floated in a government Consultation Paper,[5] had to be thrashed out by the politicians. What it meant in practice was that there had to be a majority of *both* traditions in favour of a particular decision, initially about the processes used in the the negotiations, and then about the structures of the Assembly.

'Do you ever listen to both sides separately?'

All the political parties were involved as negotiators, so ostensibly it wasn't their role to mediate – that was the responsibility of the British government, the Irish government, George Mitchell and his team. All the same, most parties represented by the interviewees found themselves acting as go-betweens. David Ervine explained that he would talk separately to Gerry Adams (President of Sinn Féin); he found that they had in common being associated with paramilitaries, but that was as far as it went, because, as Ervine said, 'I am a Unionist'; similarly with David Trimble (Leader of the Ulster Unionist Party): they would have an understanding because they both came from a unionist tradition. But again, that was as far as it went, because, he said, 'I am associated with people with guns'. Ervine went on to say that 'in both cases we speak their language, but we don't have their trust'.

Sean Neeson instanced another Alliance negotiator and himself meeting with Sinn Fein on Maundy Thursday to hammer out the guarantees that would make it possible for them to agree to being part of the Assembly. McGuinness acknowledged that the Unionists were the group that Sinn Fein had the hardest job convincing of their sincerity. Over many years Sinn Fein's strategy had been to build a bridge to the Unionist political leadership, through establishing relationships with others including the Protestant churches and the Protestant business community. When it came to the talks themselves, the British Government, the Irish Government and the SDLP all played a role. McGuinness said:

> certainly other parties had a role to play. I'm not so sure it was like an intermediary role or . . . a structured thing, in as far as we would be *using* the SDLP. It was a matter of us, in our relationship – with the Irish Government, the SDLP, the Unionist business community and the churches – it was more a question of them explaining where we were coming from, and hoping that the right signals would go to the leadership of the Ulster Unionist party.

But throughout the pre-Good Friday Agreement negotiations, the Unionists and Sinn Fein didn't talk to each other. McFarland argued, in circular fashion, that the Ulster Unionist Party wouldn't talk to Sinn Fein because they didn't trust them, and they didn't trust them because they had no relationship with them, and they had no relationship with them because they didn't talk to them . . .

In addition to the similarities here with the peer mediation process – the need for trust and the importance of talking separately – there were a number of major differences. Peer mediation only works if parties agree to meet together in the same room. Furthermore, deadlines and time frames have limited relevance, although the impending school bell can concentrate the minds at the end of lunch hour. There is no doubt about the level of coercion towards the end of the talks that led up to the Agreement, with the British Government and the Irish Government putting on the pressure. It could be argued that their role was one of arbiter rather than mediator. The role of the two Governments was significant; according to Farren, 'Really, if the parties themselves had been in control of the negotiations we would still be there yet'.

The importance of relationships
Fundamentally, peer mediation is about restoring existing relationships, whereas a great deal of the work of the Peace Process inside and outside the negotiations was in building confidence and developing *new* relationships.

Sean Neeson alluded to a trip the politicians made to South Africa in 1997:

> It was supposed to be secret but as we drove through the gates of the place we were staying in, there were the television cameras. Sinn Fein flew out separately, the Unionists wouldn't even travel on the same plane with them – I well remember that first day at the dining table, I was there with David Trimble. Martin McGuinness came over to shake Trimble's hand and Trimble just turned away from him. Over the next couple of days, when we got into the social environment some of the barriers were broken down. I think that nothing of huge political significance came out of the South African experience, but I think the most important thing was that it was the first time that senior Unionists shared the same room with senior members of Sinn Fein. I think that is what this whole process has been about . . . it's not a question of overnight people changing their attitudes towards one another; but it has been a process, and I know that prior to the suspension of the Assembly there were occasions when jokes would be passed between leading members of Sinn Fein and leading members of the Unionists. To the extent you can get out of the formal situation into the informal environment, you find the barriers become broken down.

Just as the nature of relationships in peer mediation is key, the relationships at an individual level between the negotiators were vital to the the dynamics of the process. Sean Farren found it easier to get on with the UUP, even though he was a nationalist, than with Sinn Fein, as is explained later in the chapter. Both McFarland and Ervine made the point that you need to know your opposition's position in order to understand them better.

'Did all the disputants talk to each other?'
Farren pointed out that 'the Ulster Unionists and Sinn Fein didn't directly negotiate with each other *at all* during the

negotiations. They talked through others, through the two Governments in particular, and across the table at each other – *at each other*.' Ervine, concurring with Farren's perspective, said 'The two Governments had essentially negotiated by proxy for us. There was some direct negotiation [between parties] but not a lot.'

'Has brainstorming ever worked when you are negotiating?'
'In mediation we learn to give and take and to bargain. Can you use these tools in your discussions?'
Mo Mowlam, who was British Secretary of State for Northern Ireland in the months leading up to the signing of the Good Friday Agreement, is reported as using brainstorming when looking at previous negotiations for inspiration:

> [When] they brainstormed ideas for a solution they could look back to earlier attempts and discover whether it had worked or not. Experience taught lessons quickly. Once, when [Mo Mowlam] was faced with an enormous problem, someone observed that she should treat it like a boulder on the street – go around it, then look back on it, and it may look smaller.[6]

It was clear that there were a number of tools used during the process. McFarland referred to 'parking', whereby: 'You deal with the easy things and you park the difficult areas; you put brackets round it and say "This is parked". We can't find agreement to this – we shouldn't destroy the rest of it, so we park it.' Ervine stressed the need for 'give and take'. It was a question of 'recognising that there was little point in attempting to take the bus fare off your opposite negotiator – everybody has to retain an element of dignity'.

All the interviewees acknowledged the need to be inclusive, and the fact that knowledge and understanding of your opponent's position was essential if he or she was to be part of the solution.

The role of the 'mediators' in the Peace Process
A frequent challenge for peer mediators is having to mediate

their friends. On a macro level this was at least a perceived problem for some of the interviewees. McFarland maintained that:

> whereas the Irish Government was firmly locked in with Sinn Fein and the SDLP in what was termed at the time the 'Pan Nationalist front' our Government, our natural allies, had removed themselves into the referee's position, were refereeing like mad and paying no attention to our problems. Yet the Irish Government were linking daily to John Hume and Gerry Adams.

He did, however, concede that: 'Having said all that, when we got to the end of the process and things were in a tight corner, Tony Blair did stand by us, and was direct and honest . . . he was the first prime minister who stood by us for a long time and said "No, we can't sell this to the Unionists".' For his part McGuinness said:

> The most important Government to us was the British Government. I'm not saying that in any disparaging way towards the Irish Government, but the Irish Government knew what was wrong in the North and knew what was needed to put it right. The British Government had to face up to all of that, and of course the Blair government did show particular courage in participating in the negotiations – Blair himself coming to the negotiations and being part of the Good Friday business. It was always part of our belief that if Blair hadn't appeared on the scene we wouldn't have got the Agreement.

Ervine said both Governments were too close to the respective groups and actually got in the way: 'We witnessed the process being destroyed day after day after day, by the very people supposedly involved in the process – where the process here [in Belfast] has been massively undermined by trips to Dublin by Nationalists and trips to London by Unionists.'

It was certainly held that the Governments were or would

be advocates for each side, rather than an impartial third party. In a speech identifying ten peacemaking lessons from the Good Friday Agreement, Mo Mowlam cited one as: '*Keep the momentum but give people space to think.* Mowlam constantly set deadlines to indicate she wanted to make progress. It encouraged the negotiators, even if they did not meet a single deadline on time.'[7] Ervine maintained that: 'The Governments' approach (which I thought was quite masterful at the time) was, if you can't get them to agree, throw down something and get them to negotiate away from it. In that case the methodology wasn't as important as the outcome.'

George Mitchell

On the day that the Good Friday Agreement was signed, all the political leaders present at Stormont paid warm, specific praise to the chair of the Peace Process, George Mitchell. For the television viewer, it added to the historic moment of the Agreement that here were political opponents united in their praise of the mediation skills and values that he had brought to the Process. In their explanations about his role, the interviewees made the following points. 'When the talks began in 1996 with George Mitchell as the chairman,' Neeson said, 'some Unionists found it difficult even to accept an outsider, or trust an outsider as an honest broker. The reason they found it difficult was simply because of the fact that he was American and they didn't trust Americans.' Neeson went on to say that Mitchell gained trust through his patience, his even-handedness and his respect.

McFarland, having identified the shortcomings of the two Governments as 'referees', said of Mitchell:

> You need a very good referee. I think we were extremely fortunate in finding George Mitchell. Because both sides are then able to 'whinge' at him, for want of a better word; but knowing that he's not going to take sides. He's going to soak up whatever you want to say, and is then able to point out to the other side that it may be very difficult for us, and is there any way they could temper [their demands]?

Fearon, too, appreciated Mitchell:

> He always treated people with respect, he would acknowledge people by [saying] 'I recognise Dr Paisley' or 'I recognise Mr McCartney.' He was always friendly to people without favour and allowed people to speak as long as they liked, which was sometimes frustrating. He didn't get in their way. He was valuing every contribution, and not giving any indication of what he thought of their contribution. He allowed everybody the space and the opportunity to do that.. He was really 'steady as she goes', he never got excited. He hardly ever smiled either . . . I'm not saying he was sour but he was very, very serious. He was interested in new ideas and ways of thinking about things.

She also acknowledged the role that the rest of his team played:

> Whilst George Mitchell worked with the parties inside the room, the rest of his team would work extensively with the ones outside. His team members would go to the parties on a one-on-one basis and find out their views and do all that sort of intelligence-gathering for him. It was a team effort – he was brilliant in his own right, but it was a team effort.

Farren said:

> Our process demonstrated a rather crude approach – and it was one which depended a great deal on the two Governments and on George Mitchell – reassuring the two parties that most needed reassurance, Sinn Fein and the Ulster Unionists, that they could make an agreement and retain the integrity of their basic position. And so it was a process of gradually bringing those two in.

McGuinness's perspective was:

What was needed and what George Mitchell brought, was decency and quietness and determination and an ability to gain the respect of all the different participants. And he did that, he gained everybody's respect, everybody liked him and he had the right personality, he could crack a joke, he could make people feel at ease, he could slowly and gently bring people to a position that we could accept and acknowledge that the plan before us was the only plan before us, and any rejection of that would be disaster.

Poacher turned gamekeeper

In previous chapters I have alluded to the transformation of children from being the causers of conflict to being the resolvers of it. The importance of including 'troublemakers' in peer mediation training is mirrored by the vital role that individuals who previously espoused violence played in the Peace Process. Ervine stressed this point:

> I think that one of the ways to explore conflict resolution is actually the case study – because you begin to see yourself in the case! Knowing that you are not alone, knowing that the process of conflict resolution in its own inimitable way is being practised all the time, but yet isn't the science that I think it can and will become. But *not being alone* is vitally important . . . for example, I've listened to Mac Maharaj of the South African Government who was actually the senior Army member of the ANC. His job was to escalate war and then when things began to move politically they came to him and said they needed him to explain to the soldiers why they were going to end the war. Something very similar happened to me. The resonance that had with me . . .

Martin McGuinness responded to the point that young people who have a history of conflict actually often make the best mediators by commenting:

> I do subscribe to the notion that the people best able to participate in a conflict resolution situation are the

people who have been directly involved with the conflict – that also includes the British Government . . . I do think people like David Ervine and Billy Hutchinson [of the PUP], Gary McMichael, and David Adam [of the UDP] and ourselves within Sinn Fein made our own particular contribution, which . . . is a huge contribution to the peace process, and to the success of the Good Friday Agreement.

For Sean Farren, only by Sinn Fein's 'inclusion being guaranteed was there any prospect of the violence being ended'. Alan McFarland said: 'We all have pasts . . . each side has got something murky in their past. Let's live with that and find a way forward.'

'Do you find it hard to listen to the other side and to appreciate what they are feeling?' 'Is it hard to put your own feelings and background to one side when you are trying to find mutual agreement?'
To this Ervine responded, 'It is hard to listen to the other side without wanting to stop them at certain junctures, with an "Ah, but . . ."', but what tested him more was being seen as a traitor by his own tribe, as he put it:

I feel that I've learned a lot about me, about my own people, and that's not easy, that's very painful, to be [seen as] a traitor to your own tribe. I don't think I'm a traitor, so it's not so bad . . . You don't need to make peace with your friend, but you most definitely need to make peace with your enemy . . . you cannot make peace without engaging with your enemy.

McGuinness said that in practice this was bound to be difficult – for everybody:

When you get into the type of process that we went into, there had to be a recognition within ourselves and publicly that compromises would have to be made. And if compromise is part of the equation, that essentially means within yourselves you have to consider everything in relation to what you stand for and what you believe. I think you can still do that and maintain the integrity of your political position. I mean, I am still an Irish Republican and leading member of Sinn Fein, I'm still a representative of a community that desperately wants the Peace Process to work. They are prepared to support me in my efforts within that. Knowing that you have that support and they are prepared to support the compromises that I am prepared to make, is a great comfort, and I think that knowing that gives you opportunities within the Process to stretch out the hand of friendship to our political opponents.

He didn't understate the struggle involved in the continuing dialogue:

But there's an awful lot of pain in that, because once you make that connection, everybody has to face up to all sorts of realities and there has to be the skill of not just articulating where you are coming from, but being prepared to listen to other people and where they are coming from. And in the listening to try and create a set of circumstances in which you could persuade them that they too had to listen to what we had to say, and face up to the issues which were difficult for us.

Farren said that 'even those people [in his party] who had misgivings believed it was the right thing to do, despite the fact that they might have felt the pain of doing so more acutely'. However:

it always irked me that they [Sinn Fein] came from the same broad political tradition [as me] but had represented the violence of that tradition . . . In that sense I was uneasy and also I always felt that as a Nationalist the people I really had to reach out to were Unionists, and the success of an accommodation depended on making it possible for easy working relationships to exist.

Skills needed in the Peace Process

The children who had asked some of the questions also said what skills they thought were needed for peer mediation: 'Patience; good listening skills, and good memory'. The politicians were asked what skills they thought were necessary for the Peace Process.

Farren replied, tongue-in-cheek, that a capacity to look as though you were listening was required. McFarland said, 'Patience, and the ability to see things from "the other chap's shoes".' Ervine felt that the skills were intuitive, but that he had gained a lot from reflection (in prison), and had gone into the process with a commitment to resolution. McGuinness made the point that the skill was 'in accepting first of all that there had to be a peace process . . . awareness and recognition that we had to move along that road was a skill in itself!'

Neeson also echoed the children, with the word 'patience'. He said that he had first entered politics as a local councillor, but that he was aware that the skills of a 'counsellor' were also needed. He alluded to the fact that, as well as the content of political issues, the emotional context too had to be listened to, before the facts could be dealt with. This last comment reinforces the value of that part of the peer mediation process when each disputant is asked in turn how he or she is feeling; it underlines the need for children to develop a vocabulary of feelings.

The benefits of conflict-resolution education

McFarland acknowledged the benefits of conflict-resolution skills training; his previous experience in the Army and in business had led him to an understanding of Republicanism combined with a knowledge of negotiation. However, he was firmly of the opinion that, in day-to-day life – given adversaries of roughly equal stature – conflict resolution should only come into play when the natural order fails. Somewhat tongue-in-cheek, he suggested that the interventions of mediators in everyday disputes might prolong a process that could be quickly and easily sorted by a more summary method. This was more a criticism of third-party intervention; he felt it better that two youngsters should sort it out themselves, even if it meant them fighting it out.

Ervine mentioned an occasion in a public debate when he had rather mischievously, although genuinely, agreed with the points of each of the political opponents, in the process wrong-footing both of them.

What should be taught in the curriculum?

Ervine talked with passion of the need for children to understand about 'power and morality' – which will be echoed by Hilary Cremin in Chapter 11 of this book when she encourages people to reflect on the nature of power in the context of peer mediation programmes. Neeson, who was a schoolteacher before he became a politician, after reflection replied that the only way of passing on peer mediation skills was to model them. McFarland was wary of a 'nanny'-type intervention before the children had a chance to sort things out for themselves, but acknowledged that it was 'good for children to know that here is a system of solving things that exists if you cannot resolve it yourself'.

McGuinness stressed that:

> in ten or twenty years from now people will look back on this period with incredulity and fascination as to how it all came about. Within it lies a huge debate and an educational programme which can be applied to the resolution of conflict, not just here in Ireland but in almost every country in the world. And the key to it is a recognition that if there is a problem and a difficulty, if people are losing their lives, if there is conflict, if there is injustice, if there is inequality, the only way to sort it out is to get people to the negotiating table and to get people to face up to what is required to resolve it.

Sean Farren echoed McFarland's earlier point that the capacity to see something from the other person's point of view was a key skill; whether or not it could be taught was a different issue, but some allowance should be made for it on the curriculum.

In interviewing these politicians individually, I was aware that in addition to the political answers were personal statements, emanating from the experience, often painful and frustrating, of having been part of a process, a continuing process, which didn't have pat answers and which did have difficulties. Empathy, the ability to understand your opponent and a willingness to listen, were all skills and values that the politicians identified as being key – and that are clearly relevant to peer mediation. In a circle time training video, one of the adult participants makes this point: 'It does change the way [the children] relate to one another, and for some of them it is the first time that they have thought about how someone else might feel. It takes a long time for children to put themselves in other people's shoes.'[8]

7. How to Respond to Resistance

'How do you [grown-ups] deal with *your* conflicts?'

'I like peer mediation to help me if I have an argument because children understand children better and they listen to you and you feel that what you have to say about what happened is important. Teachers are too busy and don't listen like that. They just decide on the spot who was in the wrong and give them lines.'[1] *(Peer mediators talking about their experiences)*

While adults have their concerns about children's ability to handle conflict satisfactorily, children can also have low expectations about the ability of adults to model effective responses to conflict.

'It is a common mistake for teachers to ignore, belittle or resist solving the very real problems which exist in children's lives, whether at home, in the classroom or in the wider community.'[2] On the one hand, as adults we tend to trivialise children's conflict, ignoring the link with the emotional fall-out that can leave a child unable to learn anything for the rest of the day; on the other hand, we think mediating is placing a heavy burden on young shoulders. The reality is that, within a well structured and supported programme, mediating and being mediated are empowering experiences, heightening self-respect. It is worth repeating part of the quotation above: '[Children] listen to you and you feel that what you have to say about what happened is important.'

Why is there resistance to children being trained to mediate their own conflicts, and what form does this resistance take? One answer lies in the values and methodology of the peer mediation process itself, which challenges the traditional way in which conflict is handled in schools. This is why the question about how *adults* handle conflict is so pertinent. As noted earlier, 'schools are essentially hierarchical institutions where disciplinary procedures are rigidly established and documented,[3] with an individual adult acting as an arbitrator; whereas mediation is based on a different system of values. Norwegian educationalist Kjell Andberg lists the differences between mediation and arbitration from a pupil's perspective[4] (see Figure 7.1 on pp. 164–5).

Although some teachers do endeavour do hear both sides, and to facilitate a mediation process so as to resolve a conflict, inevitably what results is arbitration rather than mediation. The left-hand column of Andberg's table illustrates that during arbitration the arbitrator is in charge, and it is at his or her discretion whether the disputants have a say. Arbitration involves apportioning blame and deciding on suitable sanctions; whereas mediation is more often about *restoring* relationships.

If we take each issue in Andberg's diagram separately, it is possible to begin to understand the underlying concerns that give rise to resistance.

Distribution of power

Some teachers perceive giving children responsibility for resolving some of their conflicts as letting go of control. Helena Davis, a founder member of the San Francisco Community Boards peer mediation scheme, was asked whether teachers feel their authority is being taken away because the mediators are doing such a good job. She responded:

> It has happened in a few cases [that the teachers have felt that way]. But . . . teachers are so overloaded and so harassed – when you have 35 children in a single classroom, and no help, if you can find a way to get them to take care of their own conflicts, it is so much the better for you. There was an interesting study done in the State of California in 1980, and it was discovered

Arbitration	Issue	Mediation
Arbitrator A has control over both process and result.	Distribution of power	The parties decide both development and result. The mediators guide them through the process.
A is in a position to demand that the parties accept the result. A decides if it is just.	Control of outcome	The parties agree upon a result that both feel is acceptable, or they stop the mediation.
Ideally, A is neutral, but is meant to distinguish right and wrong from school rules.	Impartiality	This is a main issue for the mediators – or the mediation is likely to fail.
A has to have opinions and is supposed to give a 'verdict'. A must consider the school rules when giving his or her verdict.	Third-party judgement	The mediator is not supposed to reveal his or her opinions about who is right – preferably, not even if asked.
A has the power to decide if and how disciplinary action is to be taken. School rules are important here too.	Discipline	Mediation is non-punitive.
Often the main focus is on what happened and who started it.	Time perspective	Solutions for the future are most important. Actions in the past are discussed only to establish a basis for mutual understanding.

	Arbitration	Mediation
Winners and losers	After arbitration there is often a loser – maybe two both are still unhappy.	It is important to find a winner and a solution in which there is no losers, if loser. No agreement is worse than one that is dissatisfying for one of the parties.
Voluntariness	The process is normally compulsory. The parties have to accept whatever outcome.	Mediation has to be voluntary. If not, it might be impossible to mediate.
Definition of the conflict	A defines the conflict according to rules and his or her own judgement. A will often choose the issues, ignoring those that are the most important for the parties.	The parties are led by the mediators to reveal the core of the conflict. The parties decide to what extent underlying issues are brought up.
Scope	A wants to discuss the issues that are the reason for the dispute; likes to define the scope and not let the discussion be sidetracked.	The issues raised by the parties are normally considered relevant, and mediators are trained to handle all such issues.
Confidentiality	A often neglects to raise this issue. The parties are normally uncertain how confidentiality is going to be handled.	This is discussed and it is made clear that confidentiality is significant in mediation. Exceptions are to be agreed upon.

Table 7.1 Differences between arbitration and mediation in pupils' conflicts (Source: Kjell Andberg (2000))

that the classroom teacher spent between 50 per cent
and 80 per cent of his or her time playing referee in the
classroom. 'Did he hit you first, or did you hit him
first?', or 'Be quiet there!' The teachers are more than
willing to give this up so that they can do what they are
trained to do, and what they are paid to do (i.e.,
teach).[5]

Individual teachers have feared that peer mediation would
undermine the traditional role of the teacher. At School D in
our survey, the principal was aware that the class teacher
had such reservations:

The [Primary 7] class teacher had not had the benefit of
the Train the Trainer course. [It] was a clear management decision [to involve him in the peer mediation
programme], given that he had personal misgivings
about the venture, which were not [being] addressed to
his satisfaction, and he therefore entered the programme less than fully engaged at a personal level. It
was the principal's judgement that the Primary 5/6
teacher [also involved in the programme] was more
receptive to the methodology and the rationale behind
the programme, and that he would support his colleague and ultimately sustain the programme. The project had learned from previous experience that a
teacher's active participation in such programmes
depends very much on assent to a vision of education
that attaches high priority, alongside academic achievement, to the development of children's self-esteem and
interpersonal skills; in addition, it requires familiarity
with and some level of assent to the use of interactive
learning processes. The class teacher's colleague, however, was most supportive of him and, with the help
also of project staff at pre-workshop planning meetings
and in the workshops themselves, he became somewhat
more comfortable with the process, to the point of
facilitating component activities very effectively. This
significantly enhanced his relationship with the children
during the period of the training programme.[6]

In the case of School D, the individual teacher was supported and encouraged and his misgivings were taken seriously.

Control of outcome

The issue of teacher control also relates to concern about the outcome of a mediation. A frequently asked question is 'What if it doesn't work?' Other concerns that teachers have are to do with inappropriate outcomes, perhaps where an agreement makes unrealistic demands on absent third parties – for instance, 'I'll give you your football back if you get your Mum to mend my coat.' The job of the mediators is to verify with the two disputants whether they really do agree, and also at a later date (usually about a week later) to check that they have kept their sides of the agreement. It is at this stage that it is possible to renegotiate the agreement if it has failed. The fail-safe mechanism is that if the mediation doesn't work, then the dispute is dealt with by the school's existing discipline policy.

Impartiality

Mediators are chosen by a selection process involving their peers and teachers. For each individual mediation they have to be acceptable to both disputants. Often there is resistance from other teachers to an individual child being chosen as a mediator because they don't think he or she will be fair. Unlike arbitrators, who tend to be self-appointed or appointed by the staff, mediators depend on their reputation as to whether individual disputants will choose them. Consistently, mediators are valued by their peers for their 'fairness' (impartiality by another name), and in practice this means they take the time to listen to and affirm both sides. In Chapter 1 a child was quoted as saying that mediation 'is not about giving advice or taking sides or blaming people or forcing them to agree'.

The nature of the mediation process, with its emphasis on the disputants taking an active part, means that if an individual mediator favours one side or the other, it will soon emerge that he or she is not doing the job properly. Because mediation is a *voluntary* process, if a mediator is not acceptable to his or her peers, the situation will need to be addressed quickly. Teachers have expressed concerns that in choosing mediators they might come in for abuse for being 'teacher's pets', or 'special'; perhaps even be bullied. When this concern has been put to children they have been quick to say that, as long as they do their job well, they are accepted. However, as previously argued, if the mediation service is perceived as being run by children who are never seen to be in conflict themselves, it will have little 'street credibility'. When adults perceive mediators as being like prefects – that is, children who are given extra responsibility and *power over* other children – they become concerned about mediators *exploiting* their position.

If anything, the mediation process empowers the disputants, and the role of mediator is to facilitate that process. It could be argued that the job of the mediators is to empower the disputants to solve their own problems.

Third-party judgement

In the case study at the end of this chapter, a teacher expresses a concern that children will have different values from adults, implying that an adult needed to be present to referee. Adults fear a *Lord of the Flies* outcome – that if you leave a group of children to their own devices for any length of time, the law of the jungle will take over. In reality, as already mentioned, adults have been impressed by the integrity and the responsibility with which children carry out the tasks of peer mediation, and the value they put on their role.

Running through nearly all mediations of children of this age is the need to *restore relationships* rather than just the obeying of rules. There are no two ways about it: mediation requires a child-centred approach, with school rules taking second place to child welfare.

If rules are based on the need to provide a safe, secure learning and teaching environment that upholds mutual respect and support, then restoring relationships will help to reinforce these rules. For example, if Peter knocks Susan over because he is running down the corridor, which is against the school rules, and Peter and Susan resolve that conflict, it is likely simultaneously to reinforce the need to validate the school rule.

Discipline

Perhaps this is where the greatest resistance comes. As Figure 7.1 shows, mediation is non-punitive. In a comment that inspired the EMU-Promoting School Project to question its own assumptions and gave rise to a series of workshops exploring restorative justice principles, one teacher responded thus to a demonstration of peer mediation: 'This is all very well, but what about blame and punishment?' In other words, unless there is some element of punishment, children won't know they have done wrong. Behind this question lies the requirement that the child who has behaved inappropriately be made aware of the consequences of his or her actions, take them seriously, and that he not repeat the misdemeanour. This underlying concern is shared by teachers who promote peer mediation; the difference is that they would recognise that the process of hearing the other person's point of view and how what they have done has upset them, plus being heard themselves, helps to ensure that both sides take responsibility for their actions.

With each of this teacher's concerns, it is tempting to be dismissive, as if once she has seen the light, she will see sense. To continue the metaphor – if the promoters of peer mediation (or any other strategy) think themselves the sole guardians of the 'light', they may become blinded to the light of others. If there is to be a whole-school approach, then scepticism has to be recognised, even encouraged. It certainly deserves to be listened to and taken on board. In a chapter entitled 'Complexity and the change process' Michael Fullan, who has researched and written extensively about school improvement, writes:

> As Maurer (1996)[7] observes, 'resistance' is an essential ingredient of progress. 'Often those who resist have something important to tell us. We can be influenced by them. People resist for what they view as good reasons. They may see alternatives we never dreamed of. They may understand problems about the minutiae of implementation that we never see from our lofty perch atop Mount Olympus.[8]

Time perspective

This follows on from the issue of discipline; in arbitration the focus is on who did what to whom – that is, it is about the past, and the future is about retribution. In mediation the *process* creates the climate for transformation. Although at the outset both disputants are usually arguing about what happened, there comes a critical point when attention shifts from the past to the future. At that point the energy which was previously expended in shoring up their position begins to be used in a more constructive way to generate solutions; such solutions are geared to addressing the issues of each disputant, and often represent a greater understanding of each other's needs.

Winners and losers

Mediation gives equal status to the two disputants in the sense that both are able to tell their side of the story, say how they are feeling and share ideas about possible solutions. If one child is perceived as being in the wrong and the other is seen as the victim, for example in a situation of bullying, teachers may question the appropriateness of mediation. The school needs to have clear guidelines for the mediators about what is, and what is not, mediable. In cases where physical abuse has been involved, it is unlikely that mediation will be appropriate. However, in a case where two girls have upset another girl by excluding her from their friendship – a particularly invidious form of bullying – mediation can work.

It is, of course, vital that neither disputant is pressurised into agreeing to something that he or she later regrets, and the mediators have a role to play in ensuring that this doesn't happen. However, as Andberg states, whereas arbitration can end up with both disputants unhappy, i.e. losers, mediation simply can't continue unless there is an agreement that all are happy with.

Voluntariness

In the school context mediation has to be voluntary; pupils can't be *sent* for mediation. Teachers may think that because it is voluntary, conflicts will only be dealt with at the whim of the disputants or of the mediators. However, if either of the disputants doesn't want to take part, then the conflict reverts back to the school discipline system – which in effect means it goes to arbitration where all parties have to accept whatever the outcome is. In schools which run peer mediation services, disputants are given the choice of having their conflict dealt with by mediation, or by a teacher.

Definition of the conflict
A classic example of the difference between mediation and arbitration is the story of two children fighting over an orange.

They both wanted the orange and both had hold of it. A teacher came up, immediately quelled the fight, and took the orange off them. She brought them into her classroom, went to her cupboard, got a knife and cut the orange in two and gave each child half. This was a solution to the problem, but it wasn't the solution needed – it transpired that one child wanted the *juice* to drink, and the other wanted the *skin* to make marmalade.

As adults, we tend to treat the symptoms of children's conflict – anger, distress, tears – with more seriousness than we treat the issues that give rise to them, more often than not describing those issues as 'trivial', perhaps not realising that from a child's point of view we too are seen as getting 'upset over nothing' when we become emotionally involved in a conflict. Peer mediation, by children for children, challenges the often myopic adult view of their world.

Scope
A key part of the mediation process is the 'listing of problems' by the disputants. The children in the dispute each decide what is relevant. In arbitration it is the arbitrator who defines what the issues are, and usually requires that these are stuck to. The definition of the issues usually comes within the parameters of the school rules. Teachers have raised doubts about the amount of time spent by mediators on unimportant issues. But it's worth remembering that mediation doesn't happen in a vacuum; the alternative to time spent mediating is often time spent on conflict in a

classroom. As one anonymous teacher wrote, after an in-service training session: '[Peer mediation] would be a great time-saver for the teacher in the long term. The children's big problems are often viewed as our "little" problems when the same problems/conflicts are occurring every day and never seem to be solved. This leads to frustration by both children and teacher.'

Furthermore, children can be trained to differentiate between what is and what isn't mediable. One principal remarked that the pupils had 'demonstrated their capacity to identify those types of conflicts which they should not try to mediate, e.g. when one party presented with marks on his neck'[9]; as already mentioned, mediation is not likely to be appropriate where physical abuse is concerned.

Confidentiality

A question that is often raised about mediation is the degree to which it places unfair burdens on young shoulders. It needs to be stressed that normal codes of child protection still apply, and mediators cannot promise complete confidentiality – they will keep 'good secrets' (see pp. 61–2), but other information will be relayed to the teacher in charge. Some mediation schemes are unequivocal about the need for confidentiality – 'If there is no room for confidentiality in a school's discipline policy, there is no room for peer mediation.'[10]

Sometimes doubt is expressed about the ability of children to keep secrets. But we have had consistent feedback from teachers indicating that they are impressed with how seriously children take their responsibilities, and this includes confidentiality. As with other expectations, we really don't give children sufficient credit for what they are capable of doing.

Dealing with teachers' general concerns about peer mediation

Other concerns are raised by teachers, in addition to those arising from the differences between mediation and the more traditional ways in which conflicts are resolved at school. One such is the issue of when and where mediation takes place; and what happens if it spills over into lesson time. Chapter 5 demonstrated that the skills of mediation are directly relevant to 'speaking and listening' in the curriculum; so it could be argued that the children's learning in this respect during mediation is significant. As has been previously pointed out, it is also supporting the teacher by allowing him or her to get on with teaching.

When you are trying to promote a particular programme there is a tremendous temptation to see all resistance as negative and/or to get defensive. In the early days of peer mediation in Northern Ireland, the EMU-Promoting School Project made mistakes, and perhaps didn't take on board the concerns of teachers, even those actively involved in the programme. Comments from teachers such as 'Have adult evaluations been taken on board from last year?' 'Workshops have not changed.' 'Are we being listened to?' indicated a lack of listening on our part. It is important that teachers are demonstrably treated as professionals, and that means that an external agency has to be professional in its dealings with them.

> [The programme] has been very professionally done. I would have reservations if I thought that it wasn't well organised [and] well programmed. It is, and it has been from the very beginning, and things have changed because you took heed of the difficulties that arose or areas that you felt needed further insight into. Professionalism is important. Teachers need to see that it is professional – and it has been.[11]

Resistance can also be symptomatic of teachers' own lack of confidence, or personal feelings of uncomfortableness with peer mediation skills training. One vice-principal of a primary school said to the external agency that he was not happy with having to play 'silly games', and made it clear in advance of a staff training day that if he was required to participate in such activities he would remember a prior engagement and leave. The agenda took on board his misgivings, and those of others of his colleagues; ice-breaker games were omitted, experiential activities were discussed and approved beforehand, and as a result the day was successful, full participation and interaction. This experience, while exceptional, illustrates the general need to build up trust and confidence.

It is a common experience that teachers are not prepared in their initial teacher training for a workshop approach to learning and teaching; and there is a growing awareness that they should be. For example, one action-research project in Belgium, entitled 'To become one's own mediator', reported: 'Most of the teachers regretted not [being] prepared [for] this type of intervention. According to them, training in communication and . . . conflict management should be part of their basic training.[12]

'Our school doesn't need peer mediation because we haven't got problems'

In recent years there have been a number of school improvement programmes in Northern Ireland. If a secondary school has been identified as underachieving, this can have a knock-on effect on its feeder primary schools, *irrespective of their own level of achievement*, with the concomitant detrimental effect on staff morale; but it has also led to money being made available to support initiatives like peer mediation in primary schools. This has perhaps been responsible for the misperception, sometimes encountered, that peer mediation is only relevant for schools that need extra-support programmes.

In fact, this book is endeavouring to make clear that for peer mediation to work there has to be good communication, a supportive atmosphere and a child-centred ethos.

Sometimes the rationale for associating peer mediation with problems is the notion that, since peer mediation is about resolving conflict and the existence of conflict is sometimes seen as a sign of failure, then peer mediation is only needed when there is a problem.

The reality is that peer mediation is valuable as a *proactive, preventive strategy in dealing with conflict*. Professor John Darby was the first director of INCORE (Initiative on Conflict Resolution and Ethnicity), a joint project of the University of Ulster and the United Nations University. He articulates an aspect of conflict that underlies the value of peer mediation: 'Conflict is neither good nor bad, but intrinsic in every relationship from marriage to international diplomacy. Whenever two or more people are gathered, there is conflict or potential conflict. The real issue is not the existence of conflict but how it is handled.'[13] Again we come back to the question that opened the chapter, How do we adults handle conflict? If we wish children to be able to respond creatively and constructively to conflict on an individual, societal and global level, we are talking about *life skills* rather than about an 'add-on' a programme or project. In Chapter 10 the need for change in school cultures will be analysed, and proactive rather than reactive approaches to conflict championed. The relevance of peer mediation skills training to citizenship education has already been underlined in Chapter 5.

What about resistance from children?

There was some resistance [to peer mediation] from friends, because after all mediating conflicts was unfamiliar, and was described as weird or a joke, 'however, once these other children actually saw the process work and understood that it was an alternative to getting into trouble with adults, most of them decided they liked it and often soon came back for additional services.[14]

Change and resistance
Dealing with resistance is about managing change; and if a peer mediation programme is to be tailor-made rather than off the peg, a whole-school approach is necessary. A prerequisite to starting a programme, before any work has been done with the children, is to build up trust with the entire staff, including the ancillary staff. In the survey of peer mediation agencies, one of the questions asked was: 'Some research indicates that the greatest challenge to schools in embracing a whole-school approach to peer mediation is in relation to managing the necessary change in ethos. Is this your experience?'*

*See Appendix 2.

The response was consistent.

'Not all teachers are comfortable with the responsibility taken by children. In some cases it can be their own lack of confidence or a fear of exposing children to too much responsibility. They [nine- and ten-year-olds] are too young to learn about equal opportunities. They are only children for such a short time.'

'Yes, the attitude of head and staff is crucial.' (Disinterest and/or cynicism can negate a programme.)

'Many staff failed to appreciate the philosophy behind peer mediation. They still held on to their low opinions about children.'

One comment reflected the very real pressures on teachers in dealing with change, 'In a way, [this is my experience], but the greatest challenge is to allocate to teachers time to carry out supervision/co-ordination of the mediation scheme.'

One agency wrote to say that it had 'a very stringent process of agreeing to work with schools. We have this [because] peer mediation can only work in a climate where schools are suitably positioned to hand over responsibility to young people. It's important to work with schools where this is in place but [also] to be able to support schools to get to a position where peer mediation is possible.'

Supporting schools to get to a position where peer mediation is possible

One of the difficulties that the EMU-Promoting School Project came up against was that, by the time the staff heard about peer mediation, it was sometimes a *fait accompli*, with the principal having made the decision – with or without the involvement of the senior management team, let alone the teachers – to go ahead.

Since one of the hallmarks of peer mediation is that it is a voluntary programme, our research has demonstrated the need for there to be a consensus among staff to go ahead. This is easier said than done, since the politics of the staff room are such as to make it difficult to voice dissent openly. Fullan maintains that 'consensus would be pleasant, but actually impossible to achieve except through superficial agreement'.[15] Just as, in Chapter 6, the term 'sufficient consensus' was used to describe the decision-making process of the Northern Ireland Assembly, taking cognisance of the needs of a divided society, so it could be argued that 'sufficient consensus' would be a more appropriate approach in some staff rooms, in order to acknowledge divisions – not divisions of a sectarian nature but, often, historical ones.

Part of the process of preparing a school for peer mediation is illustrated by the case study that follows, showing an attempt to ensure that consensus is more than just a superficial 'toeing of the line'. In this case study we were aware of the principal's determination to introduce peer mediation, but knew that for this to be sustainable there had to be general agreement. We therefore deliberately introduced an exercise ('Challenging Adults') which we had been using in workshops at conferences and training events, but never previously with an actual staff team. We wanted to try and get a consensus based on giving a voice to scepticism, and encouraging people to see things from each other's point of view. We wanted to support the principal, but were prepared for the consensus to be against peer mediation – which is the way it eventually turned out.

Developing a strategy to deal with resistance

So far in this chapter we have concentrated on the specific trademarks of peer mediation as a means of dealing with conflict. But there is also a more general case to argue about the impact of peer mediation as a process requiring whole-school change, and the nature of resistance, as will be touched on at the end of this chapter.

In Chapter 8 it will be demonstrated that an 'exit strategy' is needed to ensure that the programme becomes sustainable and doesn't remain dependent on the external agency. This exit strategy needs to be identified from the outset.

The EMU-Promoting School Project became aware of the myriad reasons why schools might want to 'do peer mediation'. Having had the experience of being invited into a school by an individual teacher, only to be made aware later that the senior management team was unhappy with the invitation, the Project had learned, the hard way, to check that the person making the decision had the authority to do so. Equally, it was important to be wary of principals who were known for their enthusiasm for new programmes, and for the frequency with which they left one to start another. Sometimes a keen principal fails to carry the staff with her, and in this instance a breakdown in communication can lead to individual staff feeling inadequately informed.

A case study: school H

Achieving consensus about peer mediation
In Northern Ireland in 1999 an Education and Library Board (an ELB – one of five local Education Authorities in the province) organised a two-day workshop on peer mediation and circle time, led by the EMU-Promoting School Project (EMUpsp). This workshop followed the 'Training the Trainer' pattern described earlier, with teams of three adults from each of five schools being trained to lead workshops.

School H followed this up with a request for more support, the principal being very keen to introduce peer mediation into the school. By this time, however, EMUpsp was wanting to work strategically rather than with individual schools. It was important that work done at School H be in partnership with the ELB. Negotiations were started with the school and an ELB officer. It was hoped that this could be a pilot project for other schools in the area to follow. EMUpsp, as an action-research project, was keen to apply the learning from its bank of experience (see Chapter 9).

The single most important lesson from this learning was that peer mediation in itself was not the answer. If it was to be sustainable, it was not appropriate as a starting-point in a school; work needed to done first with the staff.

In the early stages of the negotiation between the Project, the ELB and School H, the aim of the in-service training sessions (INSETs) was agreed.

Aim

As explained in a letter to School H's principal:

> The aim of these INSETs will be to work towards creating an environment where work with pupils can begin. This initial stage will address issues that the school has identified as important ... It will focus on the whole-school adult relationships and the environment necessary for any educational initiative to take root and have success.

The initial stages of the programme were planned to train the adults only – not the children. The programme was to start with teachers, with ancillary staff joining in, followed by parents. From the outset EMUpsp was clear that peer mediation would not necessarily be on the agenda until some considerable way down the road. Interactive styles of learning, such as circle time and a focus on staff relationships, would provide the context for the work. The anticipated outcome would be, the letter continued, 'that the staff will have strategies for creating a co-operative atmosphere in the staff room and the class room. A key outcome will be to ascertain what, if any, further work needs to be done with the staff in order to prepare for training the pupils in peer mediation.'

The dynamics – and politics – of any primary school means there is inevitably a spectrum of responses to new initiatives. And, as already suggested, for any whole-school initiative to work, particularly one involving an external agency, the principal needs to be actively involved in forms of commitment, making staff, time and financial resources available for training, planning and delivering workshops. There also needs to be a supportive senior management team (SMT) to provide positive leadership, and co-operation in the logistics of organising the programme.

The rest of the staff have to be prepared and at least to suspend their disbelief – and what this means in practice is reserving judgement about peer mediation's likelihood of success. And finally there needs to be an enthusiastic teacher, for he or she will find him or herself giving up time to promoting the work, and to planning and evaluating workshops.

Inevitably, when a new idea is introduced to a school

staff, there will be different levels of enthusiasm – all of which are tempered by the realities of other, ever-increasing demands on teachers' time, such as assessment of pupils, reading initiatives, and so on.

For a programme like peer mediation to be sustainable – that is, maintained by the school beyond the involvement of an external project – it is doubly important to achieve a consensus about going forward with it. If it becomes identified merely as yet one more initiative of the principal's, or perceived as the latest flight of fancy of an individual teacher, this will seriously undermine its sustainability. For, EMUpsp whether the ultimate decision was for or against peer mediation, was not as important as getting a consensus.

In October 1999 two INSETs were arranged for the staff, with a gap of two weeks between them.

INSET 1 – challenging adults

At the first INSET, the overall aim was 'to explore the dynamics of introducing a change into the school environment that gives more responsibility to pupils'. The aim had been refined, deliberately omitting any reference to peer mediation. Part of the reason for this was to be able more easily later to reinforce the fact that *change* is an inherent part of the process of introducing peer mediation.

The goal of exploring the dynamics of change reflects the difference between peer mediation training being seen as a *programme* that children do, and peer mediation training as a *process* that transforms the culture of the school. It also acknowledges the outcomes of action-research since peer mediation was introduced in Northern Ireland in 1993. These outcomes will be explored in depth in later chapters. In the meantime, a look at the objectives of this first INSET demonstrates how it was intended to meet the overall aim.

Objectives for participants

- *to receive an introduction to peer mediation*
- *to experience circle time and conflict-resolution skills training*
- *to be able to hear, and articulate opposing views.*

As mentioned earlier, we had learned from experience that it was all too easy to prejudge scepticism as opposition and see resistance as negative. In the past we had had a tendency, in our enthusiasm, to see teachers as being either with us or against us – forgetting in the process that our role is to be *with* teachers, or at least to acknowledge where they are coming from.

If a programme was to achieve a whole-school approach, it would require *listening* to all the staff, to their concerns, their enthusiasms, their misgivings – and, where possible, answering them. Peer mediation, particularly when it comes as an initiative from outside, requires of the school staff a common sense of purpose, working as a team. This avoids initiatives becoming the preserve of the principal, an individual member staff or an exclusive clique. Another issue for EMUpsp was to avoid creating a dependency, something that is difficult to avoid if you are seen as being the only ones with the answers. Faced with the questions of how to ensure that all staff, particularly those with doubts, were heard, and how to address concerns without appearing to be seen as experts, we developed a workshop exercise that became known as Challenging Adults (see Figure 7.2 on p. 182).

This exercise enables participants to articulate and respond to opposing views. The first INSET provided an opportunity to put this into practice. It included a fairly typical group of staff, at least in relation to their knowledge of peer mediation: one or two of them had seen it in practice, one had been on a two-day training programme, while the majority had only watched a short video. Figures 7.3 and 7.4 show the feedback and responses to the feedback.

The 'Challenging Adults' exercise proved beneficial on a number of levels. It encompassed the values of mediation, encouraging the airing of different, opposing perspectives; it called for listening, in order that each side could hear and respond to the other's concerns. It was also a consensus-seeking exercise, and proved to be a way of ensuring that an initiative would go ahead, or not, on the basis of an informed decision.

The outcomes set out in Figures 7.3 and 7.4 (pp. 183–4) indicate that, while some questions were unanswered, a

Part 1

The participants are split into two groups. This can be done in one of three ways:

1. at random
2. ensuring that each group contains a mixture of people likely to be in favour and likely to be against the introduction of peer mediation
3. asking people to get into the groups that represent the *opposite* to their own view.

Group 1 is told that it is *in favour of peer mediation* – they have to come up with reasons to introduce it into schools.
Group 2 is told that it is *Against the introduction of peer mediation* – they have to come up with concerns that they have about it being introduced.

The two groups go into separate rooms for 10–15 minutes, having been told to pick a rapporteur and to write their feedback up on a flip – chart sheet.
The groups then meet, and each reports back.
(Facilitators should be taking notes in order that each group has a copy of the other's feedback.)

Part 2

The two groups then reconvene separately.

Group 1 *responds to the concerns of those against*
Group 2 *reflects on what they need to hear from those in favour, in order that their concerns are addressed*

The two groups report back to each other, and in the remaining time there is a debriefing, allowing for people to say what it was like taking part in the process.

Table 7.2 The Challenging Adults exercise
(*Source:* Jerry Tyrell (2000))

Feedback from the 'Peer mediation sounds great' group	Responses from the 'We have our doubts' group
1. Children have more time than adults for peer mediation.	1. When and how often will peer mediation take place?
2. They hear both sides of the story without 20 different perspectives from onlookers.	2. Other contributions are valuable, so as to find out the truth.
3. Any solutions are more likely to work because they are the children's own ideas.	4. Teacher intervention is necessary to establish values.
4. Children are on the same level of thinking (e.g., they know how important a pog* is!)	
5. Mediators develop personal skills that can be applied in other situations.	
6. Children are more likely to be honest if the teacher is not there.	6. Children should be encouraged to be honest all the time.
7. Peer mediation saves teachers and supervisors time.	7. When/where/who? and what about monitoring the mediations?
8. Understanding of feelings, needed in peer mediation, is essential as a life skill.	
9. Children become more responsible for their own behaviour.	
10. Peer mediation creates better understanding of what acceptable behaviour is.	

Table 7.3: The Challenging Adults exercise – outcome 1

*A pog is part of a playground game that was in vogue in the 1990s, often being a cause of conflict.

Feedback from the 'We have our doubts' group	Responses from the 'Peer mediation sounds great' group
1. What about children who won't accept training . . .?	1. If a child is unco-operative, it's time to involve the teacher.
	2. At lunchtime?
2. What about the time factor. . .?	
3. What about supervision . . .?	3. Designate a specific area for mediation? (within sight, if not hearing, of the teacher).
4. Who is trained?	4. Upper KS2 children as mediators – KS1/KS2 for skills training meaning
	5. Keep the teacher on hand till everyone has cooled down.
5. What about aggression . . .?	
	6. Lunchtime
6. What about the mechanics? When?	
7. Will there be a time limit?	7. 10 minutes
8. What if it doesn't work?	8. Then involve the teacher or postpone it.
9. What if the mediator isn't impartial?	9. Can't remain as mediator (need to reinforce the importance of this role)
10. What about trust . . .?	
11. What about continuity?	12. Inform and get on board
12. What about parents?	13. Make a list of circumstances when mediation would or wouldn't be suitable
13. What dictates mediation?	
14. At what level – One off or constant?	

Table 7.4: The Challenging Adults exercise – outcome 2

dialogue had started – and that an attempt had been made to respond to people's needs.

INSET 2 principal of school A

Two weeks after the Challenging Adults INSET, the staff of School H, including the ancillary staff, met the principal of School A (a school that had been involved in peer mediation for four years). We reminded the participants of the first INSET programme and of the feedback from the 'Challenging Adults' exercise (we handed out sheets so that everybody had a copy of the latter), and then the principal of School A was introduced.

He explained that when he was first approached by EMUpsp he had already read about peer mediation when studying for his Master of Education degree, so it wasn't completely new to him. He liked its child-centred approach. By the time he had met up with EMUpsp he was already doing action-research in the playground, using video cameras to identify the types of conflict happening there. It was clear that there was a lot of kicking and fighting going on. A lot of problems were landing on the teachers at the end of lunch breaks, and often these were referred on to him. He introduced a training package for the lunchtime supervisors, including material from Newcastle University, and the *You're Only a Dinner Lady* video and training package,[16] a Manchester-based resource.

He arranged INSET meetings for EMUpsp with the teaching staff; they agreed to go ahead with peer mediation and reserve judgement for twelve months. He felt that peer mediation was only relevant for Key Stage 2 – problems with Key Stage 1 were more manageable. Key Stage 2 children, by contrast, 'brought their histories to school with them'. Running the programme has depended on having two staff volunteers. He has never had a problem getting those volunteers.

Peer mediation was a *process*, he said; for the teachers concerned, it had led to a 'transformation in their teaching styles and in how they relate to children'.[17] The various initiatives including peer mediation had 'changed the culture of our school'.

Interestingly, he was not keen on peer mediation *per se*: 'I have witnessed children carrying out a peer mediation rather badly.' (EMUpsp would maintain that this might point to a need for structured support and supervision for mediators, rather than a weakness in peer mediation itself.)

The principal of School A went on to describe the development of the supervisory assistants' (SAs') training. The idea is to 'engage the children in purposeful activities'. Each SA has a box of resources. Although there is no organised training of SAs he had the help of the ELB, their Physical Education dept and Exceptional Closure days (special days for staff training). He had supervised his SAs, met regularly with the chief SA, as well as being involved in the playground and in the canteen. Finally, they had told him that 'they would operate better if I withdrew'. He was delighted to be able to do so.

He gave an example of the effect of the various peer mediation initiatives at his school: prior to these he had to deal with 10 to 12 behaviour reports a week, whereas now he has one or two a fortnight. He had noticed a change in culture, leading to a very good rapport between the teacher and the pupils.

He did underline the cost in terms of commitment of the staff.

Questions from the school staff to the principal

'How did you get the support of the parents?'
The principal had informed parents of what the school was doing, invited them to an assembly presented by the class doing peer mediation, and written peer mediation into the discipline policy of the school. He stressed that the children had the option – it was just an option – and put out leaflets in language that the parents would understand.

'When do the children do the peer mediation?'
Twenty minutes was the shortest time a mediation took. The usual scenario involved a supervisory assistant finding two children squabbling, and asking them if they wanted peer mediation or an adult intervention. If the choice was peer

mediation, then the peer mediators were contacted. They were easily identified because of their baseball caps. The mediation started immediately the bell went, so it was done in class time. Classrooms had access to practical areas, so that it was carried out in view of the teacher.

Peer mediation did reduce the amount of conflict, the principal said and the peer mediation ground rules had a powerful effect if they were used in class as well as workshops. He cited the example of teachers apologising to a class if they had made a mistake, and that was accepted, because 'It's okay to make mistakes'.

'How quickly did you see the benefits?'
After the first run-through of the full training programme, it became clear that behaviour was changing. 'Some of the worst-behaved children in my school became mediators.' There was a cumulative effect. But he was concerned about the fact that children have these skills in Primary 7, and then leave primary school to go on to secondary school and lose them.

'How do you deal with persistent misbehaviour?'
He instanced five boys whose persistent inappropriate behaviour had led to their having a programme to themselves. The peer mediation training had helped them to reintegrate with their former classmates. Children judged fairness very rigorously, more rigorously than adults. Peer mediation did not have to have an adult input in order to maintain values. The time and integrity that children brought to the process more than matched that of adults.

'Are there any circumstances when mediation can't be offered?'
Where 'teeth, skin and hair' were involved, he said, then the principal or vice principal had to be brought in.

Teachers do need to take ownership of the programme for it to be meaningful, he said; the involvement of Key Stage 1 teachers in the Primary 7 peer mediation workshops meant that they could adapt some of the exercises to their own classrooms. Peer mediation needs a lot of space, a lot of adult input, and a definite ethos of co-operation. Staff need to be honest, and, if they feel very sceptical, it is unwise go ahead. Peer mediation training, for his school, resulted in a transformation of its culture.

After this INSET the staff of School H had time to reflect, and as a result they asked to learn more about circle time. The EMUpsp people attending and the ELB officer suggested that a vice principal who had introduced circle time in her school be contacted and invited to lead an INSET with the staff on circle time.

INSET 3 – circle time

So the vice principal from the third school led a two-hour workshop, using circle time. It was the first time she had worked with a group other than her own staff. Because she spoke directly from her experience, as a vice principal and Primary 2 teacher, and because she introduced circle time in a gentle way, she soon had everybody participating. She demystified it and used hand-outs to encourage staff to follow it up. Circle time was not about therapy, she said, but she had used it to help individual members of her class to deal with difficult issues.

Earlier that year, during the summer holiday, the father of one of the girls in her class had died. She had two other siblings at the school, and so the vice principal had visited the girls' mother and asked her and her children how they would like their friends at school to be told. The girl in her class had said that she wanted to tell them soon, while her brother and sister decided they wanted to wait a while.

That week when it came to circle time, the vice principal asked her class to share a time when they were happy. The little girl in question talked of a time when she was out playing with her daddy. The vice principal continued round the circle asking each person in turn if they wanted to tell of a time they were happy.

When everybody had had a chance to speak, the vice principal asked if they would like to share a time when they were sad. When it came to the little girl's turn, the vice principal asked her if she wanted to tell them, or did she want her, the vice principal, to do it. The little girl asked her to tell them, and so the class was told that the girl's father had died. A number of children were moved to tears, the death was acknowledged, and the responses round the circle continued.

This powerful story, along with the light-hearted activities, including passing round a cuddly toy as a microphone, demonstrated the value of doing circle time regularly.

During questions at the end of the workshop, one Key Stage 2 teacher said, 'The benefits to Key Stage 1 were clear, but wouldn't it be too young for Primary 7s?' For the EMUpsp staff present, it was refreshing to hear this comment; the opposite perspective – of the work only being relevant to Key Stage 2 – was the more usual one.

As a result of these three workshops, a consensus was reached by the staff of School H that they weren't quite ready for peer mediation, but they would like to start circle time on a whole-school basis. As the school principal was later to write:

> We feel that circle time has a very important part to play in the development of pastoral care in our school. We seek to promote an ethos where children can feel they are in a safe and caring environment . . . [As they begin to feel comfortable] in discussing problems affecting the whole class we hope that we are laying the foundation for the next stage in personal development – i.e., the use of conflict-resolution strategies and the maturity to use these to defuse difficult situations.[18]

Conclusion

Conflict, diversity and resistance are potentially positive and absolutely essential forces for success, Fullan has argued, and he stressed that:

> respecting those you wish to silence is a good rule of thumb[19]. You often learn more from people who disagree with you than you do from people who agree, but you underlisten to the former and overlisten to the

latter. You associate with people who agree with you, and you avoid those with whom you disagree. Not a good learning strategy . . . it is better to incorporate differences early in the process of change (when there is a chance to address problems) than to avoid conflict only to have to face it later when it is unresolvable . . . if you avoid differences you may enjoy early smoothness, but you pay the price because you do not get at the really difficult issues until it is too late.[20]

It is beyond the scope of this book to explore the dynamics of schools that make them resistant to change, beyond acknowledging that 'schools are much more a conservative agency for the status quo than a revolutionary force for transformation'.[21] Nevertheless, in Northern Ireland, education is changing whether we like it or not, and with an emphasis on citizenship. 'Education not only makes democracy possible, it also makes it essential. Education not only brings into existence a population with an understanding of the public tasks; it also creates their demand to be heard.'[22]

The principal of School A pointed out that change was inevitable, and in the survey of UK agencies this view was reinforced. 'In my initial contact [with schools] I issued a 'health warning' to heads – this will change things in your school – and change has a cost and can be painful! I say that we are "giving the children a voice" '[23]. The challenge for peer mediation is to take the necessary time to identify and encourage resistance, provide space and time to address it, and with the knowledge gleaned from that process to encourage a school to make an informed decision as to whether or not to go ahead with peer mediation.

8. How to Create a Self-sustaining Programme in Schools

In Northern Ireland in 1993 peer mediation was such an unknown quantity that a great deal of persuasion was necessary in order to get it into schools. Chapter 4 described in detail the strategies that were used to achieve this. However, once a peer mediation programme was up and running in a school, word spread – usually by one principal talking to another. Requests started coming in to the EMU-Promoting School Project from other schools, keen to have peer mediation in their school. It became progressively easier to 'sell' the idea to schools. By 1997 the Project was working in a dozen. Originally the challenge was how to get into schools, now the challenge had become how to get *out* of them, once the essential groundwork had been done.

This chapter examines the need for external agencies to have an exit strategy if schools are not to become dependent on them. This requires a genuine partnership, that builds in-house teams of confident and competent adults. After the agency has gone, this team is then in a position to adapt the training process and implement it themselves, and become self-sustaining.

We describe a case study focusing on a state primary school.* We also draw on research into five other primary schools, one Catholic and four Integrated. All these Northern Irish schools (designated here School A, School B,

---

*In Northern Ireland State (or voluntary) schools tend to be predominantly if not exclusively Protestant.

etc.) were involved in peer mediation training for periods ranging from one to four years during 1993–97. The external agency, the EMU-Promoting School Project, researched the experience of the schools in the months after its last direct involvement, as part of an overall self-evaluation.

The Project's original objectives included researching:

- the feasibility of Key Stage 2 children helping their peers to deal with their conflicts
- the prerequisites, as regards the practices and policies of a school, for embarking on such a programme
- the approaches and strategies to be used by the Project to ensure that a school can assume ownership of the programme and sustain it by itself in the long term
- how the programme can serve to support the overall (academic and personal-development) objectives of the curriculum, by enhancing the teaching/learning environment of the school and classroom.

In the course of developing and trialling the programme, initially in two schools, and exploring strategies for promoting the schools' ownership of the training provision, the Project published the report *Peer Mediation in Primary Schools* in 1995.[1] Besides indicating the benefits of the programme for children, in educational and personal-development terms, the report found that children aged 10 to 11 *can* help each other to deal with their conflicts. It also established that such programmes provided an effective means of delivering a component of Education for Mutual Understanding (EMU) – the statutory educational theme in the Northern Ireland curriculum (see Chapter 5) – and a useful foundation for subsequent EMU work in the teenage years.

Issues of school leadership, adult relationships, school ethos and training in the use of interactive teaching methodologies, however, were key to the long-term viability of such programmes, the report said. When the Project's workload expanded to 12 primary schools, the work focused not just on refining the programme content but also on addressing these issues.

In the course of this work between 1995 and 1997, and

despite substantial efforts to support them, it became clear that some of the 12 schools, including one of the original pilot schools, were unlikely to be able to achieve the environment necessary to sustain the the peer mediation programme. The most common reason for this in these schools had to do with leadership – including *changes* in leadership – which affected the schools' capacities to address issues and training needs concerning ethos and whole-school relationships. The net effect was that some schools expected the Project to come in and 'do' peer mediation every year, with little or no taking over of responsibility for it by the school. As already mentioned, a key issue for the Project as an external agency was to avoid a situation where the relationship with any given school was based on dependency. When a school relied on the Project coming in each year to train the staff and the children, it indicated that the programme wasn't sustainable in the long term.

In the summer term of 1997 the Project staff recognised the need to be proactive about this state of affairs, but this was easier said than done. There were individuals in each of the schools who were making valiant efforts, and who had built up a good working relationship with Project staff. The Project was aware that disengaging from the schools might seem like abandonment, and so it was important to develop an appropriate exit strategy. The Project staff recognised that whatever the exit strategy, without the Project's continuing support in some schools the programmes would probably falter and indeed fail. Nevertheless, in advance of the 1997/8 school year the Project indicated to schools that, following a training course for adult teams in early September, Project assistance with training workshops for children at the schools would only be available in the autumn term. (This training course is described in detail in Chapter 2.)

As well as creating an exit strategy for the Project, this approach created the opportunity, from January 1998, to research the *outcomes* of the training in the schools concerned.

The exit strategy as a means towards creating a self-sustaining programme

With hindsight the Project recognised that even before it had engaged with each school it should have had a well defined

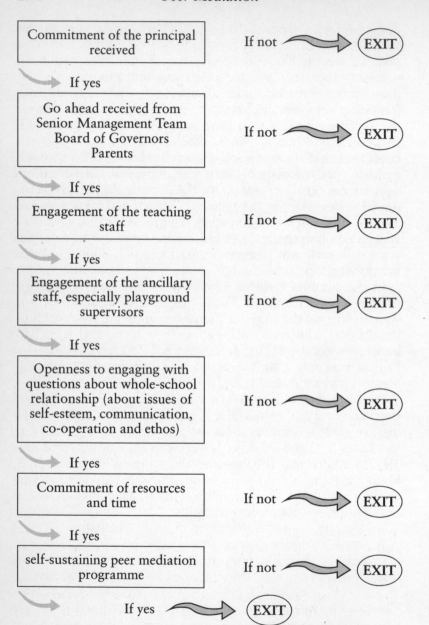

Fig. 8.1: Stages towards establishing a self-sustaining peer mediation programme in partnership with the school

exit strategy, agreed with the school from the outset. Instead, the exit strategy (see Figure 8.1) only evolved in 1997. It provided a model for disengagement by the school, or by the Project, at any stage if essential criteria for the success of the peer mediation programme weren't being met. The ideal scenario was disengagement of the Project because all the criteria were being met and a successful sustainable programme had been established.

There is an interdependence between all the various components in a successful sustainable programme. As discussed in Chapter 7, there needs to be a committed principal, a supportive senior management team, one or two enthusiastic teachers, and the rest of the staff needs to suspend their disbelief. The principal's commitment isn't sufficient on its own, of course; the staff perspective could still be – and was in at least two cases – 'Oh no, not another initiative', and a sense that they were being mandated rather than consulted. So it is important to meet with the senior management team, and also to get the approval in principle of the board of governors.

Similarly, the programme won't reach first base without the engagement of the teaching staff. What this usually means in practice, as we have seen, is a presentation with a mini-workshop for all the teaching staff of Key Stages 1 and 2. Chapter 7 has shown that gradually, through the experience of dealing with teachers' resistance, the Project came to realise that suspension of disbelief was not enough and that there actually had to be *consensus* to go ahead. In theory, at every stage of the journey represented by Figure 8.1, the Project – and indeed the school – could exit. In practice, that journey meant that working relationships developed, camouflaging the seemingly black and white 'yes' or 'no' answers of Figure 8.1. To put it another way, it was very difficult for the Project to say no to a school when there were two or three very keen staff creating a climate of affirmation in their classroom once a week, even if they were having to battle away in isolation within a school culture that wasn't supportive or even particularly interested. (The 'Challenging Adults' exercise described in Chapter 7 is one way of ensuring consensus).

Nevertheless, in June 1997 the Project staff wrote to all the schools with which it was working on peer mediation, giving six months' notice of its intention to quit. The schools responded in different ways. One had been involved in the programme for a year, and had hardly had time to get started. For four others it marked a natural moment to bring the programme to a close, and for a sixth school it was more difficult for the Project to let go because it had built up a strong relationship with it. This last school was unable to sustain the programme without the significant involvement of the Project. (Two years later, however, through the initiative of one of the teachers, supported by the principal, a whole-school approach to circle time was achieved.)

The net result was that only six schools were still involved at the start of the 1997/8 academic year, Schools A, B, C, D, E and F.

The biggest challenge of the exit strategy for the Project staff was letting go; allowing schools to make mistakes and do things differently, the natural process of taking ownership. 'Schools learn by their mistakes and it's difficult, but it's worth allowing them to make mistakes, e.g. when they forget resources like the tape recorder,' one member of staff wryly noted after a workshop. In the process of letting go, the Project staff learned from the teachers new ways of developing the work. Project staff and teachers had to model what the teachers themselves would subsequently model for the peer mediators.

By June 1997 the Project staff had been responsible for training hundreds of children and tens of teachers, ancillary staff and other adults. In the process, as described in Chapter 7, the Project had developed a format of INSETs, half-day and full-day workshops that followed a set pattern, with the expectation of a peer mediation service being set up at the end of them. From the point in September 1993 when the external agency had been learning the process on the Tuesday and delivering it to a school on the Wednesday, it had became an expert.

The difficulty with this model is that in demonstrating its proficiency and authenticity, the external agency can be off-putting. Instead of modelling a way of working that was accessible and replicable, a situation began to arise in which a teacher would say, 'You make it look so easy, but I couldn't possibly do it' – a succinct example of the way that 'teachers flatter us and put themselves down'.[2] It became clear that after the initial training a mentoring process had to take over, so that an individual teacher would gain in confidence as well as competence. One of the reasons it is difficult for an agency to leave is articulated by US educationalist Tom Roderick: 'Even if you give people a good amount of training and a curriculum, there are many pressures that teachers are under, and fears they have about teaching in a different kind of way. They appreciate someone who comes in and holds their hand, demonstrates a few lessons, co-plans lessons with them, and provides support.'[3] But the mentoring had to be done diplomatically. Teachers as a rule do not associate being observed in their classroom by another adult as support, but as inspection, as a form of intrusion. The exit strategy had to address this issue if it was to ensure that the school staff had a good enough working relationship to sustain the programme. If the programme was to encompass a genuine whole-school approach, then effective relationships between all staff, teaching and ancillary, were vital.

A whole-school approach – involving the ancillary staff
One way of gauging the potential working relationships of teaching staff and of ancillary staff was in the make-up of the adult teams who came from each school for the 'Training the Trainer' sessions. In the case of School B, for example, the principal, the Primary 6 class teacher and a parent representative of the board of governors attended a two-day 'Training the Trainer' course; and School C was represented by the principal, two teachers, a parent governor and a playground supervisor. (Eight months later another teacher and two playground supervisors/parents attended another 'Training the Trainer', course from School C.) The principal had earlier expressed concern that the children did not show lunchtime supervisors due respect and felt that their direct involvement in the peer mediation programme would help to address this issue. His enthusiasm for

engaging ancillary staff occasioned a session following their lunchtime duty. The workshop was evaluated very positively indeed by the participants. Project staff found them extremely articulate and capable, with a very positive attitude towards the children. Several had already attended a session with governors, teachers and parents. One lunchtime supervisor in particular showed clear potential as a workshop facilitator.

A second teacher INSET on the same day was also attended by the supervisors – further evidence of the efforts of School C's leadership to promote collaboration and teamwork between the various sectors of its adult community. There appeared to be potential here for a genuinely whole-school approach to the development of the programme.

The bulk of this chapter is drawn from the experience of the peer mediation training programme in the remaining six primary schools (A–H) in which the Project was involved. We decided to omit further reference to the other two schools because issues already identified in this chapter were also very much to the fore in the six remaining schools.

Maintaining an effective school environment is a dynamic process. Apart from the vagaries of staff changes, schools face ongoing challenges to do with the provision of effective leadership, adequate training and an enhanced culture of teamwork. All the schools that feature in this chapter were initially judged to have met the basic school-environment prerequisites to justify proceeding with the peer mediation programme; but the findings show that the programme's long-term viability in each school depends on *continued* enhancement of the school environment and on the leadership necessary to support this process. In practical terms the research outlined in this chapter helped to clarify the schools' position in terms of being able to commit resources and time, and create a self-sustaining peer mediation programme (the last two areas of the exit strategy).

Until December 1997 the focus at these six schools was on the training element of the programme – the design of the training workshops and strategies for promoting ownership by schools themselves of the training provision.

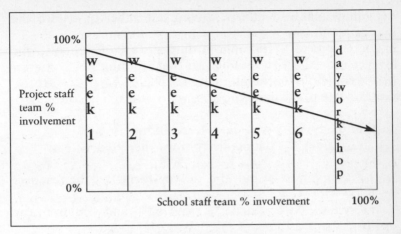

Fig. 8.2: Percentage of Involvement
moves from 90% project/10% school to
50% project/50% school

During this time project staff were heavily engaged in facilitating workshops with children, initially as principal facilitators and then as co-facilitators with teachers and other adults from the schools.

As demonstrated in Figure 8.2 the idea during the course of the first series of workshops was that the leading role would shift from being 90 per cent from the external agency to 50 per cent external agency, 50 per cent adult school team.

This process of letting go was difficult both for the Project and for the teachers concerned. The significance for the adults of the 'You may pass', 'Encourage one another' and 'It's okay to make mistakes' rules didn't go unnoticed. It was important that everybody involved recognised that getting it right didn't mean slavishly following a prescriptive model. Equally, it was critical that the essential ingredients in the process were understood and internalised, and above all *modelled* by the teacher. The timing of the handover of the responsibility of training from the Project to the school was often delayed unless circumstances forced the issue. There was at least one occasion at an assembly to launch the peer mediation service at a school when a Project staff member was unavoidably detained, leaving a teacher to rise to the occasion and lead it as if to the manner born.

On completing training in one group of schools, the Project moved on to another, so that training work continued throughout each school year. There was therefore no opportunity to evaluate the *aftermath* of training formally.

Methodology: how was the research done?
A dual strategy for data collection was adopted:

1. the completion of monthly survey forms by the teachers involved
2. interviews with teachers, principals and children, by Project staff.

Care was taken to ensure that survey forms would not prove excessively burdensome to overloaded teachers. They consisted of a single A4 sheet, with one side to be completed and the other containing guidance notes. Each teacher received a pack containing forms and stamped addressed envelopes for easy return of the forms each month.

The survey was launched through initial visits to each school in January 1998, to secure the approval of the principal and to introduce it to the teachers concerned. Project staff again visited the schools at the end of the spring term and at the end of the school year. Interviews by Project staff examined the impact of the programmes at two levels:

1. training outcomes
2. mediation service outcomes.

Rationale
On the basis that research evaluation by teachers is good education practice, this research project provided an opportunity to promote the concept of the 'reflective teacher',[4] through which teachers continuously monitor, evaluate and revise their own practice. Several purposes were identified, both for the school and for the project, and are outlined below.

Benefits to the school
As schools become autonomous in their peer mediation training, evaluation

- helps them to customise their training programme and the management of their peer mediation service
- helps to identify those for whom the programme has proved significant or otherwise
- serves to identify additional staff training needs in support of the programme's continuance
- helps to locate the programme in the context of the curriculum, the school's ethos, and the broad objectives of education.

The survey report provides each school with an overview of best practice and serves as a consultation document for later school development in this area.

Benefits to the project
As an action-research project, the Project depends on feedback to help it evaluate; it sees the teachers with whom it works as its practitioner research colleagues. Such feedback benefits the project in the following ways:

- it informs the Project of what works and what doesn't work in the realities of schools
- it provides an overview of the similarities and differences in how a programme is taking shape across a range of schools
- it helps to identify additional training needs for staff in support of programmes in the relationships and conflict-resolution field.

Data
The Project sought feedback, through the class teachers involved, from:

- staff-teachers (including those not directly involved in the programme), playground supervisors and other ancillary staff

- parents, other adults and, of course
- children

about the programme's impact, positive or otherwise

- within the school
- outside school
- as regards conflict, conflict resolution and relationships.

Opinions and observations were sought from the staff as to whether the programme impacted, or not, on:

- discipline and behaviour
- relationships among the children
- whole-school relationships
- the teaching and learning environment.

The Project suggested to teachers that a useful process for gathering feedback from children would be circle time in the classroom, with discussion of questions such as:

- Who has used their mediation skills? Where?
- Have the skills proved useful?
- Has anyone talked to their parents or friends outside school about their skills?

When launching the survey, the Project stressed that it was seeking information regardless of whether a school had a functioning peer mediation service or not. Where there was such a service, schools were asked to maintain records for an end-of-year analysis of the numbers, types and outcomes of mediations which took place.

Where the research was done
The research was conducted in six primary schools which were broadly representative of primary education in Northern Ireland. They included controlled (state), maintained (Catholic) and integrated schools. Locations included two main cities in Northern Ireland (Belfast and Derry), three of the six counties (Londonderry, Antrim and

Fermanagh), and three of the five Education and Library Board areas (Western, North-Eastern and Belfast). They represented a mixture of middle-class and working-class catchment areas, and urban and rural locations.

The following case study concentrates in depth on one school, while drawing on the experience of the others. It illustrates how the evidence was gathered that helped to lead to the conclusions indicated elsewhere in the book. A report of each of the six schools was written up in a similar fashion.[5]

A case study: school A

Background
This Project-school partnership was the first extension beyond the two schools involved in the original peer mediation pilot scheme. Social indicators for School A's immediate catchment area – an urban estate of 1,000 houses – included unemployment levels in the region of 65 per cent, a high number of single-parent families, and attendance by the principal at child protection case or review conferences twice per month on average. Conflict in the playground was frequent and very often developed a physical element. Games were characteristically aggressive in nature. Parental communication with the school was often confrontational, and the principal had on occasion been subjected to threatened or actual violence. Reflecting on his initial decision to explore the peer mediation programme, the principal said, 'I was immediately attracted to the idea of peer mediation since I felt that the notion of children taking direct responsibility for their own behaviour fitted neatly into the positive discipline arrangements we, as teachers, were pursuing in the school.'

Initial training
INSETs produced a useful picture of the nature and extent of conflict in the playground and elsewhere in the school. Substantial numbers of conflicts originated within family and community situations, and those involving adults

(parents, neighbours, taxi-drivers etc.) intruded massively on the time and energy of the principal, proving extremely difficult to deal with. This information suggested that the partnership should aim to involve the local community as much as possible, all classes and teachers and the playground supervisors. However, the work began, and would remain, largely focused on peer mediation at Primary 7 level.

The programme was increasingly acclaimed, from within and beyond the school, as significant. The teachers and principal reported that, in combination with the purposeful engagement of all children in a games programme with playground supervisors during the lunch break, the peer mediation scheme had reduced 'aggressive interaction among the children' and effected 'a significant reduction in the classroom time required to sort out lunchtime problems'.

From a broader educational perspective the programme greatly increased the children's self-confidence and had a profound and positive effect on the classroom and playground environment; and also on relationship of the children with their teacher and with playground supervisors. This in turn had numerous benefits in terms of teaching, learning and the delivery of the curriculum. In professional terms, teachers found it transformative; the conventional emphasis on maintaining control in the classroom was balanced by a focus on fostering a climate of mutual respect. One of the teachers at School A stressed: 'My involvement in this programme has transformed the total way I teach.'

The Primary 7 teacher who had been central to the programme from the beginning transferred to another school in the summer term of 1997. The programme was resumed in the September with a firm resolve on the part of the school to achieve self-sufficiency with regard to it.

Research results (spring term 1998)

Interviews

When analysed the research data clearly shows that from the introductory meeting (8 January) between the Project staff and the school, the new Primary 7 teacher did not need to be convinced of the value of reflecting on practice. In view of how energising and enjoyable the workshop programme had been for the children, she had begun to schedule periods of circle time in her class. She had also begun to plan the peer mediation workshop programme for the current Primary 6 class – to take place in the summer term.

Project staff met again with the Primary 7 teacher and the principal on 27 March. The school had been addressing serious behavioural problems among a group of five Primary 6 children, which had rendered teaching virtually impossible in that class and created problems throughout the school. (The problem could be traced back at least to when the boys were in Primary 4.) The school's special needs teacher had been released from all other duties for the rest of the school year to work with this small group.

The teacher continued to run circle time sessions with her class, though these were prone to disruptions. Also on Fridays she had a programme of her own creation which she called 'It's not-fair time' – an opportunity for everyone, including herself on occasion, to say what they wanted on issues of 'not-fairness'.

This teacher had an obviously good relationship with her class – and the children valued it. She played a lot of sport with them – hockey, football, etc. – a good context for building relationships. But a concern she had was that, though while they were with her the children were 'great', with supply teachers, other teachers or playground supervisors, they often behaved very inappropriately. She was conscious of the need for consistency among the adults concerned in how they related to the children – of the need for a whole-school approach.

There was very little contact with the playground supervisors as regards the peer mediation service; they didn't generally refer conflicts to the mediators. But the Primary 7 teacher herself had a good relationship with the supervisors and, through the peer mediation programme, had become acutely aware of the importance of teacher-ancillary staff relationships. Relationships between pupils and ancillary staff remained conflictual.

Survey

The monthly survey forms filled in by the teacher showed the programme's ongoing value for both the children and the teacher herself. Among other teachers and ancillary staff there were some signs of their coming to recognise its value. However, there was limited feedback from parents. The following comments about pupils, staff and ancillary staff were written by the Primary 7 teacher as part of the survey.[6]

The pupils

The children value their rules and the fact that the teacher also observes them – especially 'No put-downs'. They value working together. During the [Department of Education] Inspector's visit he asked them how they felt to be mediators and they said 'Important' and 'Sort of proud'. Isn't that great! I think the mediators would like to have a greater number of disputes to mediate!

Class teacher

I am working with the children more in groups. I talk with the children more about co-operation, sharing and about why we are doing something. We do circle time. I feel that the children would benefit from occasional reminders' about the rules and how to respect each other etc. As well as games etc. in circle time, I'm also going to get discussion going about some issues around how to treat others.

Other staff

Supervisory assistants were initially somewhat sceptical but are now a bit more positive. Similarly with other teachers, but in general I think that those who had no contact with the programme had no opinion one way or the other. But [in February] before the Inspector arrived we discussed each Performance Enhancement Programme initiative as a whole staff; after the peer mediation had been discussed at least two members of the Key Stage 1 staff approached me and commented on how they felt it was benefiting the children and the school. I found these comments very encouraging, especially coming from Key Stage 1 staff who I felt knew least about the process.

Outside school

Feedback has been limited. Parents are mostly in touch with the school about problems. But I do hear children saying things about 'getting on better' [with brother or sister] and 'I tried to talk to X about our disagreement.' When the [Department of Education] Inspector was present, one of the children told him that he had mediated between his small brother and sister; he claimed that it had worked quite well.

Research results (summer term)

Survey

Class teacher

I ran a refresher workshop for my own class at the beginning of the summer term, on the theme of bullying. There is one boy in particular who bullies others in the school – and terrorises some younger children, both inside and outside school – in fact just about everywhere except in the classroom or where another adult is present. I wanted to try to bring to the attention of everyone how it feels to be bullied (and to be the bully) and to explore what we can do about it. I suppose my objective is to promote the idea of thinking first before using fist or tongue. It was also a chance to recall and reinforce the ground rules and also to restore the habit of being openly affirmative of one another – both of which have lapsed somewhat of late.

She provided details of this workshop programme which, while drawing extensively from the peer mediation programme, was substantially and impressively her own creation: 'I'm happy to report that there hasn't been any report of the particular boy bullying since the workshop – five weeks ago. I felt refreshed and ready to tackle the new term.

It did me no harm to be reminded myself of the ground rules. I'm ready now for another refresher – and reminder!'

Staff

My classroom assistant helped me with this workshop. She had been through the process a couple of years ago and although she doesn't express her opinions readily, she was clearly pleased to take part.

Pupils

The children really enjoyed the workshop. They surprised me with the ideas they came up with during the group discussions. They want another workshop before the end of term – which is very encouraging. It was amazing how well they kept the rules during the workshop, although they had lapsed somewhat in the class before it.

Outside school

'As mentioned earlier, there have been NO reports of bullying by a certain star in my class. YIPEE!!!'

Primary 6 training programme – summer term

The teacher reported separately in June on the Primary 6 training programme, which at the time was nearing completion. It began on 30 April – facilitated by the Primary 7 teacher and assisted by the Primary 6 teacher and her classroom assistant. Two Key Stage 1 teachers helped with the workshops that they could attend. The Primary 7 teacher involved children from her own class in the Primary 6 training workshops, for example in role-plays, assigning one or more of them to each small group.

One reason for training the children while still in Primary 6 was that they would be in a position to offer the peer mediation service from the beginning of the next school year. Another was that the workshops could help in the process of reintegrating the five boys who had been withdrawn from the class, though they would not return fully to the class until the following September. There was evidence from the very first workshop that they were enjoying the programme and were keen to participate in it.

Feedback on Primary 6 training programme
The Primary 7 teacher provided the following comments on the training programme for the Primary 6 class that was carried out in the summer term in readiness for when the children would be in the Primary 7 class the following September.

Pupils
I hear mutterings of 'It's OK to make mistakes' in the classroom, playground etc. We are encouraging an environment of mutual understanding! Considering that there are so many problems in the Primary 6 year, they listen, behave and respond just like other years. The workshops have been very beneficial for the five boys from the class who had been singled out for special attention on account of behavioural problems.

Primary 7 teacher (Training programme leader)
We have had to run the workshops more or less weekly because the term is so short. I feel the concepts raised at workshops are not being emphasised enough back in the classrooms. [With] hindsight I would have had one or two of the workshops before the Easter holidays. Unfortunately the team planning meetings have been very rushed and often with only three facilitators present; I have had to fill the others in, in spare moments, on what's happening. This problem is being addressed for next year.

Staff
The Primary 6 teacher is already trained and the classroom assistant has some training. There is also the teacher who takes the five Primary 6 boys with behavioural problems. Two Key Stage 1 teachers have also been coming, when possible, to facilitate. It has been great to show them what goes on at the workshops. They are both very positive and have plans to use the circle time process in their own classes. It's a pity everyone hasn't the same attitude.

Outside school
  'I have even heard a ground rule being muttered at the school gate!!!'

Interview – summer term (end)
At the meeting with Project staff [11 June], the Primary 7 teacher reflected that the training workshops with Primary 6 should have started earlier, so as to have a fortnightly interval between workshops. This was because extra time was needed. Time proved to be insufficient in practically all the workshops, so that some, often very important, work was left unfinished. Not being the class teacher, the team leader had no opportunity to complete it in class time. But she will be their teacher from September and will begin with one or more recall (refresher) workshops. She also acknowledged that trying to use the 30-minute space created by the Friday assembly to plan each workshop was 'crazy'; an alternative and longer space must be made available. She expressed satisfaction with how the workshops had been for the five boys with behavioural problems.

Project staff had the opportunity to view the agreement forms that had been completed in relation to formal mediations during the year. These indicated that the peer mediation service was well used and proving useful, with encouragement from the teacher for both service providers and users. (The agreement forms from the schools established a peer mediation service were analysed and assessed in Chapter 3.) The teacher's evaluation of the service is positive, though she would view it as secondary to the value of the training workshops (and the process which these initiated in the classroom). 'You might as well have [peer mediation] as not, since the training makes it immediately feasible. It's an added bonus – and a worthwhile one.'

The agreement forms from this school contain quite specific details in writing about what each disputant has agreed to on a quid pro quo basis. These details indicate that some of the issues were quite serious and with a potential for escalation that the mediations may have defused; there was bullying, name-calling involving family background, and threatening to get a gang or brothers to deal with the other person. As mentioned elsewhere, a very common issue, especially for the girls, is that of one person having taken away the other's friend(s); for both boys and girls there is also exclusion from a group and from games teams. At the same time, beyond the 'give and take' details of the agreement, there is equal emphasis on 'making friends, saying sorry etc.', – though occasionally the agreement is about staying away from each other.

This case study highlighted what was to be a common perception from each of the six schools. On the one hand the schools perceived an expectation on the part of the Project staff that the programme would only be complete with the establishment of a peer mediation service; on the other hand, they felt that the training programme was worthwhile in itself and a peer mediation service was icing on the cake. The Project staff were aware that danger threatens when the launch is over and mediation, and the responsibility for it, become a reality. When the training programme, which has been well structured and supported, comes to an end, the peer mediation service often experiences, after the initial novelty, a dwindling clientele.

Time

Equally, it emerged that time was a critical factor in the ability of schools to sustain the programme. The planning of workshops, while seen as essential, often had to be crammed into short periods, and it was often difficult to get the key members of staff present at the same time. The involvement of the Project staff helped to create that time, and the fear was that if the Project was no longer involved, the other varied and conflicting demands on the school's time would squeeze out peer mediation.

How have schools sustained the peer mediation programme?

In the case of School B, this Primary 6 class had been trained in the spring and summer terms of 1997, with the help of the Project staff. As Primary 7s and with the full support of their new teacher, the children resumed their peer mediation service in the September. The school adult team, without assistance from the Project except in the concluding all-day workshop, provided the training programme for the Primary 6 children in the autumn term. Significantly, they used the expertise of some of the Primary 7 mediators to help with some of the workshops. Following a refresher workshop in April 1998, the Primary 6 children joined their Primary 7 colleagues in providing the peer mediation service in preparation for taking full charge of it from September.

An important practical expression of a whole-school approach by School B was the development *by the school itself* of a programme for the Primary 3 children, drawing on the peer mediation programme but creatively adapted for Key Stage 1. (The school had identified discipline issues in Key Stage 1, one aspect of which was the fact that the Primary 3 boys were particularly rough at play.) By April 1998 four workshops had been conducted, by the principal and the Primary 6 and Primary 3 teachers. Outstanding programme resource materials had been designed by the principal at School B for each workshop, such as, for Workshop 1, 'Good games/bad games', using smiling/frowning faces and 'Tom and Jerry' cartoons. And in Workshop 2, rules were devised to ensure that no one got hurt or had a bad time, using the 'Jack and Jill' and 'Humpty Dumpty' stories. For instances, discussion would ensue from such questions as 'Could it be that Jack fell because he was pushed?', 'What co-operation is needed to put Humpty Dumpty together again?'

The workshops took place mostly in small groups around tables. But there were also some larger group sessions. Department of Education Inspectors discussed the workshops and were very impressed, describing the programme as 'one of the school's strengths'. From the comprehensive set of ground rules of the peer mediation programme were selected 'No put-downs' and 'One person speaking at a time', plus of course the 'Quiet Please' sign. The Primary 3 teacher expressed delight with the programme, feeling that the children had benefited greatly from the workshops.

Sometimes the perceptions of the teacher, the Project staff and the children about a programme would be very different. In School C it became apparent in conversations with the Primary 6 teacher, and subsequently with the principal in June 1998, that adult-relationship issues were the critical factor in relation to the programme. Project staff had previously gained some sense of difficulties in this area, but the June meetings gave a much clearer indication of these and of their potential to abort the programme. By contrast, a meeting with the children in June reinforced the previous evidence of its benefit to them and of their positive evaluation of it.

Divergent views about the programme are of course valid ones: the Primary 6 teacher did not attach particular value to the programme, and did not become fully comfortable with the interactive processes on which it is based. She did not see it as having significantly enhanced the children's self-esteem.

Apart from having held three or four circle time sessions in the final term in response to the principal's encouragement of all teachers to do so, there was no real follow-up to the training workshops. There was no visual 'legacy' in the classroom either of the training programme or of the mediation service (e.g., posters, a list of the ground rules, a mediation service rota and so on). Asked about how it might have supported teaching and learning in the class, the Primary 6 teacher said: 'This has always been a very nice class; they get on well together; boys and girls mix well and play football together, and classmates visit each others' homes etc. Three children who came new to the school were immediately welcomed and integrated into the class. I wouldn't particularly attribute this good atmosphere to the peer mediation programme.'

However, an opportunity for Project staff to meet with the class indicated that for the *children* the training programme was *very* significant. They vividly, excitedly and fondly recalled the workshops – the role-plays, games, small- and large-group work and so on, and spoke of how useful the skills they learned had been for them outside school – in restoring their friendships after a falling-out, and sometimes in prompting them to act as mediators in disputes at home or on the street. There was therefore quite a contrast between the *teacher's* perception of the programme and the *children's* view of it.

Given that a particular feature of this training programme is that its delivery is dependent on collaborative engagement between the class teacher and other staff, parents and so on, it challenges both the conventional hierarchical culture of schools and the isolationism in the teaching profession. So it raises complex relationship issues in all schools:

- The engagement of ancillary staff and/or parents in classrooms and schools can lead to conflicting roles, as seen by teachers and principals on the one hand and non-teachers on the other.
- In a particular school, interpersonal issues and diverse perceptions and priorities as regards education come to the fore.

This case study demonstrates that the resources and talents of teachers and those available to work with them are less pertinent to the success or otherwise of a programme than is the question of relationships. Without due attention to the primacy of relationships, and to the establishment of a process whereby issues can be dealt with constructively, skills and abilities can be at best wasted and at worst a further source of conflict. In School C, while there were sufficient people with the *ability* to continue the programme (even if the Primary 6 teacher were to leave), preliminary and ongoing team-building work seemed to be necessary.

It needs to be stressed that such issues are not unique to any school (only different in each); and alongside the skills resources of this particular school there was evidence of its real will and potential for enhancing the spirit and practice of teamwork.

The experience of the EMU-Promoting School Project was often that schools would expect peer mediation with children to be the starting-point; and indeed during the pilot project in 1993/4 this was the case. As mentioned earlier, training for teachers was minimal in advance of the children's workshops themselves. However, gradually it was recognised by the Project, and later by the schools themselves, that there was a need for substantial training for the adults, both the whole-school staff and the team that would be delivering training to the children. This balance between support and dependency has to take into consideration the demands on a school. External agencies can afford to be single-minded about their particular programme, and voluntary agencies have a tradition of developing education packs which they want to introduce to schools. (In the USA there is the added dimension of 'vendors', private companies that sell educational programmes to schools.) A peer mediation programme, like any other programme, has to fit into the logistics and vagaries of the school day.

It has been found in other countries, too, that peer mediation programmes need conflict-resolution approaches to have been established in schools prior to peer mediation being introduced.

> The Resolving Conflict Creatively Programme (RCCP) initiates the mediation component only in schools that have been participating in RCCP for at least a year and have a group of teachers who regularly use the [RCCP] curriculum. School mediation programmes are best implemented as part of a larger effort to train staff and students in conflict resolution. This is a significant strength over approaches that use only mediation.[7]

In Northern Ireland, conflict-resolution skills training in schools didn't have a tradition to draw on, unlike the USA where community mediation programmes were well established before schools mediation took root. But there was an awareness of a need to have a 'prequel' to peer mediation training that could be made relevant to Key Stage 1 classes in particular.

Teachers themselves made the connection with circle time, and as previously mentioned, peer mediation training developed organically from a circle time format. The example of School F illustrates how the two were conjoined.

School F
School F wished to continue with the peer mediation programme for its two new Primary 6 classes. The Project, however, indicated that it could not provide the

level of support that it had given in the year just ended. It was agreed that a Project person would attend both of the first sets of workshops, provide distance support ahead of the second and third, and come as a visitor to the fourth set.

At Workshop 4 (26 October 1997) it was most encouraging to find how well the school team was managing by itself, with the continued support and involvement of the principal. The pupils were clearly enjoying the programme and the recap component of Workshop 4 demonstrated clear evidence of learning. Not surprisingly, the visitor from the Project heard renewed emphasis on the need to link the programme to a foundational programme (circle time) in Key Stage 1 and lower Key Stage 2, and to follow up the peer mediation programme with circle time in upper Key Stage 2.

While many teachers were already working with circle time, it was expected that the Project could be available to support its expansion and enhancement. Given the school's wish to offer *everything* that would enhance the children's total learning and personal development, it was understandable that an overstretched staff would seek all the help it could get.

In the meantime, a limited mediation service was being offered by the Primary 7 children – limited not least by their engagement in preparing for the 11+, transfer tests. It was being used in particular by the Primary 6 'trainee mediators'. Ancillary staff were not much involved for reasons unconnected to the programme. But on the afternoon following the first transfer test, the scheduled workshop (number 5) with the Primary 6 classes was replaced by a refresher workshop with the Primary 7s, planned earlier in the day by the two Primary 7 teachers and the Project's link-person with the school. Such engagement in the programme by the two teachers, on a day of undoubted high stress for them, was yet more evidence of their commitment to it. They subsequently amended their proposed programme, following consultation with the children.

Despite the considerable time lapse since their training programme, the Primary 7 children immediately fell into workshop mode and the event was as much as anything a *collaborative* venture between themselves and the adults. Coming to this activity from the rigidly individualist and crude assessment – the transfer test – earlier in the day, they launched wholeheartedly into creating and celebrating an atmosphere of mutual affirmation, co-operation and support, easily recalling the peer mediation process and techniques. It was clear, too, that the teachers had become increasingly comfortable with the workshop approach to learning.

The Primary 6 training was duly completed. The Project link-person who attended the remaining workshops observed a real sense of unity among the children and the obvious ease of adults and children with each other. Parents, staff and the board of governors were treated at their annual meeting to a demonstration by the pupils of their peer mediation skills, which included, as the invitation to parents and staff stated, 'the "circle time skills" of affirmation and listening and conflict resolution'.

Two years later, School F approached the Project asking for assistance in developing a whole-school approach to circle time; and a refresher course for all the teachers, involving demonstration workshops, ensued.

Endnote

How should we define a 'self-sustaining peer mediation programme'? When the principals of the six schools were asked to approve the manuscripts of their respective case studies, the principal of School E returned it, happy for it to be used, with the comment:

> Something that strikes me about peer mediation – it is now so much part of us all at [the school] that we (and I in particular) use the techniques all the time – I mean on a daily basis literally – to resolve disputes, problems, allegations, etc., of all the children, of whatever age – listening to each side, repeating it back for clarification, asking how the children feel or felt, asking them about possible solutions, agreeing a resolution – I record it in the incident book.

Far from being an 'add-on', the principles encapsulated in peer mediation, in this school at least, have been integrated into the discipline procedure. Over a period of years the school has taken total ownership of the training process, and in so doing has transcended the 'Oh no, not another initiative' syndrome.

9. If Peer Mediation Is the Answer, What Is the Question?

'It is vital that teachers see themselves as equal partners in the research process, whose open and honest reflections as practitioner-researchers are listened to with total respect, and that their opinions will have equal status with those of colleagues from the EMU-Promoting School Project in influencing future action. To an important degree the same applies to Project relationships with principals, other adults and children. Such relationships are essential to ensure that both schools and Project have a shared understanding of the purposes of the venture and are working to the same agenda.'[1]

'More and more I'm realising that I don't want to go into a school with answers. What I'm trying to do at the moment is 'learn the good questions', and then from those good questions come the school's answers.'[2]

'When you are given the opportunity to look at a problem you begin to realise that you must look at the genealogy of that problem. You begin to realise that this thing has a family tree, brothers and sisters and a life expectancy. Every problem or concern that you encounter has an extended family to be considered.'[3]

Peer mediation needs to be undertaken in the context of

research. There are pragmatic reasons for this: every school is different, each workshop has its own dynamic, and individual children have different needs. Continual monitoring and evaluation are needed to respond to different teaching and learning situations. The study of peer mediation training in Cleveland, Ohio,[4] referred to earlier in this book illustrated that diverse outcomes occur when an identical programme is delivered in different schools. Mark Bitel, who has specialised in evaluating peer mediation projects, citing one such peer mediation project involving nine schools in Leicester, made the same point – 'Exactly the same programme works differently in each of the schools.'[5]

In this chapter I aim to illustrate what action-research is and why, in my experience, it has proved so relevant to the implementation of peer mediation, particularly as part of a whole-school approach. I shall use as a case study the experience of the EMU-promoting School Project in applying action research to its own practice in the introduction and development of peer mediation in primary schools in Northern Ireland.

I shall refer to recent developments in the USA, notably the Conflict Resolution Education Network (CREnet) and United States Department of Education (USDE) research and evaluation symposium held in Washington DC in March 2000. In conclusion I shall argue that the principles and values of peer mediation coincide with those of action-research. Drawing on the experience of educationalists like Professor Julian Weissglass whose model of educational change is explored later in this chapter, I shall demonstrate that if peer mediation is about change, then, 'change, whether desired or not, whether imposed or voluntarily pursued, represents a serious personal and collective experience characterised by ambivalence and uncertainty.'[6] I shall contend that action-research enables everybody involved in peer mediation to reflect on their practice: the teacher with his or her relationship with a class of children, the member of an external agency dealing with questions from a group of staff, the pupils in the playground making choices as to how they deal with conflict. The cyclical nature of action research equips each of these groups and individuals with a means of making sense of the uncertainty, removing the anxiety and achieving a sense of 'mastery, accomplishment and growth'.[7]

What is action-research?

'Action-research is the name given to an increasingly popular movement in educational research. It encourages teachers to be reflective of their own practice in order to enhance the quality of education for themselves and their pupils.'[8] Jean McNiff, who has written extensively about action research, teamed up with June Neill of the Western Education and Library Board in Northern Ireland, on a project with teachers. In their report of that project they outline the action-research steps:

- What is my concern?
- How am I concerned?
- How can I show that in action?
- What do I think I can do about it?
- What will I do about it?
- How can I gather evidence to show that I am influencing the situation?
- How can I ensure that any judgements I make are reasonably fair and accurate?
- What will I do then?[9]

Throughout this book run themes of school ownership, citizenship education, transformation and democracy. If peer mediation is to be more than an 'add-on', more than just another initiative foisted on an overworked and undervalued staff, then peer mediation programmes have to take cognisance of the reality of the school in general, and the classroom in particular.

The individual teacher himself or herself has a key role to play in reflecting this reality. Peer mediation has to be at one and the same time part of a whole-school approach and relevant to the individual teacher, as a reflective practitioner. It is actually difficult *not* to reflect on your own practice when teaching children conflict-resolution skills, as children are quick to point out any discrepancy in what is being modelled and what is being asked of them. It has to be a case of 'Do as I say *and* do as I do.' 'If we are serious about encouraging children to resolve their own conflicts by mediation, they in turn may ask us how we resolve our conflicts. There is no doubt that schools embarking on peer mediation training have to be prepared for such questions.'[10]

Peer mediation requires a consistent environment in the school if it is to have hope of taking root. Where there is incongruence between the adult relationships in a school and those being promoted among the children, the children quickly notice it and, rightly, ask 'Why?' The programme becomes saddled with a credibility problem. An example of this is the introduction of workshop ground rules. These are negotiated by all the participants, children and adults alike. This has ramifications. If the school's expected outcome is behaviour modification for only the children, then an *unexpected* outcome is behaviour modification for *teachers*.

Children often lead the way in instigating change; for example, requesting that the ground rules of the workshop – no put-downs, affirm one another, listen, it's okay to make mistakes – be implemented in the classroom; they want to transfer a safe environment from one situation to the other.

Sometimes teachers become aware of their own reliance on put-downs as a means of class-control: As one remarked, 'Pupils began to tell me when I was not treating them with the respect they ought to have. All teachers use put-downs on occasion, but the children were quick to point out that if they should not do it, I should not do it either.'[11]

So, it could be argued, and will be in this chapter, that a natural development of effective peer mediation training is that teachers reflect on aspects of their own practice.

Applying action-research to peer mediation

Phase 1 – the pilot programme

Chapter 2 mentioned that peer mediation was introduced to Northern Ireland in the context of an action-research project. In 1993 when the peer mediation pilot programme started, the project team used continuous evaluation of individual workshops, and self-evaluation, as a means of its own action-research. Later it made a more structured attempt to involve teachers in the action-research process, but at the start, although it consulted closely with teachers, this consultation concerned the *action* rather than the research.

Although the action-research project team had experience of working in general conflict-resolution training, it had limited experience of mediation. Understandably, the focus of the team's research was on its own confidence and competence in delivering the workshop programme: 'Given the [project] team members' limited previous experience of mediation skills training, the format of the training sessions consisted of [project] team members "doing" the kinds of exercises which were being envisaged for the children and then, through analysis and evaluation, designing the exercise for use in the children's workshops.'[12] So in the first year it was really a question of our action-research 'concern' being to tailor the peer mediation training programme to the individual class. We learned by our mistakes, one of which was not informing the lunchtime supervisors from the start. Since they are often key players in having to deal with conflict, their role in supporting peer mediations – as, I hope, has already been stressed – is also a vital one.

If an issue arose during the workshops, we would try to deal with it at the time, or at the next week's workshop. One such problem, already alluded to in Chapter 3, was that some children were reticent about speaking up in a large group – so work was then done with them to build their confidence.

Perhaps our view was myopic, but our objective at that stage was not so much to establish a peer mediation service as part of a whole-school approach, but to satisfy ourselves and the schools that it was possible to train children to mediate their own conflicts. So in the first years of the peer mediation programme in Northern Ireland, we were applying action-research methodology to individual workshops, and also to our own thinking. McNiff and Neill[13] give as an example of working criteria to judge progress the fact that 'we would challenge and justify our own assumptions and prejudice where appropriate'.

In the early days of the project we found ourselves doing this, although not necessarily with clinical objectivity, but often with passion and heated discussion. It is hardly surprising that in any pioneering enterprise there are doubts, anxieties and even conflicts. But as was pointed out at the time:

> There always has to be a balance between the team spirit and the task, as a focus for attention. I think we achieved the task, but I found being a member of the team stressful; and not a place where it was easy to share feelings of inadequacy or difficulties. I am excited about the work, but not about working in that team. It is however a credit to our collective professionalism that we achieved the task.[14]

From the outset we had to acknowledge the difference between the adult experience of mediation and that of children:

> [Participating in a mediation training day] helped me to identify a number of dilemmas about the training process. I knew that we would need to do role-plays, both to give the team confidence, and also to iron out problems in materials which we might later use with the children. But should we work with situations which were real to us, or the sort of problems which arise for children? Children's mediation does not mirror adult practice; they tend to do it much faster, and are less concerned with tying up all the issues in an agreement. But it would have been hard for us to enter into that – aping pseudo-P7 mediators would not have helped anyone.[15]

These two quotations indicate that we were challenging and justifying our own assumptions and prejudice, but not in a systematic way; and often such interactions became heated, as we did not always implement the working criteria that Jean McNiff and June Neill were advocating:

- We would listen to each other with courtesy and respect, and try to understand an alternative position.
- We would value the person although we might not agree with the opinion.
- We would acknowledge the legitimacy of an opinion even if we disagreed with it.[16]

To sum up, we were very task-orientated, and constantly evaluating our practice in order to improve the workshops. With hindsight we would also have benefited from substantial time spent on team-building. The action research focused almost exclusively on how the project team planned and delivered the workshops. It was a sharp learning curve: practising a workshop on a Tuesday, and delivering it on the Wednesday and Thursday to different schools. We were basing our programme on US models; and although we knew peer mediation worked in other countries, we weren't sure if it would work in Northern Ireland. We needed to know that peer mediation was a viable option in terms of children's capabilities; exploring the ramifications of making it part of a whole-school approach came later.

The process of writing a report of that first year, *Peer Mediation in Primary Schools*,[17] led to an explicit recommendation for a higher action-research profile. The full pilot programme recommendations are given below.

Pilot programme recommendations in relation to research
The service's development crucially requires an action-research process. Interested schools should be made aware of the research requirements of the agency, and necessary contractual arrangements in respect of these should be negotiated at the beginning.

1. Research instruments must respect the confidentiality of all parties in all mediation cases. There must be clear and agreed guidelines about the confidential nature of all records.
2. Research instruments must be teacher- and pupil-'friendly'

and be developed in consultation with the teachers.

3. It is necessary for the agency to have a person specifically assigned to research co-ordination so that a proper balance between action and research is maintained.[18]

Other broad recommendations included:

- A peer mediation service should be established in schools in Northern Ireland.
- Schools should be fully aware of what was required of them, and a contract between the school and external agency agreed and signed before the start of any programme.
- As many children as possible should be trained, and careful attention paid to the selection procedure for mediators, in order that those not chosen are still able to play meaningful roles in the peer mediation service.

In addition, the findings of the action-research into the project team's own dynamics led to recommendations that:

1. any team of people from an external agency should include trained teachers
2. adequate time should be spent in team-building activities to build up co-operation and communication within the team
3. adequate time should be allowed to the team to develop its confidence and experience in, and practice of, the mediation process, before starting to train children
4. there should be a commitment from all team members to using mediation in resolving intra-team conflicts
5. there should be clear procedures for leadership within the team.[19]

Phase 2 – peer mediation gains ground

It helped when we were working with people who had experience of action-research and understood the methodology. I remember being struck by the clarity with which the principal of School A gave an example of action-research. His concern was that behaviour in the playground was not satisfactory; fighting would regularly occur between pupils. His concern led him to undertake a piece of research.

He had security cameras in action, trained on the school fence to prevent people breaking into the school. He decided to turn the cameras round on to the playground, and immediately saw that the children did not have enough space or support for games, and that fights were starting from boredom. This led to a whole series of initiatives, including peer mediation, as part of a whole-school approach.

This principal started with a concern about playground fights; as a result he began to develop a preventive programme that engaged children and lunchtime supervisors in providing enjoyable and meaningful activities, which in turn prevented or resolved conflict. He was therefore already engaged in his own response to this concern when the project approached him at the start of the second phase of the peer mediation programme.

In 1995, two years after the first phase began, it was decided to expand the programme beyond the two original schools. *Peer Mediation in Primary Schools* had concluded that there was substantial evidence that the concept of a peer mediation service in primary schools in Northern Ireland was 'indeed feasible, given certain conditions'.[20]

In addition to the project approaching individual schools, it began to be approached by schools themselves. Word had got around, usually by recommendation from individuals who had seen demonstrations of peer mediation: 'Children who have trained and practised as mediators are a special resource in "selling" the peer-mediation idea. They have impressively demonstrated the process and competently fielded the questions of adults and other children.'[21] But as we saw in Chapter 6, the children's ability to sell peer mediation became a double-edged sword. It was often inspiring to hear them talk in a matter-of-fact way about the skills they had learned and their experiences of using them. The honesty with which they responded to questions, the way in which they wouldn't be drawn on the details of a specific mediation because it was confidential, the seriousness and pride with which they took their role as mediators – all this created respect and made peer mediation very attractive. But it also blurred the fact that this was the end result of a considerable journey for a school, and not the starting-point. There was a great temptation for principals to see peer mediation as the answer to their problems, and to want the product rather than the process of getting it.

The concerns that led schools to ask the Project for peer mediation were many and various, and often fell into one of these two categories:

1. 'We have a problem with . . .'

The problem could be, for instance, a class that lacked self-esteem, or bullying in the playground. The teacher or principal might or might not have been actually looking for a quick fix, but nevertheless there was an expectation that peer mediation might help solve a specific problem. In a US context, where violence is a prevalent problem in schools, Bickmore acknowledges: 'It is tempting to respond to educational problems with quick fixes, and thus to respond to the social problem of violence with "negative peacemaking" strategies that put the lid on the symptoms of the problem.'[22]

In other cultures where the problem of violence may not be so extreme, the response may still be dealing with the superficial rather than the underlying cause of the problem. This response is explored further in Chapter 10.

2. 'We've heard that such and such a school is doing peer mediation and they speak highly of it . . .'

This was more likely to result in an effective engagement – provided that the person on the end of the phone had some kind of mandate from the school to request outside involvement.

Even when a school was being proactive in terms of wanting a programme to improve existing relationships rather than reacting to a particular situation, it was usually a package they were looking for, rather than a process. And invariably, whatever the motivation of the school, they wanted us to come in and 'do peer mediation' and to do it with the *children*.

There's an old joke about a couple in a car pulling up,

asking a man in the street for directions and getting the response, 'If I was going there, I wouldn't start from here.' The parallel with the pedestrian's comment is that there needs to be a very compelling reason to *start* a peer mediation programme with *children's* workshops if the end result is meant to be a whole-school approach. Our research illustrates overwhelmingly that work needs to be initiated with the staff beforehand – if only because, as has been illustrated, the greatest resistance comes from the staff. (A caveat here would be that in secondary schools there have been examples of a 'green shoot' approach in which a pilot programme is inaugurated with young people as an exemplar for the rest of the school.)

As we saw in Chapter 3, Seamus Farrell wrote an extensive report on a 'Training the Trainer' course in which he concluded:

> This report represents a new approach to our action-research. It is the outcome of:
>
> a: a *range* of creative approaches to securing feedback from participants – written personal goals, rolling evaluations, closing circles, and an opportunity to offer comments freely (i.e. not tied to specific questions as was the case with designed evaluation forms)
> b: an in-depth staff evaluation of the entire process – from planning, programme design and materials production through to assessment of the event itself.[23]

Farrell acknowledged that this intensity of evaluation 'clearly signals an effort to take action-research more seriously, [but] it is appropriate to consider if it is worth the expenditure of time'.[24] A key element of action-research is that it is put in the public domain in order that it can be challenged – that is, it is published. The Project initially tended to rely, perhaps too heavily, on workshops as a means of disseminating its learnings, rather than publishing in journals. Nevertheless, it began to gain a reputation in the peer mediation field.

As the Project continued we became more and more

aware of a paradox. In Northern Ireland we began to gain a reputation for being the 'experts' on peer mediation, and yet our response to every request was becoming similar to the pedestrian in the joke.

Why was this? There were a number of factors. In the course of ten years peer mediation had gone from being an unknown quantity which we had to *sell*, to being one which (while still being largely unknown) was beginning to be *in demand*. Initially grateful just to *get* into schools, we tended to go along with the idea of delivering a package rather than thinking through the ramifications of cultivating a process. It was because of the contradictions that were thrown up by the contrast between the ethos of the workshops, based on co-operation, communication and problem-solving, and the ethos of the schools, which had a more hierarchical and punitive approach to conflict, that we realised that a process was necessary to build a bridge between the two.

Jean McNiff[25] contends that the starting-point for action-research often occurs when a practitioner perceives his or her educational values being denied in practice. A moment when this became clear to the Project has been described in Chapter 7, when a teacher asked, 'What about blame and punishment?' in relation to peer mediation. That moment happened at a time when we felt sufficiently confident with the training programme – we had helped train children who were delivering an effective peer mediation service – that we could begin to look beyond the training programme to the schools themselves.

Returning to McNiff and Neill's action-research steps, it became clear that, in the process of implementing peer mediation, we were already becoming over-reliant on the establishment of a functioning peer mediation service as evidence that we were 'influencing the situation'. One area we needed to expand into was the direct involvement of teachers in the action-research process. But it was the goal of achieving a whole-school approach, and the inherent need for transformation, that challenged the Project in terms of action-research. This was particularly true even if, on the surface, everything seemed fine: 'A clear and accurate picture of the issues affecting the capacity of schools to enhance their practice cannot be arrived at quickly. It takes time to get behind external images of collaboration, collective leadership and team-work to identify the gaps that may exist between theory and practice.'[26] The process of using the peer mediation training programme meant that the Project had to build up trust with the adult school community, while often simultaneously becoming aware of the obstacles to the application of peer mediation. Trust-building is a lengthy process, and:

> the investment of time and resources involved could in no circumstances be justified either in terms of its useful findings for an individual school or for the development of a specific programme such as peer mediation. But the cumulative findings from a range of engagements in schools are extremely relevant to the search for ways to promote good educational practice in general, *throughout* the school system.[27]

This explained the rationale for an action-research project to become involved in peer mediation, as the investment of resources could be justified in terms of the impact it might have in developing the work strategically, through disseminating the learning. Such learning could help to stress the 'critical importance of whole-school relationships issues and indicate the strategies needed to address these. In these terms they further demonstrate that investment in educational research is neither a luxury nor an optional strategy.'[28] The EMU Promoting School Project and its predecessor, the Quaker Peace Education Project, set out to be action-research projects, so this defined the research process they brought with them to the peer mediation programme. In other parts of the world, different types of research were also going into peer mediation programmes.

The effectiveness of peer mediation: experience in the USA

In the past years, many conflict resolution educators

have been asked by peers, colleagues and critics to provide evidence that what we do is effective. We often reflect on what we still need to know about the impacts of conflict resolution education on students, teachers, diverse populations, and school climate. And, many of us grapple with questions about processes of institutionalising these programs and wonder which approaches are most likely to make our work central to the educational mission.[29]

The Conflict Resolution Education Network (CREnet) and its forerunner the National Association for Mediation in Education (NAME) have been consistent in advocating evaluating and research processes. In *Mediation Is Great . . . But Does It Work?*[30] in 1994, Dan Kmitta recounted his responses to phoned inquiries from journalists who were often looking for statistical evidence of the effectiveness of peer mediation, and usually in terms of reducing violence in schools, with a narrow definition of violence as being interpersonal. Establishing baselines for such research is time-consuming – 'at least a month of daily observations'. Kmitta made the point that at that time the conflict-resolution and peer mediation movement was barely out of its infancy, and that little evaluation or research had been done.

NAME had been instrumental in producing guides such as *School Mediation Programme Evaluation Kit*,[31] *The Impact of Conflict Resolution Programs on Schools*[32] and *Recommended Standards for School-based Peer Mediation Programs 1996.*[33] In March 2000, CREnet convened a research symposium in Washington DC, sponsored by the US Department of Education (USDE). Its purpose was threefold:

1. examining the results of current research and evaluation of school-based conflict resolution education programs . . . in relation to identified needs of educators;
2. identifying on-going research needs; and
3. developing a product or products based upon the conclusions (drawn from (1)).[34]

A very thorough process was undertaken by the members of the symposium, with issue papers written by members: 'These issue papers would serve as a foundation for the discussion but would also be a valuable resource for the field because they would summarise the current state of the art.'[35]

There was a systematic attempt to survey educators and practitioners in the field, throughout the USA, in order to identify key issues. The symposium was geared to 'providing a forum in which researchers, practitioners and educators could learn from and with each other'.[36] Consequently the teams of writers who wrote papers addressing each issue had at least one member from each of the three categories.

The article in the CREnet journal *The Fourth R* which describes the preparation, organisation and format of the symposium demonstrates that the *process* of consultation was inclusive, accessible and democratic, and made best use of the experience of the 43 participants, as well as of those consulted beforehand. It is an outstanding example of collaborative research. It has to be stressed that the subject matter was conflict-resolution education, of which peer mediation is just one component. The point was made during the symposium that 'there is a tendency to use and evaluate only peer mediation programs because peer mediation programs are tied to disciplinary systems'. Conflict-resolution education is more amorphous, less easily quantified; nevertheless, a significant finding was that conflict-resolution education increases:

- academic achievement
- positive attitudes to school
- assertiveness
- co-operation
- communication skills
- healthy interpersonal and intergroup relations
- constructive conflict resolution at home and school
- self-control.[37]

Other findings show that conflict-resolution education has a greater impact on the school climate in elementary schools than in middle or high schools; and that it has a positive impact on classroom climate in terms of constructive conflict behaviours.

In terms of future research needs, the most urgent were in relation to the need to incorporate multiple perspectives – particularly relevant to multicultural settings; to instigate a national research survey; and to 'conduct research using more standardised methods and measures, not necessarily quantitative, but replicable measures and procedures; and finally to include effects on parents and the wider community that schools serve'.[38]

In several chapters of the report there are calls for more action-research in future work, and in the final chapter, a summary of future directions across topic areas, this call is repeated. Action-research is clearly recognised as having a key role to play.[39]

Experience in the UK

In London in September 2000, a meeting of agencies involved in promoting peer mediation in the UK was organised, to provide 'an opportunity for practitioners to meet one another and share good practice, discuss issues of common interest and concern and much more besides!'[40]

Monitoring and evaluation was seen as a key issue, and Mark Bitel's presentation, 'The Rough Guide to Monitoring and Evaluating Peer Mediation Programmes in Schools'[41] used 'Weaver's Triangle' (see Figure 9.1), to illustrate that evaluation 'isn't an "add-on" extra but part of your programming'.

Self-evaluation was now recognised as legitimate by the UK Government, he said, as long as it was systematic. He urged people to make time for routine and participatory evaluation systems, not simply for the benefit of funders, but 'as a tool which will help you communicate your message'. During the course of his talk Bitel mentioned 'empowerment evaluation', which has a lot in common with action-research. Empowerment evaluation has been defined as 'the use of evaluation concepts, techniques, and findings

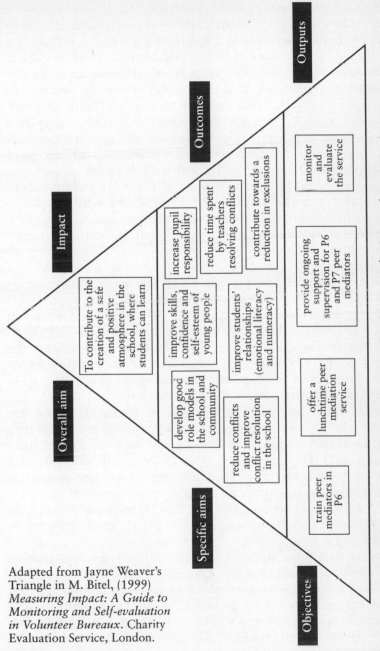

Fig. 9.1: Anytown School peer mediation project

Adapted from Jayne Weaver's Triangle in M. Bitel, (1999) *Measuring Impact: A Guide to Monitoring and Self-evaluation in Volunteer Bureaux*. Charity Evaluation Service, London.

to foster improvement and self-determination . . . [it] has an unambiguous value orientation – it is designed to help people help themselves and improve their programs using a form of self-evaluation and reflection.'[42] Bitel argues a strong case for the involvement of young people in the design of monitoring and evaluation strategies, and in the collection of data. (This point reinforced the value of existing practice in some schools, where a maths project had been done to identify the frequency and type of conflicts mediated.) He gave an example of one school that had adapted the layout of the Rosenberg self-esteem scale[43] – a tool that could be used as part of a 'before and after' survey – by using graphics to make it more child-friendly.

He made the point that young people were 'switched on to data collection and the use of ICT [information communication technology]'.

Bitel explained that anecdotal evidence was gathered in a reactive way, and suggested becoming more proactive by asking yourself, 'What are the questions that I want to ask?' An excellent example of such a question cropped up when he was talking about questionnaires to follow up individual mediation. In a follow-up questionnaire designed by the peer mediators themselves, the disputants would be asked a series of questions including 'What do you think would have happened if you hadn't gone to mediation?'

The participants at the conference immediately saw the importance of this question, particularly after one person had said that responses to it included 'We would never have made up.' The evidence gathered from such a question serves to illustrate that mediation is a vital component in enhancing the teaching and learning environment.

A substantial part of the day was, significantly, spent on monitoring and evaluation, and the participants at the meeting felt it was beneficial.

Barbara Curtis spoke about the lack of a central database of peer mediation in the UK. In an attempt to get an overview and an awareness of what was happening and where, she decided to do some research. She wanted to know how people were working – examples of good practice, problems to avoid.[44] There was a consensus at the meeting that a national network was vital, and funding for a 'peer mediation person' should be sought.

Other issues that were discussed in workshops were marketing, sustainability and accreditation.

UK peer mediation agencies

Questionnaire 2 has already been referred to. Several of the participants at the peer mediation meeting had recently completed my survey. Of the twelve respondents, all bar two replied to question 13, 'How do you measure the effectiveness of your programme?'

One answered, 'With great difficulty. Easy to collect subjective material on changes, harder to tie down to hard facts.' The majority relied on feedback from teachers and children, after individual workshops and/or the full training programme. Responses included this, from the deputy head teacher of a primary school: 'Quite noticeably the majority of the children have gained a great deal from the training and from the experience of actually mediating. Their communication skills are improved, their confidence and self-esteem are noticeably raised.' And from children: 'School's a better place to be' and 'My teacher is kinder now – they have more time since we can go to the mediators to sort out our arguments.'

Two of the respondents mentioned follow up, one saying, 'Schools are approached again after six months to ask for their views on the effectiveness of the workshops, whether they have observed long-term benefits, whether they have incorporated the workshop practice with everyday activities, etc.' The other indicated a more proactive subsequent involvement: 'In peer mediation work we visit a few months after the implementation of the programme to deal with any problems.'

Having acknowledged the difficulty of getting hard-nosed evidence, one agency was 'going to try comparing statutory tests of peer mediators and a control group before and six months after training in the hope it shows – across three schools – that the mediators have improved more!'

Monitoring and/or evaluation was mentioned by nearly all the respondents who answered the question – they said they used:

- pre-start monitoring
- evaluation questionnaires
- 'before and after' evaluations
- self-esteem questionnaire
- staff questionnaires.

In addition to self-evaluation, three agencies used external evaluations – by the National Lottery Charities Board, a university, and the Charities Evaluation Services. Another respondent was currently working with a university on a research protocol.

It was clear, then, that these agencies, mainly new to the field, were taking monitoring and evaluation seriously. Other agencies, including those featured in Chapter 11, have also seen its relevance and value to peer mediation. For example, Hilary Cremin, who has been at the forefront of developing and evaluating peer mediation, has recently finished her PhD on the effectiveness of peer mediation in schools, in which she evaluates the effectiveness of a peer mediation programme in three primary schools in Birmingham, using pupil questionnaires and teacher interviews.

What do action-research and peer mediation have in common?

The long and distinguished relationship that efforts in conflict resolution have had with educational reform is illustrated in a wide-ranging article in *The Fourth R* by Harry Webne-Behrman, himself a veteran in the field of conflict-resolution programmes. The next chapter explores in greater detail the potential for peer mediation to transform education. 'Mediation is a metaphor for the empowered classroom community, a learning environment in which teachers, students and parents come to perceive conflict as an important challenge to be embraced, an opportunity to learn non-violent strategies for resolving differences.'[45] The idea of a learning environment of partners, with the teacher as facilitator providing a structure, and conflict providing an opportunity for growth, fits in with the dynamics of action-research as a way of implementing, measuring and managing change: 'action-researchers are deliberately encouraging change. Any form of change is unsettling and controversial, and some questions about the research design and results are sure to arise.'[46]

If conflict is 'a signal for a need to change,[47] then conflict resolution, like action-research, is concerned with the *management* of change. Webne-Behrman cites Montessori, Dewey, Holt, Illich, Freire and Gandhi as people who challenged traditional notions of schooling, arguing for experiential learning and the practice of democracy. The collective wisdom and experience of these visionaries is sometimes dismissed simply as Utopian – the demand is to 'get real'. However, in the real world, research continues to indicate that disaffection from schooling amongst young people is a major issue. The research cited in Chapter 5 carried out amongst a cohort of 3,000 pupils in Northern Ireland, which found that schooling was not relevant to their every-day lives beyond being a means to get qualifications, underlines this. Chapter 5 demonstrated that citizenship and human rights education and democracy are challenging schools to adapt, albeit belatedly, to the needs of the twenty-first century.

In Britain successive governments have used education as a political football, and in the implementation of policies teachers are often the last to be consulted, if at all. And yet teachers are key. This situation has been lambasted by writers such as Marian Dadds:

> The wisdom and insight of the educational practitioner has been savagely scorned, abused and ignored in the processes of government educational reform ... The practitioner's voice has been negated in all but the technicist reform discourses. Only when centrally controlled educational changes ran aground on [its] own internal inconsistencies and inefficiencies were teachers and head teachers allowed into the debate. ... the consistent devaluing of teachers' judgements at a macro-political level has become a national scandal. Negating

teachers' informed and thoughtful professional voices constitutes a waste for children. Further, it damages teachers' self-esteem and endangers their willingness to see themselves as responsible, experienced and competent knowers. A nation cannot care for its children by abusing its teachers.[48]

The still, small voice of the teacher reflecting on his or her practice, collaborating with colleagues, learning from each other's experiences and publishing these learnings in a variety of forms, is the missing ingredient in educational reform. Many teachers join the profession with a sense of vision and a desire to be part of changing society. Such high aspirations are worn down by a tired cynicism in too many staff rooms, by the hard grind of being part of an overworked and undervalued profession.

Chris Woodhead, former Chief Inspector of Schools in Britain, offers little encouragement, despite the title of an article quoting him, 'Learn from each other, says chief inspector'.[49] In the article he is reported to have referred to the 'cult of the reflective practitioner', saying that teachers should not be seduced into becoming researchers, 'as such a role is unnecessary'. It is important not to 'exacerbate the debilitating belief that there are experts out there in the universities and town halls who know more than good teachers already know,' he concluded.[50] Few would argue with that. However, he doesn't show how this practical knowledge can be shared and disseminated without increasing the self-esteem and self-confidence of teachers and providing opportunities for them to reflect on their practice, and communicate it with one another.

This book argues that neither teachers, nor indeed universities, operate in a vacuum. Action-research hinges on the recognition that practice informs research which informs practice, and the 'expertise' of teachers is a crucial element in that cycle. As regards 'experts', as McNiff says later in this chapter, knowledge cannot just be measured as a commodity, and disseminating expertise depends on a collaborative approach. Good practice in research shares the values of good practice in educational reform and good practice in conflict-resolution education:

> Action-research and Education for Mutual Understanding are ideal companions; they share the core values of tolerance, care, and respect for others as equals; both have an explicit social intent; they are about transformation and change; they seek to promote movement from the rhetoric to the practice of collaboration; they are about participative democracy.[51]

Webne-Behrman advocates the creation of safe environments to build 'peaceable' communities within schools. He quotes Deutsch,[52] one of the world's most respected figures in conflict resolution, as identifying four key factors for education for a peaceful world: 'co-operative learning, conflict-resolution training, the constructive use of controversy in teaching subject matter and the creation of dispute settlement centres within schools'[53]. If these *are* key factors, perhaps they should be given higher priority in teacher training. Webne-Behrman advocates a pedagogy of conflict-resolution education: 'Synthesis of *concepts* (informed by theory), and *experience* (informed by the cultures of the learners) must occur within an *affirming environment* (informed by *skills* and *potentials* of teachers and learners) within a larger "peaceable" organisation'.[54] He presents a blueprint for conflict-resolution education that takes in everything from transforming the teacher-learner relationship to establishing a community of learning and a creative approach to teaching mediation. He acknowledges that, as true learning is informed by practice, peer mediation *training* isn't sufficient in itself. But although he is formulating a blueprint, it is processes rather than outcomes that capture his imagination.

Seven years later the Washington symposium recognises the need for collaboration, inclusion and, implicitly, transformation. The next step is to involve the teachers and the pupils as participants in the research process – and here we come back to Bitel's advocacy of 'empowerment evaluation'. A hallmark of many peer mediation programmes is that children fill in simple evaluation forms after every workshop. The purpose of these is to gain some idea of their understanding of the point of the various exercises; and by asking them what they enjoyed least and what they enjoyed most, their answers also evaluate the workshop itself. On more than one occasion teachers recognised that this was a rare, sometimes unique, opportunity for children to be asked what they thought of a lesson, albeit an unusual one.

Chapter 10 will explore further why it is so short-sighted to perceive peer mediation merely as a way of achieving behaviour modification. In resolving conflicts, children have demonstrated skills that adults have been aware they possess – the same is true of their capacity to improve what adults are trying to deliver, and in the process improving the teaching and learning environment.

Encouraging teachers and children to reflect on their own *and* each other's practice is a logical step in the process of monitoring and evaluating peer mediation.

The challenges facing action-research

McNiff acknowledges that 'a common challenge to action-research is that it is [perceived as being] subjective and therefore unreliable, that is, the solutions that it claims to generate cannot be universally tested and are therefore invalid'.[55]

She eloquently answers this challenge by exploring three steps: self-validation, peer validation and learner validation. In a telling chapter in her book *Action-research: Principles and Practice* she articulates the common reservations that people have about the validity and legitimacy of action-research. In response to comments and queries about its value, ranging from 'It's not proper research' to 'How can you measure anything without specific scales?', she states, 'Action-research is about people explaining to themselves and others why they behave as they do, and enabling them to share this knowledge with others.'[56]

One of the attractions of action-research is its accessibility. This was brought home to me at a conference on the subject when a team of action-researchers gave reports on their

experience. In the group was a woman who had an adminis-
trative role, and who had never done research before or spo-
ken in a large group. She delivered an enthralling report on
how she had used an action-research process to deal with a
recurring issue – the chaos in the stock room. The way she
involved colleagues in solving this problem, and tried out
different solutions, was inspiring. Her report illustrated that
everybody could and should be involved in the process.

The case study in Chapter 7 involving a teacher who
elicited from his class a concern about bullying shows the
start of an action-research process, and the challenge is to
have a genuine collaboration between pupils and staff. We
have already touched on the difficulty created when the
external agency is seen as the 'expert', and the need to
ensure that all 'expertise', the children's, the teacher's and
the external agencies', be identified and harnessed in a common approach. In answer to the comment, 'If you are a
researcher you must claim to have some expertise in your
field. Yet you say you are not an expert. Please clarify,'[57]
McNiff replies:

> I am not an expert in the way perhaps that you mean.
> Perhaps you are thinking of someone who has amassed
> a quantity of knowledge and skills and has developed
> an expertise in applying them. This person is acknowl-
> edged to 'know' more than others. He follows the pop-
> ular notion of knowledge as a commodity, like money
> or cake, and he has more of it than other people.[58]

She goes on to explain that action-research in this context
is not research *on* other people, but rather it is about studying our own educational development in responding to the
needs of pupils.

Engaging in educational change

In putting the case for action-research as an integral part of
a whole-school approach to peer mediation, a case is simultaneously being made for educational change, at the level of

the school both as an institution and as a community. This requires teachers in particular to be agents of change. Weissglass contends that there are four integral elements to educational change – getting information, reflecting and planning, obtaining emotional support and taking action. All too often teachers are given inadequate information, little time for planning or reflection, no expectation of emotional support and yet are still expected to take action in implementing curriculum changes. Weissglass's model (see Figure 9.2) is designed to encourage teachers to clarify their thinking and evaluate new information in the light of their own experience.

Weissglass's model for educational change

In the UK awareness is growing of the need for newly quali-fied teachers to have time for reflection and planning built into their timetable. The concept of emotional support here is controversial, yet it could be argued that, in its simplest terms, this means the opportunity to be listened to. A stan-

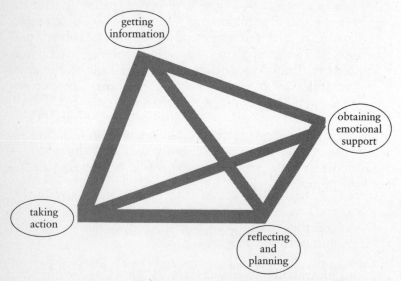

Fig. 9.2: Weissglass's model for educational change

dard exercise that we use in workshops with children and/or adults is 'Listening or Not'[59], which consists of people working in pairs. During the first phase they talk at each other, in the second phase one ignores the other, and in the third they take it in turns to listen to each other. The three phases in total last just fifteen minutes, but they graphically illustrate different qualities of listening. Participants remark that during the final phase they really feel listened to – and yet it lasts only two minutes. Weissglass based much of his work on dyads (pairs), coining the term 'constructivist listening':

> 'Constructivist listening' involves the listener in neither interrupting the talker, nor paraphrasing, analysing, giving advice or breaking in with a personal story. It stresses confidentiality because 'one's feelings are not representative of one's rational thinking (or perhaps even of one's feelings five minutes later)[60]. The talker doesn't criticise or complain about the listener.'[61]

The relevance of Weissglass's approach to educational change in the context of peer mediation became apparent to the EMU-Promoting School Project during one initial after-school INSET with the staff of a primary school. The Project staff were impressed with the level of engagement amongst the staff. They shared ground rules they had already negotiated with their classes, all of which were framed in positive language and were presented as ideals being brought into reality. One outcome of the training session was this question from teachers:

> How can teachers deal with feelings of anger, revenge, frustration or hurt with regard to a child, so that such feelings don't sit in the teacher, leaving him or her stressed and unhappy, poisoning his or her relationship with that child and seriously impairing his or her relationship with the whole class?[62]

This led the facilitator to comment, 'I cannot think of a more amenable environment for introducing the Weissglass model of dyads for teacher support . . . The expressed need is related to a comment in the evaluation, "I know I will probably still lose my temper with the children sometimes".'

In response to the teacher's question, the Project decided at its next INSET with the school to incorporate Weissglass's dyads in the programme. Bearing in mind that the whole staff were present, including ancillary staff, this was a new experience for them. And it proved to be very effective in enabling staff, if they wished to, to support each other with a listening ear.

Wellbeing

The EMU-Promoting School Project regularly starts workshops with the question, 'What do you need from your colleagues to work at your best?' Invariably teachers respond with requirements like 'trust', 'encouragement', to be valued', all of which contribute to a sense of wellbeing. The answers generated by that question, if put into practice, would create a climate where action-research, conflict-resolution education and educational change would converge and synthesise. This environment would not be bland or static, or indeed conflict-free. It would be dynamic, where conflicts would be explored creatively, and where support would be forthcoming.

Teaching is a difficult and stressful occupation; it can be very isolating, and a struggle. It is even more of a struggle to ask for help, as the notion that 'weak teachers should be weeded out' helps to create a climate where it is risky to acknowledge difficulty.

Conclusion

This chapter has traced the development of an approach that started with a request to deliver peer mediation as a package and evolved through action-research to adopting a whole-school approach. In the process it has become clear that peer mediation was embarked upon *with* schools rather than being done *to* them, or *for* them. The same follows for the research.

The chapter demonstrates why the peer mediation training of *children* should not be seen as the first step for an external agency that wishes to become involved in work in schools; or, indeed, as the first step when a school is instituting its own programme of peer mediation.

Action-research should be built into any engagement involving schools and peer mediation. This is for the sound educational reason that peer mediation requires teachers to be 'reflective practitioners' – otherwise, it will become just an 'add-on' rather than a sustainable programme congruent with the school ethos. There is also the pragmatic reason that funders require the monitoring and evaluation of programmes. Sometimes unrealistic targets have led to resistance to effective evaluation, in case they are not achieved.

There is a growing awareness in the USA and the UK at least for a strategic approach to monitoring and evaluation. At a basic level it is an attempt to provide evidence of the transformative nature of peer mediation. One of the points forcibly made at the September 2000 peer mediation network meeting in London was that, amongst the responses from young people to questions about the benefits of peer mediation, the statement 'It has changed my life' would consistently appear.

The interweaving of peer mediation and action-research as means of educational change is essential. This chapter asserts the need for methodologies to be adopted that support teachers as agents of change.

10. Is Peer Mediation Always the Answer?

'If [peer mediation] is misunderstood, or misapplied, its benefits may be lost, and at worst, children may be set up for failure. In [my] experience children make wonderful mediators. It is invariably adults who need to review their attitudes towards conflict, power and control if peer mediation in a school setting is to thrive.' (Hilary Cremin)[1]

Peer mediation has a huge potential, but it also has limits in its application in current educational settings. We have already noted that:

- peer mediation training fits into the curriculum
- children make excellent mediators
- work has to start with the staff
- self-sustaining programmes are possible
- it is important for teachers to reflect on their practice.

Taking all these elements into consideration, I shall now propose that the major obstacle to peer mediation's progress is a lack of child-centred approaches in education.

The concept of peer mediation in schools gained favour initially in conjunction with the wave of enthusiasm for the development and use of mediation techniques in the broad arena of human conflict – at international, community, intergroup and interpersonal levels. The experience of their use at all these levels has now provided a sufficient basis for researchers and practitioners to investigate the effectiveness of peer mediation, and the way it has become institutionalised.

One example is the work of Baruch Bush and Joe Folger, mediators working in the USA to promote the need for mediators to reflect continually on their practice.[2] While remaining advocates of the mediation process, they argue that its value is distorted when structured so that 'solving the problem' becomes both its objective and the measure of its success or failure. It is important that the disputants remain in charge of the *outcome*, which itself may be secondary to the effect of the *process* on transforming their relationship. To put it another way, 'Our emphasis on the agreement as the desired outcome of mediation neglects the importance of the experience of conflict and disagreement as a learning opportunity; there must be explicit value given to the *being* of the mediation experience, not just the *doing*'.[3] The perception that peer mediation is solely about problem-solving has sometimes led to the erroneous notion that it is only for schools with 'problems', and particularly for 'problem schools'. I shall argue here that peer mediation is only sustainable in schools that take a proactive approach rather than a reactive, 'quick-fix' approach to conflict resolution. I shall also draw heavily on research by Professor Karen Bickmore advocating that 'comprehensive infusion of co-operation and conflict resolution into *both* school processes *and* core curriculum is more likely to yield significant and lasting learning, compared with more limited intervention'.[4]

Ideally peer mediation is for schools that see conflict resolution as an integral part of citizenship education, as a means towards creating democracy within the school. Conflict-resolution skills training should be higher up the agenda in schools, in addition to being for adults as well as children. There are sound educational reasons for this, which include the need to ensure that citizenship education, in whatever form it takes, is part of a commitment to *democratic education*.

A *child-centred* approach to mediation rather than just a *problem-solving* approach is called for, if mediation is to be experienced as authentic in schools. Hilary Cremin argues:

Twenty years ago teachers were familiar with the concepts behind humanistic psychology and education. They were concerned to create a 'child-centred' classroom and to ensure that learning is built on the interests and abilities of individual children. In the current educational climate this is becoming harder to achieve, with a standardised curriculum and an emphasis on content and results detracting from more process-orientated methods. Peer mediation is often set against the prevailing school culture.[5]

Peer mediation faces an uphill battle in getting established in schools, because of issues of control, power and an agenda of 'negative peacemaking' that is more about ensuring children behave properly than giving them skills of conflict resolution and opportunities to practise such skills. Children at primary schools remain a largely untapped voice, whose potential is measured in limited ways and rarely fully utilised, despite the best efforts of teachers.

Peer mediation – obsessed with problem solving?

There is a growing movement in the USA to encourage mediation centres to use 'med-arb' (mediation–arbitration), so that if settlement isn't achieved through mediation, arbitration can be brought in. The parallels with peer mediation are stressed later in this chapter.

The human inclination to want to rescue situations, to get things fixed, can distort the mediation process into one more 'top-down' strategy, similar to arbitration and adjudication; such strategies do not involve real change. As I've stressed throughout this book, mediation, long before it is about problems to be solved, is about a *process*, and is posited on a fundamental optimism about people – that they can move from a focus on self-defence to taking account of others, from self-absorption to responsiveness.

A relational or a problem-solving approach?

Chapter 3 showed that the majority of conflicts in primary schools occur when friends fall out. Peer Mediation is a *relational*, before it is a *problem-solving*, process. As such it is more circular than linear. If it is structured it tends to get locked into a linear process of movement – from problem to solution. Restoring relationships is a journey, backwards and forwards, between the past (what happened) and the present (how each of the parties is affected by, feels about and has opportunity to express, what happened). Solutions to particular problems of the moment may emerge from this process.

The integrity of the mediation process is maintained only when the resolution of conflict occurs in *consequence* of the *relationship* being restored or established. Hence it is a *restorative* process, restoring relationships rather than punishing wrongdoers. Folger and Bush talk about mediation as transformation – transformation of people to improve them, leading to a change in 'the consciousness and character of individual human beings'.[6]

Is peer mediation training too rigid?

A linear process of fixed steps, from introduction to agreement, is very attractive in a training context, and in particular commends itself as a process for primary schools. But to use the analogy of teaching English, it is important that children continue to use their imagination and write creatively while learning the grammar. Grammar is essential, but it is, after all, just an aid in making sense of writing; it is part of the process rather than an end in itself. It is interesting to note that in many countries in Europe, as well as Japan, Korea and New Zealand:

> children are not introduced to the formal teaching of reading, writing and mathematics until they are considered developmentally ready, at about six years of age. Research indicates that children who are introduced to *formal* reading and writing at this later age not only catch up with, but within about 10–12 weeks begin to outpace, children who have begun formal reading at the age of four, with significantly less incidence of failure.[7]

This mirrors the experience of EMUpsp that there should indeed be a focus on conflict-resolution skills training in

early education, but that it should be less about structures
and more about guided interaction, such as circle time.

Chapter 2 showed that although mediation is a linear
process, the training – while incorporating the various steps
chronologically – is not didactic, and incorporates a lot of
supporting activities. It is succinctly summed up by a peer
mediator herself: 'To become a mediator you have to know
the process, you have to be good at brainstorming, good at
learning and be able to co-operate with everybody around
you. To help us do this we did role-plays and played lots of
co-operative games. I am very proud of the responsibility I
have in being a mediator.'[8] Even though, as this eleven-year-
old implicitly acknowledges, the training involves fun and
games, mediation is a bit like a dance – learning the steps is
awkward, but after a while it becomes intuitive. But should
this description of mediation, apt though it is, be turned
around? It begs the question as to whether enough research
is being done into how children already deal with conflict
intuitively.

Is peer mediation child-centred enough? How do children resolve their own conflicts?

We get a picture of the conflicts that children *can't* resolve.
They come running to us with them – or, worse, they don't
and they store them up, and/or they escalate. As a consequence the question arises, 'Is conflict seen as natural and
relational, or are those who get into trouble blamed individually for their problems and marginalised as somehow
bad?'[9]

But, if we accept that conflict *is* a natural part of relationships, including those of children gathered in the playground
or the street, shouldn't we be celebrating the conflicts they
resolve without third-party intervention as much as being
perturbed about the ones they don't? After all, this is the
bedrock of experience that children, and adults, use to take
one step further with mediation training.

Equally, we should take cognisance of, and value, the
informal benefits of peer mediation training. Children inter-
nalise their mediation skills and in addition to, or instead of,
a formal mediation service, put their skills into practice: 'My

mother and my brother fight – he's not washed his hair; he's not brushed his teeth, and I use mediation then,[10] 'I helped two of my friends in the street sort out a fight over their Barbies.'[11]

Peer mediation may not be necessary unless direct approaches fail

Underlying this is perhaps the assumption that peer mediation is '*the* way to handle conflict' – when in fact it applies only to circumstances where other ways have failed or not been tried and where third-party involvement is required. Alan McFarland in Chapter 6 sounded a cautionary note when he counselled against third-party intervention before the parties have had a chance to sort it out themselves. Belinda Hopkins (whose own work incorporates a whole-school approach to conflict resolution) will refer in Chapter 11 to Richard Cohen's 'ideal system of conflict resolution' (see Figure 10.1).[12]

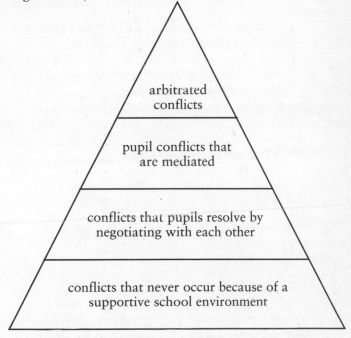

Fig. 10.1: The ideal system of conflict resolution

Cohen graphically demonstrates where peer mediation should fit, ideally between the bulk of potential conflicts that get diffused because of the nature of relationships in the school, and the few that have to be arbitrated.

What is your problem?

There is a tendency to focus on conflict in isolation from its context – as a factor, albeit important, in human interaction. When conflict is viewed as a separate entity, attention is drawn to the problem and its resolution rather than to the parties and the relational dynamics at work between them. This focus is compounded when, for example, a child with behavioural difficulties is perceived as *the problem*, rather than *having* a problem. (Even this may not be the whole picture, as often it is the school that *has* the problem – with the child.) But when viewed in the context of relationships, process assumes priority over problem, and its resolution (if any) is posited as an outcome of that process.

Where has peer mediation been part of the answer?

Inside the Gates: Schools and the Troubles[13] is a report into the ways in which schools support children in relation to the political conflict in Northern Ireland. Specifically, the report focuses on the way in which the political conflict has impacted on the sample schools in four main ways, namely:

- ongoing tension and disturbance
- traumatic community incidents
- specific incidents affecting pupils and their families
- attacks on the school and its personnel.[14]

This study investigated eight schools as examples of good practice and 'identified as providing active support in response to the needs of their pupils', the criteria being:

- a whole-school ethos
- pastoral care support structures
- initiatives associated with EMU, cross-community contact and prejudice-reduction programmes.[15]

Two of these schools had undertaken peer mediation in partnership with the EMU Promoting School Project. A group of peer mediators were interviewed by a researcher without any other adult present, and in the section of the research report entitled 'Pupil responses', she wrote:

> What emerged as impressive was that they could communicate their grasp of the basic values, rules and principles involved in the peer mediation process and how these applied not only to the classroom but also outside in the playground and beyond. There appeared to be genuine interest and enthusiasm for this aspect of schoolwork.[16]

She went on to say that the summary statements by peer mediators quoted in the report itself 'showed little or no evidence of . . . being over-interpreted or presented in a parrot-like fashion, but rather appeared to be the natural and spontaneous words of ten- or eleven-year-old. olds.'[17] The children demonstrated a clear understanding of the mediation process, of the rules that mediators had to keep, and of how difficult that sometimes was. They also valued the trust that the teachers had in them: 'The teachers trust you to go out of the classroom and they trust that you can sort the actual fight out, otherwise you wouldn't have been picked.'[18]

Peer mediation was just one of a range of strategies adopted by these schools, and only forms a small part of the report. However, what is particularly heartening is that *Inside the Gates* identifies the *existing good practice* that Bickmore describes as being more noticeable by its absence in schools generally. It concludes that 'best practice' was exemplified by:

- the positive ethos
- the inspirational role of the principal
- the whole-school involvement
- the team approach
- training opportunities
- the allocation of time

- supporting and challenging through EMU
- sustained and meaningful cross-community contact
- listening to pupil voices
- provision for developmental counselling.[19]

Although this report was focusing on how schools responded to traumatic events, it made this more general point:

'The best practice' identified may be equally applicable and appropriate to schooling in relation to addressing other issues, arising as it does from the best attempts to respond to the social and emotional needs of young people. Indeed the research outcomes highlight the need for schools:

- to pay much more attention to the social and emotional needs of pupils
- to be genuinely concerned with the society in which young people live and with which they wish to be engaged
- to involve young people and children in the development of pastoral and curricular initiatives.[20]

The recommendations fall into four categories:

- school management
- the participation of young people
- the curriculum
- catering for pupils' social and educational needs

and stress the need for a positive, child-centred approach to the school value-base. They underline the importance of the development of children's self-esteem, and the need to consult and involve them in matters affecting them.

The report also recommended that the curriculum should tackle 'issues of contemporary concern' to young people, and that it should 'respond to the expressed desire to address controversial issues related to this society, the recent history of Northern Ireland and events as they happen'.[21] (The young people had implicitly acknowledged how conflict issues of this kind tend to be avoided.)

The recommendations recognised the need for additional training for teachers in facilitating discussion of controversial issues, as well as the need for them 'to be able to recognise behavioural signs associated with emotional distress in order to distinguish between discipline issues and those occasioned by personal and community disruption or instability'[22]. This last point flags up an issue that is central to applying restorative principles. Certain behaviours of individual children are often defined as 'misbehaviour' because they do not fulfil the needs of the teacher, or indeed the rest of the class, in a learning situation, although they may be fulfilling the needs of the child at the time. For example, a child may 'not be paying attention' because she is preoccupied with the fact that her house was raided an hour before she came to school.

This research overtly addressed child-centred issues, so it is no surprise that it has come up with child-centred recommendations.

Where has peer mediation been part of the answer?

Safe schools

In March 2000 a conference was organised in the Netherlands entitled 'Conflict Resolution in Schools'. It was set up to influence a national campaign for the promotion of nonviolent conflict resolution and a culture of peace in Dutch schools – the 'Stop Fighting, Start Talking' campaign. It is interesting to note the echo in this title of David Ervine's contention in Chapter 6 that the first step in conflict resolution in Northern Ireland is conflict management – that is, the violence has to stop. The conference, attended by a small number of experts from 12 countries, heard that:

> In New York City the level of violence in schools led to it being declared a public health emergency in 1993. This led to the Centre for Disease Control giving partial funding to conduct a two-year study evaluating the effectiveness of a 'Resolving Conflict Creatively

Program' in 15 public elementary schools in New York City.[23]

One survey [in South Africa] in 1991 found that 84% of students had had one of their schoolmates killed in the political violence and 87% reported having been directly and personally affected by violence while at school.[24]

In parts of the world such as the USA and South Africa, violence in schools is a major issue, and one that has to be addressed before a learning environment can be established, or indeed before peer mediation can begin to be effective.

Iole Matthews of the Independent Projects Trust, working in KwaZulu Natal in South Africa, introduced a peer mediation programme into several schools. When it was evaluated it was found that, on the one hand, nearly all of the participants in the training programme thought it had been useful, but on the other:

> the programme had had no noticeable affect on the level of violence within the schools. Further research indicated that this was because the violence was largely caused by outside gangs coming into the school premises. The response of the external agency was to do a 'reality check' of the level of violence affecting schools and to talk to anybody who would listen – journalists, politicians, educationalists – to try and raise awareness of the issue. Out of this grew 'guidelines for principals and school governing bodies which provided a useful resource in terms of school security, community ownership, democratic management of schools and training and education'.[25]

Without this support in place, peer mediation was akin to applying a band-aid to a running sore, since peer mediation within a school could have no impact on violence from outside.

Meanwhile in Durban, as outlined in Chapter 1, Valerie

Dovey was coining the phrase 'peaceable schools'. She preferred the word 'peaceable' to 'peaceful' because the latter implied that the process was already complete. Her external agency had to undergo a rethink in 1996: 'Many of the educators we had trained were not committing to implementing processes. We were not seeing the kind of "ripple and rumble" effect we dreamt about. Were we really "equipping and empowering" as we sought to do?'[26] As a result her agency embarked on programmes that applied the following criteria:

- Is the proposed involvement strategic in terms of building capacity, potential influence, geographical area etc.?
- Are clients willing to engage in long-term committed partnerships with the project?
- Is involvement likely to be sustainable, i.e. grounded in a strong, supportive infrastructure, e.g. a whole institution or a cluster of schools?[27]

This need to think strategically was echoed by others present at the conference, as was an understanding about the need for the establishment of safety. As one delegate said, 'The need for quality improvement in schools requires safe learning environments.'[28] Children need to be, and to feel, safe. There was a consensus that safety is a necessary but not sufficient ingredient in creating democratic education.

Does peer mediation reinforce 'negative peacemaking'?
Bickmore maintains that:

As public concern over violence increases, school leaders often respond with what has been called '*negative peacemaking*' – the premature use of bargaining or settlement procedures, before underlying problems have been solved or understood. The goal of negative peacemaking is avoidance, not problem-solving. For example, educators may take short-term safety measures emphasising control, exclusion or segregation of disruptive students, and avoidance of sensitive topics. From these models, students may learn to hide their true feelings, to blame others for problems, and to censor uncomfortable topics or viewpoints.

'Negative peacemaking' has a certain resonance in Northern Ireland. There is evidence that in the early 1970s in inner-city areas of Belfast and Derry, where there would be regular gunfights between the British Army and the IRA, schools were seen as 'oases of peace'. The order of the school day gave a security, a safety, as if little existed outside. This wasn't true just of areas where there was a high level of conflict; in turbulent times many schools, with their timetable and order, created a safe place for young people, psychologically and physically. As mentioned in Chapter 5, the legacy of this is that controversial issues about the current political situation are rarely discussed in staffrooms, let alone in classrooms.

Just as peace is not merely the absence of violence, peacemaking requires the confronting of conflict, and it is here where the biggest challenge lies. Negative peacemaking is about reinforcing control and order, and often schools become concerned about conflict only when it breaks the surface and creates disorder, rather than having built in systems and relationships that create wellbeing and constructive ways of handling conflict. This sense of wellbeing, defined as an environment where you are able to work at your best, is a central part of restorative justice, holding out a positive goal that everybody can identify with and aspire to.

A focus on disorder can lead to a quick-fix approach, one that tries to solve visible problems rather than either deal with underlying issues or attempt to recreate wellbeing. At a school community level, or individual class level, there is huge investment in control. This can lead to an emphasis on young people learning skills so that they can be better behaved. As Bickmore explains:

In common with a negative peacemaking emphasis, many conflict-resolution education materials emphasise teaching students to be polite and non-disruptive, rather than assertive and active in handling conflict. On the other hand, conflict skills can be powerful tools for positive liberty,* with which students become more able to solve their own problems and to express their interests in ways that can be effectively heard.[29]

Chapter 7 argued that the values of peer mediation (inclusiveness, self-determination, and so on) run counter to those of arbitration – a traditional method of school discipline. But there is a degree of coercion in mediation in schools that mirrors the debate about 'med–arb', or mediation–arbitration. Diana and John Lampen bring their considerable experience in Northern Ireland, Britain and elsewhere to bear in their book *'What Ifs?' in Peer Mediation*. They acknowledge the influence of existing discipline policies in their advice to peer mediators: 'So if you do break off a mediation, it's only fair to tell [the parties] if you are going to have to pass the problem on to a teacher to sort out. Sometimes telling them this is enough to get them to solve their problem with you.'[30] It is naïve to expect anything other than coercion ready and waiting in the background. Schools are hierarchical institutions, and 'traditionally emphasise adult control more than development of students' autonomous self-control: discipline is usually managed by adults, in ways that may foster neither learning nor democracy'.[31]

This leads to the question, 'To what degree can a voluntary peer-assisted process for handling conflict flourish within a basically coercive system?'[32]

The experience of the EMUpsp was that a great deal of work had to go in to starting from where the school was at, and this was exacerbated by the fact that teachers would, understandably, see the notion of their being part of a coercive institution as an attack on their professional integrity. In an extensive evaluation of a peer mediation programme in Britain, University of Teesside evaluator Colin Webster points out the difficulties of:

*Bickmore uses the following definition of 'positive liberty' – procedures and encouragement for broad involvement in handling community concerns and conflicts – as a guiding principle of democracy.

implementing controversial programmes within schools that are initiated and 'led' by agencies outside the school system, as well as the contextual pressures on schools that lead to suspicion of 'external research' that scrutinises school life in ways that might be perceived as casting doubt on the integrity and efficiency of teachers and schools in keeping order, were such research to find its way into the public domain.[33]

The answer can lie in encouraging teachers, principals and others to reflect on their practice. Teaching is a vocation, and many people enter it as such, with a sense of vision and a desire to change things for the better. Teachers are sometimes perceived as being cynical and set in their ways, impeding their own progress as well as those who wish to make change. But often, when this resistance is listened to and heard, that cycle of cynicism and obstruction is broken. So the professional development of teachers could mean continually being reinspired by that vision to change and improve practice. Above all, there has to be partnership and recognition that this learning journey requires collaboration between the mediation community and the education community. This may involve a rude awakening – an unexpected lesson learned by one mediation agency responding to the Follow-up Survey (on p. 281) was:

> Teaching culture [is] different to mediation culture. Teachers can undermine mediation principles with their intervention. Teaching staff under pressure do not prioritise planning and evaluation. Not always open to feedback. Not enough thought given to putting learning into practice.

Another respondent wrote, 'Children are often better than adults at picking up mediation skills after training.'

Democratic education
In an article based on an evaluation of a peer mediation project in six elementary schools in Cleveland, Ohio, Bickmore argues that democratic education should be made up of three interconnected elements, each of which is neces-

sary, and none of which is sufficient alone. They are

- modelling nonviolent community
- critical reflection and analysis
- students sharing authority.

The aim of her study was to explore the elements necessary to support 'sustainable change towards nonviolent and democratic school climates'. Her findings make fascinating reading. The same programme was instigated in several different ways. The variety of approaches to the selection of mediators included the example of a school where children were chosen from a gender and ethnic group that would seldom 'get into trouble', thus reinforcing existing gulfs between able and less able students. 'Planned citizenship education programs, including peer mediation, sit somewhat uneasily with the hidden curriculum of prevailing interaction patterns in schools,'[34] she concluded.

In the survey of peer mediation agencies carried out for this book the final question related to democracy in schools:

Should peer mediation play a role in making schools more democratic, and if so, how?
Of the 11 respondents working in primary schools, three left the space blank and the others replied. Here are their answers:

- It should, but for many schools it appears to be a frightening prospect to relinquish responsibility to young students for behaviour and approach. Drip-feeding the training in schools, and ensuring that mediation is on teacher training agendas, will help to support the development of greater democracy.
- Peer mediation encourages individual co-operation and responsibility – so it surely has a role in developing the interpersonal skills which underpin civil society.
- Yes, yes, yes. By consulting children more and giving them more responsibility, by encouraging them to take more responsibility. By the introduction of things like school councils, Circle of Friends, Circle Time, initiatives

where children have a voice, a role and a responsibility.
- We encourage schools to incorporate mediation, peaceful conflict resolution, into the core PSHE curriculum – several schools now do this.
- Yes, definitely. There could be peer mediators who also work with staff mediators to resolve disputes between pupils and staff members. Perhaps they could even work with governor mediators in school–parent disputes?
- Not sure about 'should'. The end result of peer mediation programmes might result in more equality and a more democratic process. Children are more likely to given a voice, be heard and respected. More empowered ownership of decisions made, etc.
- It is one example of how children can take effective responsibility for some part of school life. Teachers have to learn to let go some of the control if the scheme is to work properly, so that might lead them to give children more participation in other things.
- Yes, input into rules of school using process of pupil-centred rule construction.

These aspirations of agencies promoting peer mediation in the UK have a certain resonance with the *Education for Citizenship and the Teaching of Democracy in Schools*[35] report of 1998 for England and Wales, which recommended:

Citizenship education in schools and colleges is to include the knowledge, skills and values relevant to the nature and practices of participative democracy; the duties, responsibilities, rights and development of pupils into citizens; and the value to individuals, schools and society of involvement in the local and wider community.

and:

Experiential learning, discussion of social and political issues as well as formal, taught learning should be part of this process, both within and outside the school as appropriate.

But there still seemed to be an underlying wish for children to conform rather than question: 'children learning from the very beginning self-confidence and socially and morally responsible behaviour both in and beyond the classroom, both towards those in authority and towards each other.'

This is just one of three factors that the report is advocating as part of 'active citizenship'. The others are 'service learning', or involvement in the community, and 'political literacy', learning how to be effective in public life. The recommendations continue: 'Experiential learning, discussion of social and political issues as well as formal, taught learning should be part of this process, both within and outside the school as appropriate.'

11. The Future of Peer Mediation

In June 1998, at the Annual Conference of Mediation UK, a panel of nine people involved in developing peer mediation in different parts of the UK (see Appendix 4), discussed 'The future of peer mediation'. Some of the issues raised, for example the need for a whole-school approach, have already been stressed. Others are highlighted in this chapter. Two years later the panel was surveyed to discover any further issues they had identified as key to future developments in peer mediation.

I also draw here on the experience of researchers in the USA, Australia and elsewhere, emphasising themes that recur throughout the literature and practice of peer mediation, and identifying areas of research yet to explored.

I conclude with a call to develop a new paradigm for intervention in schools, and stress the need to think strategically. Conflict resolution and peer mediation training have yet to realise their full potential in helping schools to adapt to the needs of education and society in the twenty-first century. The focus for the future of peer mediation will be on managing that change, and encouraging and supporting teachers as agents of change.

During the late 1980s and early 1990s the number of agencies in the UK that offered peer mediation grew exponentially. The annual conference of Mediation UK became a focal point for these agencies to share experiences and lead workshops, in themselves excellent vehicles for trying out practical demonstrations of different approaches to conflict resolution with sympathetic participants. The conference also provided opportunities for interest groups to meet, as well as the chance for individuals to meet informally.

This led in 1997 to the formation of the Education and Youth Sub-Committee (EYSC), whose main aim was to 'initiate, support and promote the development of conflict resolution and mediation among young people and those who relate or work with them.'[1] Following on from this, the EMU Promoting School Project proposed a panel discussion to look at the 'future of peer mediation' as a part of the programme of the Mediation UK 1998 conference. Seamus Farrell (then research coordinator for the EMU Promoting School Project) organised and chaired the discussion. The transcript has been published as 'The Future of Peer Mediation'.[2]

The discussion ranged from getting feedback from schools, to what a whole-school approach means in practice. A purpose in the exercise was to identify some pointers to the future.

Key issues

The following issues arose from the panel's discussion:

Whole-school approach

There was an awareness amongst the panel that, without a whole-school approach, peer mediation had a limited lifespan. What this means in practice is 'listening' to the whole school. Time spent in research, and 'taking the temperature of conflict in the school' is time well spent, as is negotiating with the school. There is need to recognise that this 'pre-engagement' may lead to no engagement, as it 'involves finding out if the school really does want the programme, and whether you can work together, because you can often find that what the school wants is different to what you can offer'. This shouldn't be seen as failure; rather it pre-empts the same discovery much later, after time and money have been invested.

Richard Cohen,[3] from his extensive experience in the USA, maintains that it takes at least two years for a programme to become self-sufficient: this amount of time and effort demands clarity of purpose, aims and objectives from the start.

Successful engagement with a school depends on a partnership, involving a number of different relationships, which take time to establish. The staff must know the nature of the process, so that they are not put off by its natural cycle.

> part of my role in managing programmes has been to signal where we are at in the process when working in a school, and to acknowledge that there are certain crisis points which we will always come up against. There is always going to be a point where people may get alarmed – about young people becoming a lot more assertive. As a person from outside the organisation, the more I can reassure people about the process that is happening, the better. It is the process of change and transformation, of course; that's what working in an institution is really about. But if you yourself are prepared for the process, can understand it and share it appropriately, then I think that helps.

There is a growing recognition within the field that peer mediation may not be the starting-point for a whole-school approach. Peer mediation 'along with reducing bullying and developing positive discipline' can be seen as part of 'issues of positive relationships in schools' strategies'. You need not necessarily go into a school with a peer mediation agenda but rather 'into whole-school transformation rather than peer mediation as such' using Cohen's model to illustrate the levels of conflict resolution (see Chapter 10):

> Using this as a model, I go in to talk to staff and get them to explore where their school (and where their classroom) is at in terms of that model. From that grows a staff awareness of where they need to work, and it may well be that they actually don't reach the peer mediation at all. What they choose rather to do is work on building up a positive ethos and their one-to-one negotiating skills.

Relationships with teachers

Work with adults first, one reason being 'the need for SMTs (senior management teams) to be positive role models for behaviour in a school'. The work of teachers, and schools, must always be valued.

> We have all come across teachers who are incredibly passionate and inspired. We have a very important role in making contact with them, and valuing who they are and what they are doing. Even if we only do a tiny little thing, through our human contact we are helping an incredibly stressed group of people just to keep going. If teachers were professionals in industry they would be much more highly acknowledged and materially rewarded.

While recognising the skills that external agencies bring into schools, it is important to recognise the skills that teachers have:

> As an organisation we understand conflict resolution very well, but the school understands teaching very well and that's what it's there to do. What characterises our relationship with the school is that we have both grown and developed together over the three years.

Not only is it important for external agencies to value the work of teachers and schools, but it is important to encourage teachers to value themselves and each other. Good practice can go unrecognised in a classroom:

> I am lucky in that I move between classes and so I can pick up the skills of various teachers. For a school to be really positive in its approach it just needs to let these new skills come in and be developed. And then for the word to get back to the teacher training establishments, through the supervision of the newly qualified teachers.

Initial teacher training

The future of peer mediation depends on a co-ordinated, strategic approach in initial teacher training.

It is perhaps a challenge to us not to be 'picking off' schools one by one but making sure that every new teacher who goes into any school has training that will enable them to run peer mediation schemes, to teach conflict resolution skills and self esteem, and to build what is part of *our* culture into being part of the culture of the education system.

Pooling energies is important:

> If some of us can get together (and some of us are lucky enough to get 'halfway in the door') I think that's where our efforts need to be directed now. With some courses that we are running in Reading University, people are saying: 'we have had nothing like this before'. The courses turn out to be a forum where they can explore their hopes, their fears, their dreams, and their needs.

However, the reality of the time constraints on trainee teachers in the UK, particularly postgraduate trainees, is such that most of their time is spent in schools. All the same there are growing opportunities for training newly qualified teachers (NQTs). But getting involved in teacher training is an uphill struggle:

> In initial teacher training a lot of the values on which peer mediation training is based are not in place, and the situation is actually getting worse as teachers are concentrating more and more on, 'How do you teach maths?' 'How do you teach English?' 'How do you teach a particular curriculum area?' We are working with a profession that is incredibly stressed and with teachers who don't often reflect on teaching and learning styles. They don't necessarily have the training in how to facilitate group work, how to develop co-operation skills, how to teach young people to listen. These all-encompassing skills don't generally tend to be taught. Certainly the pressure from government and so on is in teaching specific subjects and for education to become more and more compartmentalised.

Nevertheless agencies such as Mediation UK are 'lobbying the government to pay attention to relationships and to promoting co-operation and conflict resolution in the curriculum. We intend contacting Teacher Training agencies to discuss inputs into teacher training'.

Rooting peer mediation in educational reality

Peer mediation must be grounded in educational reality if it is to be relevant to schools, let alone sustainable:

> We have to start looking at things like the stated aims and objectives of the school and not lose sight of the fact that, under government regulations, these are public documents. Do these documents actually have anything to say which might lead you in the direction of mediation and conflict-resolution work? Do they have things to say about young people and students taking responsibility, and does the school actually set up the sort of structure that enables young people to play a full part in that way? We have then to have regard to what is actually happening in the curriculum, and where a programme can actually fit in . . .

These tentative steps towards ensuring that peer mediation is tied into government policy and is made relevant to the curriculum, indicate the work that needs still to be done. Agencies shouldn't work in schools in a piecemeal fashion, but think strategically and make best use of modern communications facilities. The fact that, for example in the UK, all school inspections reports of OFSTED (The Office for Standards in Education) can be downloaded, means that external agencies can easily access information. Consultative documents produced by Government departments and other agencies can also be downloaded and hard copies can be requested through the post. The future of peer mediation depends on it being mainstreamed, and if that is to happen and if the overwhelming relevance of peer mediation and conflict resolution to the life of a school is to be broadcast, both the overt and hidden curriculum dimensions of schools must be researched and made available.

School policies on discipline, pastoral care and so on are also key areas to address. Sometimes schools want to do work on peer mediation, 'to help them create the paperwork – the written policy – without a participative process involving as wide a spectrum as possible'. However it is also possible to work with a school authentically so that its 'overall behaviour policy can focus on building relationships of mutual respect and trust'.

Ownership and sustainability

> If you can transform the staff, then whether a peer mediation scheme will last, once you've moved out, is not a question, because they have embraced it; but I think if you leave a school *dependent* on outside support, then the job hasn't even begun.

In an extensive review of peer mediation, Hall refers to 'the influence of mediation agencies on the development of peer mediation programmes',[4] going on to point out the danger that:

> agencies overzealous in promoting a particular approach which might or might not be appropriate, . . . and some authors . . . allude to tensions between external agencies and schools, especially where the participants are volunteers, and they offer the prudent advice that external support roles be clearly defined in the planning stages.[5]

It is certainly the experience of the EMU Promoting School Project that the *promotion* of a particular approach such as peer mediation as *the* answer is counterproductive. As long as external agencies *listen* to members of the school community, and start with *their* agenda, the danger of being overzealous can be avoided:

> This work is not being *imposed* on schools; what we are actually doing is *offering* something that schools *might* want to take up if they see that it has a positive

benefit for themselves . . . there has to be ownership by the school. We have got a product; we believe that it is good and that it works but we are not compelling anybody to take it. We are saying 'take a look at it, and if you think it fits let's have a go' . . . what helps is when you get teachers who begin to realise that it actually works. That begins to generate its own enthusiasm and success.

I can remember an experience I had while doing some work with lunchtime supervisors. They themselves came to realise that in fact if mediation was to work, the whole school was going to have to adopt circle time. They insisted that I come with them to meet with the Head to insist that this happen. One supervisor started talking: 'Everyone has got to take this on board – every single adult in this school – and if one person opts out it's going to let the whole side down'. She had come to that realisation, from identifying for herself what the question was.

Finding-the-right-questions is the basis of action-research as described in an earlier chapter. The process of introducing peer mediation has, paradoxically, to allow for the option of peer mediation not being appropriate; this led to the chairperson commenting:

In terms of agencies that are considering a new engagement in this kind of work, what you are saying is 'Don't set yourselves, as the measure of your success, the establishment of a peer mediation service'. You could be setting yourselves up for disappointment and for not being able to recognise perhaps that it is the school, and how the school is, that matters, and the need to take the school at 'where it is at'.

Clear links emerged between the criteria for selection of schools, school ownership of the programme to be undertaken, dependence on external agencies, and the sustainability of peer mediation. One of the key questions (that the panel addressed) was: What type of school or educational institution would you *not* work in, and why?

One person changed the question, to schools she was 'wary of working in', then said:

> In the schools work that we have done there have been a lot of difficulties and divisions between different communities. Those difficulties are often played out in the way that the staff in the schools operate . . . Schools we are wary of working in are those where there is a significant lack of cohesion in the senior management team in terms of their approach to dealing with the difficulties that are going on in the school. Because our programmes require a big commitment from the school in terms of staff cover and time off, we are also wary about being brought in by someone who doesn't have a direct relationship with the SMT specifically in gaining access to funds and resources, or being able to negotiate staff cover and timetabling. In those situations we are more cautious about agreeing to go in and work in a school.

In the survey of agencies using peer mediation in schools (see Appendix 2), of the twelve respondents only four referred to a formal selection process in deciding which schools to work with. One of these said:

> The schools were selected by LEA (funders) on a range of criteria e.g. location, appropriateness of school, (as regards stability of staff), whether likely to sustain the programme, appropriate background and philosophy.

Another mentioned schools 'initially being referred to us by the LEA', but which subsequently approached the agency directly. Two agencies were independently applying criteria, one explaining that: 'All schools are invited to an INSET, invited to apply and selected on the basis of a whole-school commitment to the project, based partially on peer mediation readiness survey.' The other described a bidding process, where 'levels-of-readiness criteria' were applied. Apart from this, selection was on the basis of personal contact (through teachers or parents who are mediators, for example), or self-selection by schools who initiate contact in response to publicity. One agency, itself a secondary school, initiated a programme for local primary schools.

Empowerment, change and transformation
One panellist said that her research, along with that of the EMUpsp, indicated that peer mediation *didn't* transform schools:

> In my experience, occasionally teachers have found engagement with peer mediation a transformational process which completely changed their outlook and their way of teaching. But I would think that that is quite rare and I wouldn't want anyone to have the expectation that they can go into a school and transform the way that teachers work; I hope I'm not being too pessimistic! Certainly I would hope that what we *can* do is to offer teachers tools for effective teaching and thus effect change in practice.

The link between ethos and culture and the success of peer mediation programmes is made in the following observation:

> Whether peer mediation will succeed or not has very much to do with ethos and culture within a school. Mediation is a humanistic process that values individuals coming up with their own solutions to their own problems. In schools where the belief is that teachers have all the right answers and that education is about filling empty vessels – and where there are authoritarian or punitive systems – then it's clear that peer mediation isn't going to work. In my experience the only school where it did effect any kind of positive change, was one which already had such a positive ethos. Peer mediation helped that process; it was a very useful 'tool' in helping the school getting to where it already wanted to go. In other schools it perhaps helped raise awareness and

took them a little way on the journey, but it wasn't successful according to the criteria that I set at the beginning of the research.

The young people at a school which does have a positive environment are the lucky ones, and (the) schools that have a more strict disciplinarian approach are the ones which are a priority for me. It wouldn't necessarily be peer mediation, though; I might do drama work, for example.

Cameron and Dupuis[6] wrote a report on the first school mediation service in New Zealand, and it was on their findings that Robin Hall drew in her comprehensive review of peer mediation. Specifically they found that, when it was introduced in New Zealand, it had to be adapted to the culture of the school:

The different ways in which schools manage student behaviour will affect the kind of peer mediation that evolves. For example, a school with an authoritarian control structure is likely to produce a program in which mediation is *done by teachers for students*. A more patronising regime is likely to generate a service which is part of a counsellor's brief and is *provided by teachers for students*. In a more democratic school, mediation is likely to develop as a service *provided by teachers and students themselves*.[7]

Monitoring and evaluation

When asked how they met their need for feedback from schools, from both adults and children, and used it to improve practice, there was a variety of responses. One dealt with an individual workshop:

When I finish off an afternoon session, say with a primary class, the teacher, or teachers, actually stay behind with us at the end of the sessions. We go through every item that we have undertaken in the afternoon, analysing what's gone on, the responses of the children, and then discuss with the teachers the most appropriate next step. So we are not working to a fixed programme; we are working to an outline which we are continually changing as we are going along. We are using that immediate feedback and our own responses as to what has been happening in the classroom, to change and develop the work as we go along.

This is very much at the micro level, but the same panellist talked of his plans to introduce a precourse questionnaire for the children to fill in

> about conflict resolution and what's happening in the school, and their perceptions of things, and then to give them the *same* questionnaires *post*-course to see whether or not there have been any significant changes. Then there's the formal written evaluation which I am asked to carry out for my project. I know that some members of the project put in written evaluations as recording what is actually happening during a workshop and their response to it. Anecdotal feedback is very very powerful and I'm sure we have all had this. From one of the schools I'm hearing from the teachers that reading skills and general literacy skills were improving in the class as the work went on, and we put that down to the work that we were doing on communication skills. Another teacher reported improvement in mathematics, which we found difficult to claim as our own because that wasn't the focus of our work! But we put that down to perhaps the growth in self-esteem and that sort of thing. There is a lot of feedback from this work that we can use to inform and develop it.

Most panellists had some sort of system for feedback, including:

> informal evaluation at the end of each session with the children and a sort of debriefing session with the teachers at the end of each session; and at the end of the final session we also ask the children to answer three

questions: What have they enjoyed? What have they learned? and What could have been better? We have had some really good feedback from that.

One telling comment was made about the danger of people saying what they perceived as expected of them:

> When I first started in mediation I was doing the anecdotal research and I was asking teachers what they thought about how successful the programme had been, and asking the pupils what they had enjoyed and what they hadn't enjoyed. We always got very positive feedback and people said: 'I learned not to fight' and so on. After a while I began to get a bit disconcerted! I began to suspect that the 'halo effect' was operating; so much time and energy had been put into the training; they liked my coming in to work in the school every Monday afternoon. I began to be afraid that they were saying things they thought I wanted to hear.

As a result this panellist wanted to find:

> some kind of objective measures, to find out what was actually happening, to be able to measure change and quantify it. And so what I did was to ask pupils about their experiences in the previous six weeks; how often had somebody called them a name, how often had they been hit, and how often had they been excluded from games? I then repeated that three times in the middle of the programme and then again at the end of the programme so I could measure change; and I tracked individual pupils to see whether particular types of experiences had gone up or gone down; I did it with all children who were experiencing aggression and also children who were perpetrating aggression.

This led to an unexpected outcome:

> I found, interestingly, *after* the peer Mediation Training, which was Circle Time work, and a lot of the other

work that we all do in schools – developing basic skills etc. – that bullying *increased*! I also measured self-esteem, and I noticed that *after* the training it plummeted! That was surprising, given that we had spent a lot of time with the children talking about what they were good at, what they were proud of and so on. While the peer mediation training was operative it had the effect of drastically reducing bullying, and self-esteem went right up.

Subsequent research led to a possible explanation:

Pupils were reporting bullying more because the programme raised their awareness of the issue. Also, instead of just thinking 'I'm good at this', 'I'm good at that', it was encouraging them to be more realistic in their self-assessment. So they were generally reflecting on themselves. That initial dip wasn't an unhealthy thing, actually; it was about them becoming much more self-aware.

A by-product of the programme therefore, was that the children were becoming self-reflective. In conclusion this panellist pointed out the need for objectivity, and to acknowledge differences in perceptions:

So I really would encourage objective methods of measurement as much as possible because it points out so many subtle changes that might be happening. Incidentally, the teachers didn't notice the increase in bullying and at the time when self-esteem plummeted they said self-esteem had risen; so what *teachers* say about the changes they see aren't necessarily what *children* are saying.

This last comment led to someone asking 'Whose agenda does evaluation address?'

I'm just aware of how difficult I find evaluating practice without looking for things that *I* want to find (out);

evaluation forms are really *my* agenda; it's what *I* want to happen and I know that can sometimes drive the responses I get, because teachers like to see you nodding and smiling and saying 'Great' and all that kind of stuff. My questions now are trying to avoid any preconceptions about what I want to find, rather to find out *what has changed*? That approach generates all sorts of things you weren't expecting and helps the school to reflect on unexpected changes.

These frank and open responses to questions about evaluation reinforce the relevance of action-research to peer mediation. External agencies are not detached from the process; they are part of it; equally it isn't just their agenda, but rather it is the school's, especially if the whole point of the exercise is for schools to take ownership of the process. The questions identified in Chapter 9 are particularly pertinent to the responses of the panellists:

What is my concern? How am I concerned? How can I show that in action? What do I think I can do about it? What will I do about it? How can I gather evidence to show that I am influencing the situation? How can I ensure that any judgements I make are reasonably fair and accurate? What will I do then[8]?

A lot of data is produced by peer mediation programmes, but often it is neither structured nor analysed; and rarely is a control group established to verify that any changes have come about because of peer mediation.

Most of those who took part in the discussion recorded in this chapter are from agencies that have performed pioneering roles in developing peer mediation in the UK. They often had to learn from trial and error, and from the mistakes they have made. The effective future of peer mediation depends on new agencies and initiatives learning from these mistakes and successes, so that only new mistakes are made, and collective experience can grow by leaps and bounds.

Follow-up survey

In August 2000 the members of the discussion panel were surveyed by means of a questionnaire. This explored issues raised at the meeting in 1998, such as the need for external agencies to 'listen' to schools, and to become more strategically involved in the training of teachers. The survey also endeavoured to gauge the panelists' perception of the teacher as 'reflective practitioner', and their experience of peer mediation in the subsequent two years.

Question 1
What benefits have arisen from the mushrooming of community mediation programmes that have sought to be become involved in peer mediation?

Chris Stockwell, from Bristol Mediation, and Ruth Musgrave from Newham Conflict and Change, both represented community mediation services with long track records of schools' work. Both had catalogued the benefits of their involvement. Ruth Musgrave divided hers into an 'at least' list, which cited the enhancement of the confidence and skills of peer mediators, and an 'at best' list, which recorded creative ways in which schools and developed peer mediation.

John Conchie wrote that the Midlands Mediation Network, which is largely made up of community mediation services, has had a whole day meeting devoted to peer mediation. 'From this it was clear that community mediation services thought it important to develop schools work'. He added that, with some notable exceptions, not many of them have a lot of knowledge or experience of schools' work, but they were keen to learn.

According to Hall, research in the USA has identified key differences between school-based mediation and community mediation, which, arguably, would include any closed community such as the workplace. These differences include:

> limits placed on type of conflict that can be mediated by students ... attention given to educative nature of involvement ... referral process ... less confidentiality

... extra burden on being impartial ... hidden curriculum places great emphasis on distinguishing 'right, acceptable' behaviour from 'wrong, unacceptable behaviour'.[9]

Colin Webster, in his evaluation of a peer mediation scheme in an English context, refers to an inevitable, though not insurmountable, difficulty.

It became apparent that the 'ethos' and professional 'culture' of schools and those of mediation projects ... are potentially in conflict. Teachers are *in loco parentis* and as such, a defining feature of their work is the control, discipline and management of children's learning and behaviour. Arguably their relationship to pupils ... cannot be that of 'mediators', i.e. 'third-party' 'brokers' of children's relationships to other children.[10]

Arguing that the teacher's power necessarily denies the pupil's autonomy; Webster maintains that the teacher's responsibilities and duties are 'in sharp contrast to the "style" and concerns of mediation'.

As Chapter 9 illustrates, community mediation services are addressing these differences, and have a professional approach that is both supportive of teachers and challenging them to think in new ways. Belinda Hopkins, in her response to the follow-up survey, wrote that community mediation services, 'can make a huge contribution and be the "leaven in the dough" which keeps alive the issues and skills highlighted in the mediation training and process'. Hilary Cremin observed: 'Where they have worked well, they have made an enormous impact on the lives of both the mediators and the mediated'.

Question 2
What are the most frequently encountered difficulties?

In her response to the follow-up survey, Jo Broadwood was specific about the need for what she calls 'a conflict audit', 'involving one or two days of interviews with a range of interest groups within the school, asking questions about conflict'.

Hilary Cremin summed up the situation in schools thus: 'Schools are political institutions just like anywhere else'. As mentioned elsewhere, difficulties of time, remuneration and resources are obstacles. There were difficulties at the human level too:

> Staff who feel threatened by the notion of pupil empowerment. (I have been told by a fundamentalist Christian teacher that I am doing the devil's work).
> Staff who do not have the self-esteem or personal and social skills themselves to interact in a positive way with an empowered group of pupils.
> Staff who feel that they are there to teach subjects rather than children.

Jo Broadwood, although reflecting on secondary school experience made this compelling point which is also relevant to primary schools; as well as listening, agencies need to make sure they are being heard:

> Often when schools are desperate for change they see us as having quick-fix magic solutions. We need to think about the kind of 'hearing' we create in a school. If a school is desperate for remedies it can't always hear what is possible with the time and resources available. Part of our role is to educate schools about conflict and processes for change and how change happens. In order to do that well we need to ensure that the school is in a position to be able to listen to us.

Question 3
Is peer mediation an appropriate starting-point for a whole-school approach?

There were differences of opinion about this. Jo Bird said it *was* an appropriate starting-point – as long as the ethos was right and the staff and pupils were ready, although she felt that an anti-bullying programme was a more suitable starting-point. Rachel Baily responded that her agency 'only offers peer mediation as a starting-point when schools have attended an after-school session to find out about what is involved'.

Other respondents were more forthright about the starting conditions needed. Hilary Cremin said that her organisation will only work with schools that have done the groundwork. Jessica Johnston wrote that Kingston Friends were clear about not starting with peer mediation, but with 'a range of workshops identifying needs and specific strategies for individual schools to develop a whole-school approach which may include peer mediation'. John Conchie stated that it is essential to train the whole year in the skills of conflict resolution. Only then should the specific training for those who wish to go on to be mediators be carried out. Ruth Musgrave put it succinctly: 'We don't *start* with peer mediation, we usually *end* with it'! She added that work starts first with staff. Christine Stockwell said that this was a subject of debate within her agency, reinforcing the general concern of all the respondents about the need for preparatory work and the importance of identifying needs and of supporting a whole-school approach. Hopkins, having acknowledged that she didn't think peer mediation was a starting-point, wrote that she used conflict identification models to invite schools to distinguish where they wanted to start. 'I now offer a whole-school "Restorative Justice" approach, which might include peer mediation somewhere down the line.'

Hilary Cremin said that necessary groundwork involves:

- whole-staff training before the peer mediators are trained
- training being firmly embedded in the National Curriculum and the current concerns of teachers and, ideally
- there should be training for lunchtime supervisors and parents.

She added that:

> peer mediation schemes have a limited value if the trainers and consultants involved at this level do not have a background in education. Individual pupils may benefit enormously, but if the prevailing school culture

is punitive, coercive or one of pupils being 'done unto', then nothing will ultimately change.

Question 4

What about initial teacher training in relation to peer mediation training?

Although this had been pinpointed in 1998 as a key issue, the follow-up survey illustrated that it had proved difficult for agencies to engage with providers of initial teacher training. Bristol Mediation had begun negotiations with the University of West England, but these had petered out. Stockwell alluded to instances where individual trainee teachers had seen peer mediation in action while on placement.

John Conchie said that no work was being done with teachers outside schools by the agency he was involved in. Funding was an issue for Kingston Friends: 'Training opportunities have virtually ceased due to funding difficulties and the need to focus in-service training (INSET) on numeracy and literacy'. Jo Broadwood explained that conflict resolution couldn't be taught like maths, but what her agency was skilled in was facilitation skills. This raised another issue, the degree to which initial teacher training should prepare teachers for experiential work.

Everyone was trying to ensure that good use was made of INSETS and, in common with other agencies, Rachel Baily made this point:

> We always train two or three teachers alongside pupils, the idea being that the teachers can then learn new skills and transfer ideas. In the case of peer mediation they then co-ordinate the service and are responsible for cascading the training to other classes and year groups ... We usually work with whichever teachers the school gives us. But it is better if the teachers themselves get on, if they are to co-ordinate the service effectively. When teachers do get on and have an interest, the service has gone from strength to strength and they have supported each other well.

Ruth Musgrave and Jo Broadwood stressed the variety of
methods they use in their respective programmes of training
for teachers. Hilary Cremin explained that the structure of
employment at initial teaching institutions made it unattractive
for potential employees. There were virtually no new full-time
posts, and people were generally employed on a sessional,
part-time basis – sometimes just a few hours on a given day.

Question 5
To what degree are teachers encouraged to reflect on their
practice?
The question was elaborated in two parts:

(a) How accurately does the following series of questions
    describe the process of your working with schools?
    *What is my concern? How am I concerned? How can I
    show that in action? What do I think I can do about it?
    What will I do about it? How can I gather evidence to
    show that I am influencing the situation? How can I
    ensure that any judgments I make are reasonably fair
    and accurate?*

    John Conchie said, bluntly, 'They don't' (describe the
process) but went no to say that the focus tends to be on
how the children reacted to the individual workshop or
programme.
    Jo Broadwood mentioned other questions to try and tease
out what the school wanted and what the agency was able
to offer, with an emphasis on having an impact on identified
problems. She was up-front about the fact that her agency,
being an action-research project, was also interested in these
questions.

- How will working in this school add to and develop
  our learning about conflict resolution work in schools?
- Will working with this school benefit other areas of our
  work?

'If the answer to these questions is "No", then we may
refer the school on to other agencies'. This may appear

somewhat self-serving, but action-research projects aren't training providers *per se*: their strength is in building up a resource of approaches and learning, and in assisting schools to identify their own needs and to develop their own approaches. Rachel Baily explained that her research methods included asking teachers to assess the effectiveness of their current strategies.

(b) To what extent do you think it is appropriate to encourage teachers to ask themselves such question in response to conflict?

The consensus was that it WAS appropriate.

Comments included:

> Encouraging teachers to question their response to conflict is crucial in developing a whole-school approach to conflict management. Needs can be identified, as well as the range of skills available and opportunities for development.
> Yes, teachers should ask themselves these questions. It helps with strategies for changes in thinking and behaviour patterns.
> It is vital for teachers to reflect on the way they handle conflict. The activity of teaching demands that the teachers is reflective is he or she is to be successful.

Jo Broadwood struck a cautionary note:

> A teacher's ability to reflect openly on the questions you pose will depend on workload, stress levels, context, other priorities, self-confidence etc. When and how the questions are asked is as important as the questions themselves.

Chris Stockwell also stressed the constraints: 'It is essential that teachers engage in constructive self-examination of their dealings with conflict, but time and ethos are often an issue, as well as inclination.'

Jo Bird, acknowledging that the questions were 'quite appropriate, as everyone's behaviour has an impact on a conflict situation', thought they weren't the only questions that teachers needed to ask themselves, as they also needed to be able to differentiate between short-term and long-term solutions.

Question 6

What are the key lessons from your experience in the field of peer mediation and conflict resolution work in primary schools, and what would you do, or avoid doing, if you were starting from scratch?

Several overlapping suggestions were made, reaffirming points already championed by the panel. The following points addressed additional areas of learning:

- Be up-front with the school about the costs involved.
- Be clear about what the school gets for its money, (outcomes in terms of a calmer environment and so on.
- Offer a wider training than just peer mediation.
- Establish clearer links between the proposed programme and the school's plans and policies.
- Do not rely on one individual in a school as, in the long-term, a solid team of committed individuals is more sustainable than a single person, who may fall ill, move away or even reach burn-out stage.
- Work with a whole cluster of primary schools and their secondary schools to ensure that the skills of the mediators are used and reinforced in the secondary school.
- Avoid one-off events, which don't give us the chance to get to know a situation or give the school any chance to get to know us.
- Open communication with due respect for *all* stakeholders.

In Chapter 3, it was indicated that it is common practice in primary schools for all the children in a class to undertake training. This question caused Christine Stockwell to reflect:

Occasionally I have thought that not all children should do the mediator part of the training, but mostly I think they all benefit. My criterion for proceeding with only some children would be the extent to which the training is disrupted by the disaffected few to the detriment of the others.

Jessica Johnston expressed the need to 'use the skills and strategies in ways that fit individual schools'. She also came up with the reasonable, albeit radical, suggestion that since children and staff were learning mediation skills then there could be: 'opportunities for staff and children to mediate for each other as and when situations arise'. John Conchie reinforced the importance of commitment from the Principal, a common theme in this book. However, he went further by advocating the setting up of 'a contract with the school which includes a commitment from the school, and the agency, that the work will be supported over a period of time, that is, two or three years'.

If you were starting again, what would you do differently?
In the survey of agencies more recently established than those represented by the panel there was a convergence of opinion here with the panel. Two had too short an experience to comment, three made no comment, and the responses of the other seven fall into the following categories:

Sustainability

- Nail the head teacher and peer mediation co-ordinator to the floor to prevent them from leaving the school!
- Never work in school with children unless the staff are also on board. If you can't win over the skeptics, don't do the work. Ensure that staff expectations can be met.
- Budget for a greater level of support to help the scheme get off the ground.

Communication with the school

- Ensure agreement on what constitutes success

- Draw up a contract that both parties sign. Be more specific in communications with the school
- Establish, before the children are trained, how the programme will be put into practice.

Selection of peer mediators
Work out ways of making the selection of peer mediators less exclusive; maybe also train peer mentors at the same time.

Preparation
Take it more slowly; be more thorough; focus more; make use of everything learned so far.

The EMU Promoting School Project has long been of the opinion that teachers deserve recognition and, in fact, accreditation, for the skills that they develop in peer mediation training. With the increasing prevalence of a portfolio, or classroom-based, approach to postgraduate education in the UK, a peer mediation module might well be designed. It appears that no individual has yet had the time or the resources to pursue this systematically.

Schools should identify why they want peer mediation. Many see it as the answer to calmer playtimes where children's times are less structured. Fewer see it in the wider context of what it means for the whole school, including how the adults handle conflict, although some see a need for similar training for midday supervisors – rarely for teachers! Some schools work very hard to cascade the skills amongst staff and pupils, adapting peer mediation as appropriate, but most plead lack of time etc. I think that it could raise lots of issues, but there is rarely time for staff to sit back and look at the issues and how peer mediation will affect ethos and practice.

The lack of hard data about the benefits makes it difficult to sell peer mediation as something that should give overall benefit and be worth the investment. It often feels as if teachers see it as a gesture towards good practice (when there are difficulties to do with OFSTED inspections or poor reports or problems with a particular year-group). There often seems to be insufficient commitment, in terms of a whole-school approach, to support the programme properly after the trainers have gone.

Chapter 8 advocates the establishment of an exit strategy, agreed by the school and the external agency at the outset, in order to provide effective support without creating dependency. If peer mediation is to survive, the right balance between support and dependency has to be maintained. This involves the external agency being able to 'let go', just as much as it requires schools to take risks and grasp ownership of the programme. There have been occasions when peer mediation programmes have become such an integral part of a school's ethos and it has taken such total responsibility for it that when visitors come, the school has behaved as if the programme was theirs all along. As a result members of the external agency have felt aggrieved at not getting credit where they felt credit was due. While this is understandable, it is important to recognise it as a sign of good leadership when those who are being led feel as if they have done it all by themselves.

The last word

In the survey of peer mediation agencies (see Appendix 2), they were asked what was the key message that they would like to get across to the reader of this book. Their individual responses can be summarised as follows:

- Children understand conflicts and can resolve them creatively and they are capable of so much more if we give them the opportunity.
- Peer mediation needs a big commitment, and needs whole-school support. It requires time and a non-stop effort to keep the scheme going, but it is a good investment.
- Peer mediation skills are for life, and offer children positive responses to conflict.
- The skills and knowledge should be for *all*, not just for a small group of children in a school. We need to think about how to deal with the issue of pupils feeling left

out if not selected as peer mediators. Every child needs to know what to expect, whether he or she is a mediator or not.

- Peer mediation works better as part of a programme of developing good relationships and dealing with conflict. It goes together with anti-bullying policies
- Mediation is a wonderful concept; it's simple, it works, and it makes for a better ethos not only in the school, but in the community as a whole.

References

Introduction

[1]McWilliams, M. Letter to Jerry Tyrrell, Nov. 1998.
[2]ROBINSON, M. (26 Sept 1996) RTE TV News.
[3]FARRELL, S., TYRRELL J., and HARTOP, B. (2000), Six of the best – a survey on the impact of peer mediation training in six primary schools in Northern Ireland, EMU Promoting School Project, University of Ulster (unpublished), p. 20.

1: What is peer mediation?

[1]BBC RADIO FOYLE news (June 1994), BBC Radio Foyle, Londonderry.
[2]VOLPE, M. (1996), talk at Fordham Law School, New York: Fordham University.
[3]STEWART, S. (1998), *Conflict Resolution – A Foundation Guide*, Winchester: Waterside Press.
[4]*Ibid.*, p. 84.
[5]BICKMORE, K. (2000), Student conflict resolution, power 'sharing' in schools and citizenship education, to be published in *Curriculum Inquiry*, Oxford: Blackwell.
[6]COHEN, R. (1999), *The School Peer Mediator's Field Guide*, School Mediation Associates.
[7]STEWART, *Conflict Resolution*, p. 88.
[8]*Ibid.*, p. 83.
[9]FARRELL, M. (June 1994), BBC Radio Foyle, Londonderry.
[10]HARTOP, B. (21 Sept. 1997), Report of a visit to School A.
[11]MILLAR, A. (1994), 'Are you a medion?' in *Ulster Quaker Peace Education Project Annual Report 1993–4*, p. 17.
[12]BENTLEY, M. (April 1995), *Mediation in Schools – An Introductory Leaflet*, Mediation UK Schools Network.
[13]ROULSTON, M. (1995) in S. Farrell and J. Tyrrell, *Peer Mediation in Primary Schools*, University of Ulster: Centre for the Study of Conflict. p. 11.

[14]*Ibid.*, p. 78.

[15]STEWART, S. (Dec 1997), A perspective of mediation at Oakgrove and Ballysally, in *EMU Promoting School Project Annual Journal 1996/7*, p. 10.

[16]MILLAR, 'Are you a medion?'

[17]LYNAS, C. (Sept. 1998), A parent governor's point of view, in *EMU Promoting School Project Annual Review 1997/8*, p. 15.

[18]WHORISKEY, M in Farrell and Tyrrell, *Peer Mediation*, p. 65.

[19]PEGLER, L. (2000), response to a questionnaire.

[20]MILLAR, 'Are you a medion?'

[21]MURRAY, A. in Farrell and Tyrrell, *Peer mediation*, p. 73.

[22]COOKE, E. and LAWRENCE, E. (21 June 1996), 'Feeding tigers with teaspoons', in *Times Educational Supplement*.

[23]RODERICK, T. (Autumn 1990), An interview with Tom Roderick, in *Peace, Environment and Education*, 1, Malmo School of Education: Dept of Educational and Psychological Research, p. 31.

[24]JUDSON, S. (1976), *Manual on Nonviolence and Children*, Gabriola Island, B.C: New Society Publishers.

[25]BJERSTEDT, A. (Winter 1990), Peace education: An interview with Tom Roderick, in *Peace, Environment and Education*, 1.

[26]LANTIERI, L. (1995) Waging peace in our schools: beginning with the children, in *Peace, Environment and Education*, 6, 19, p. 4.

[27]BJERSTEDT, A. (Spring 1991) Peace education: a conversation with Elise Boulding, in *Peace, Environment and Education*.

[28]BJERSTEDT, A. (Spring 1993). Peace education: a conversation with Priscilla Prutzman, Children's Creative Response to Conflict, Nyack, New York, in *Peace, Environment and Education*.

[29]COLLINGE, J. (Winter 1992) Peace education in New Zealand, in *Peace, Environment and Education*. p. 10.

[30]TREVASKIS, D. K. (Dec. 1994), Mediation in schools, in *ERIC Digest*, 4, The Educational Resources Information Centre.

[31]*Ibid.*

[32]MEEKE, M. (Fall 1992), The peacekeepers, in *Teaching Tolerance 1*, p. 48.

[33]CLARKE, C. (25 Nov. 1999) Keynote speech at 'Mediation '99 – shaping the future' conference, Derby.

[34]ROY, I. (Feb. & March 1994), Conflict resolution education in Ontario, in *The Fourth* R, 49. National Association for Mediation in Education.

[35]MARESCA, J. (1996), Peer mediation as an alternative to the criminal justice system, in *Canada's Children – Promising Approaches to Issues of Child and Youth Violence*, Child Welfare League of Canada.

[36]BLOOMFIELD, D. (1989), Handling conflict in schools – towards a pilot scheme in N. Ireland, Northern Ireland Conflict and Mediation Association, Belfast, mimeograph.

[37]MORGAN, V. and DUNN, S. (1999), Evaluation report on educational programs, Education for Mutual Understanding (unpublished).

[38]NICC (Northern Ireland Curriculum Council) (1990), *Cross Curricular Themes – Guidance Materials*, Belfast: NICC.

[39](March/April 1986) New Quaker initiative – peace education in Northern Ireland, in *Friendly Word*, Belfast.
[40]DUNCAN, Y. (1992), *The Cool Schools Peer Mediation Programme*, Aotearoa/NZ: Foundation for Peace Studies.
[41]DUNCAN, Y. (8 Oct. 1999), letter to author.
[42]*Ibid.*,
[43]DUNCAN, *The Cool Schools*.
[44]*Ibid.*
[45]McMAHON, C. (1999), response to a questionnaire.
[46]*Ibid.*
[47]DOVEY, V. (24 Nov. 1999), response to a questionnaire.
[48]*Ibid.*
[49]*Ibid.*
[50]FJAEREM, A. (Aug. 1996), School mediation programme, Lecture, European Network for Conflict Resolution (ENCORE) conference, Brussels.
[51]ANDBERG, K. (1999), response to a questionnaire.
[52]BENTLEY, M. (Jan. 1999), Education advisory programme, Quaker Peace and Service website.
[53]BOWERS, S. (22 June 1994), interview by author.
[54]JUDSON, *Manual on Nonviolence*.
[55]PRUTZMAN, P. (1977), *Friendly Classroom for a Small Planet*, Quaker Project on Community Conflict, New York.
[56]BOWERS, interview.
[57]BOWERS, S. (1984), *Ways and Means: An Approach to Problem Solving* Surrey: Kingston Friends Workshop Group.
[58]BOWERS, interview.
[59]WALKER, J. (1989), *Violence and Conflict Resolution in Schools* Strasbourg: Council for Cultural Co-operation, Council of Europe.

2: How Are Children Trained in Peer Mediation?

[1]HARTOP, B., FARRELL, S. and TYRRELL, J. (1999), *The EMU Promoting School Project Peer Mediation Manual*, University of Ulster: Centre for the Study of Conflict.
[2]SMITH, V., MAJOR, V. and MNATZAGANIAN, N. (1999), *Peer Mediation Scheme*, Bristol Mediation.
[3]STACEY, H. and ROBINSON, P. (1997), *Let's Mediate*, Bristol: Lucky Duck Publishing.
[4]BICKMORE, K. (1999), Teaching conflict and conflict resolution in school: (extra-) curricular considerations, in A. Raviv *et al.*, *How Children Understand War and Peace*, Jossey-Bass, pp. 233–259.
[5]HARTOP, FARRELL and TYRRELL, *Mediation Manual*, p. 13.
[6]ROBINSON, G., BLISS, T. and MAINES, B. (1995), Coming round to circle time, (video), produced by Lee Cox, for Hummingbird Cameo Films. Bristol: Lucky Duck Publishing.

[7]BOWERS, S. *Ways and Means*

[8]TYRRELL, J. (1995), Affirmation activities used in Ireland, in *Children Working for Peace*, Unicef with Oxford Development Education Centre.

[9]JUDSON, S. ed., *Manual on Nonviolence and Children*

[10]SELLMAN, E. (2000), correspondence with author.

[11]MILLAR, A. 'Are you a Medion'.

[12]FEARN, L. (1974), *The Maligned Wolf*, San Diego. Individual Development: Creativity, Education Improvement Associated.

[13]LEIMDORFER, T. (1992), *Once Upon a Conflict – A Fairytale Manual of Conflict Resolution for All Ages*, Quaker Peace and Service.

[14]HARTOP, FARRELL and TYRRELL, *Mediation Manual*, p. 16.

[15]*Ibid.*, p. 20.

[16]*Ibid.*, p. 29.

[17]*Ibid.*, p. 38.

[18]*Ibid.*, p. 49.

[19]*Ibid.*, p. 49.

[20]HARTOP, B. (1997), Report of visit to School A.

[21]FARRELL, HARTOP and TYRRELL, Six of the best, p. 20.

[22]TYRRELL, J., HARTOP, B. and FARRELL, S. (1999) *EMU – The Games Book*, Positive Ethos Trust p. 14.

[23]HARTOP, FARRELL and TYRRELL, *Mediation Manual*, p. 94.

[24]TYRRELL, J. (1995) in S. Farrell and J. Tyrrell, *Peer Mediation in Primary Schools*, p. 32.

[25]STACEY and ROBINSON, *Let's Mediate*.

[26]*Ibid.*

[27]SMITH *et al*. *Peer Mediation Scheme*.

3: Can Children Mediate Conflicts? Yes!

[1]BICKMORE, K. (1999), Teaching conflict.

[2]*Ibid.*

[3]FERRARA, J. M. (1996), *Peer Mediation: Finding a Way to Care*, Stenhouse Publishers, p. 70.

[4]FARRELL and TYRRELL, *Peer Mediation in Primary Schools*, p. 68.

[5]HALL, R. (1996), Peer mediation in schools – a review and bibliography, Bathurst, Australia: Charles Sturt University, (unpublished mimeograph), p. 13.

[6]GIHOOLEY, J. and SCHEUCH, N. S. (2000), *Using Peer Mediation in Classroom and Schools. Strategies for Teachers, Counsellors and Administrators*. Corwin Press, Inc. p. 19.

[7]FERRARA, *Peer Mediation*, p. 70.

[8]*Ibid.*, p. 70.

[9]COHEN, R. (1995), *Students Resolving Conflict*, Good Year Books p. 115.

[10]CREMIN, H. (Aug. 2000), School mediation works, in *Mediation*, 63, Mediation UK.

[11]FARRELL and TYRRELL, *Peer Mediation*, p. 68.
[12]GIHOOLEY and SCHEUCH, *Using Peer Mediation*, p. 9.
[13]*Ibid.*, p. 9.
[14]HALL, Peer mediation in schools, p. 13.
[15]*Ibid.*, p. 14.
[16]STACEY and ROBINSON, *Let's Mediate*, p. 142.
[17]*Ibid.*, p. 142.
[18]*Ibid.*, p. 143.
[19]Principal of School A, comment at Inservice Training of Teachers, October 1999.
[20]ANDBERG, K. (2000), The pupil as a resource in school: a guide to implementation and practising of school mediation (to be published).
[21]WEBSTER, C. (2000) Evaluation of the influence of peer mediation on bullying, Research Report, University of Teeside: School of Social Sciences
[22]HALL, Peer mediation in schools, p. 14.
[23]STACEY and ROBINSON, *Let's Mediate*, p. 142.
[24]*Ibid.*, p. 143.
[25]SMITH *et al.*, *Peer Mediation Scheme*, p. 54.
[26]STEWART, *Conflict Resolution.*
[27]FARRELL, TYRRELL and HARTOP, Six of the best, p. 20.
[28]*Ibid.*
[29]STACEY and ROBINSON, *Let's Mediate*, p. 145.
[30]JOHNSON, D.W., JOHNSON, R., COTTEN, B. and LUISON, S. (1995) Using conflict managers to mediate conflicts in an inner-city elementary school,' *Mediation Quarterly* 12, 4, pp. 379–390.
[31]HALL, Peer mediation in schools, p. 14.
[32]FARRELL, TYRRELL and HARTOP, Six of the best, p. 41.
[33]*Ibid.*, p. 13.
[34]Human Rights and Education Summer School (22 June 1996), Letter to the Project. University of Ulster: Magee College.
[35]TYRRELL, J. (1997), Mary Robinson prepares for her work in the UN, in *Mediation*, 13 3, Mediation UK.
[36]FEERICK, J. (1998), *EMU Promoting School Project Annual Review 1997/8* EMU Promoting School Project, University of Ulster.

4: How Did Peer Mediation get into Primary Schools?

[1]MOSLEY, J. (1996), *Quality Circle Time in the Primary School Classroom*, vol. 1. LDA.
[2]BLISS, T., ROBINSON, G., and MAINES, B. (1995), *Developing Circle Time*, Lucky Duck Publishing.
[3]FARRELL and TYRRELL, *Peer Mediation* p. 7.
[4]*Ibid.*, p. 8.
[5]*Ibid.*, p. 11.
[6]STEWART, *Conflict Resolution*, p. 86.
[7]SMITH *et al.*, *Peer Mediation Scheme.*

[8]FARRINGTON, L. (1999), *Playground Peacemakers Key Stage 1 & 2* Plymouth: Loxley Enterprises.
[9]*Ibid.*, p. 2.
[10]*Ibid.*, p. 2
[11]*Ibid.*, p. 2.
[12]Anonymous comment (1997), Day workshop, School C.

5: Children's Needs and the Learning Process

[1]CCEA (Northern Ireland Council for the Curriculum, Examinations and Assessment) (1999) *Proposals for changes to the Northern Ireland Curriculum Framework April–June 2000*. Northern Ireland Curriculum Review Phase 1 Consultation, Belfast: CCEA, p. 16.
[2]P7 Child, HARTOP, B. (1997), unpublished report on Donemana Workshop.
[3]Dymphna, P7 child, St Patrick's Donemana.
[4]BURGESS, H., and BURGESS, G. (1999) *The Encyclopaedia of Conflict Resolution*, Santa Barbara, Ca, ABC-CLIO, p. 12.
[5]*Ibid.*, p. 262.
[6]CCEA (Northern Ireland Council for the Curriculum, Examinations and Assessment) (1999), *Key Messages from the Curriculum 21 Conferences and The Curriculum Monitoring Programme 1998*, Belfast: CCEA, p. 13.
[7]MORSE, P. S., and IVERY, A. E. (1996), *Face to Face: Communication and Conflict Resolution in Schools*, New York: Sage Publications Inc. – Corwin Press, p. vii.
[8]*Ibid.*, p. 12.
[9]Response to Questionnaire 2.
[10]CCEA (Northern Ireland Council for the Curriculum, Examinations and Assessment) (1996), *Education for Mutual Understanding, and Cultural Heritage, Guidance Materials*, Belfast: CCEA, p. 1.
[11]*Ibid.*, p. 1.
[12]*Ibid.*, p. 6.
[13]*Ibid.*, p. 6.
[14]*Ibid.*, p. 8.
[15]*Ibid.*, p. 11.
[16]NEESON, S. (2000), interviewed with Jerry Tyrrell, 13 Jun 2000, Belfast.
[17](1996/7), Report of General Inspection of Londonderry Model Primary School – inspected *EMU Promoting School Project (EMUpsp)*, in *Annual Journal*, University of Ulster: EMUpsp, p. 39.
[18](1996/7), Inspection of Donemana County Primary School, spring 1997, *Annual Journal*, p. 39.
[19]CCEA, *Education for Mutual Understanding*, p. 11.
[20]CCEA (Northern Ireland Council for the Curriculum, Examinations and Assessment) (1999), *Developing The Northern Ireland Curriculum to meet the needs of young people, society and the economy in the 21st*

Century Belfast: CCEA.
21CCEA, *Key Messages*, p. 23.
22Except in Craigavon where a different system under the 'Dickson plan' operates.
23CCEA (3 Feb 2000), Press Release, Belfast: CCEA (5,433 pupils out of a total of 17,606 who sat the exam).
24*BELFAST TELEGRAPH* (28 Sept, 2000) 11-plus – the options; Summary of the Department of Education Research Report, Belfast: *Belfast Telegraph*.
25McCANN, E. (2000), Speech at launch of Campaign Against Selection, Central Library, Londonderry, 21 Jun 2000.
26FARRELL, S. and TYRRELL, J. (1995), *Peer Mediation in Primary Schools*, University of Ulster: Centre for the Study of Conflict, p. 8.
27*Ibid.*, p. 82.
28*Ibid.*, p. 43.
29*Ibid.*, p. 69.
30*Ibid.*, p. 68.
31*Ibid.*, p. 69.
32CCEA, *Key Messages*, p. 16.
33PRUETT, P. (1997), Multiple Intelligences, in *Exploring Self Science Through Peace Education and Conflict Resolution*, The Edward Mellen Press.
34SHAUGNESSY, M. and SIEGEL, J. (March 1994) Educating for Understanding, Howard Gardner interview, in *Phi Delta Kappan*, 75, 7, p. 563 (4) quoted in Pruett, *Multiple Intelligences*, p. 40.
35PRUETT, *Multiple Intelligences*, p. 39.
36Response to Questionnaire 2, see Appendix 2.
37MOSLEY, J. (15 Jun 2000), 'Quality Circle Time' presentation, Omagh Teachers' Centre.
38FARRELL and TYRRELL, *Peer Mediation*, p. 53.
39CHETKOW-YANOOV, B. (1994). Conflict-resolution skills can be taught, in *Peace, Environment and Education*, 4, 18, Malmo School of Education; Dept of Educational and Psychological Research.
40CCEA, *Key Messages*, p. 9.
41SCCC (Scottish Consultative Council on the Curriculum) (1996), Resolving Conflict, in *Climate for Learning*, Dundee: SCCC.
42FARRELL and TYRRELL, *Peer Mediation*, p. 50.
43(June 1998) Survey form completed by teacher at School E.
44(June 1998) Survey form completed by teacher of School B.
45BICKMORE, K. (2000), Student conflict resolution, power 'sharing' in schools and citizenship education, to be published in *Curriculum Inquiry*, Blackwell.
46CCEA, *Curriculum Review*, p. 10.
47*Ibid.*, p. 4.
48*Ibid.*, p. 16.
49CCEA, *Key Messages*, p. 6.
50*Ibid.*, p. 8.
51CCEA, *Curriculum Review*, p. 25.

[52]CCEA, *Key Messages*, p. 9.
[53]CCEA (Northern Ireland Council for the Curriculum, Examinations and Assessment) (June 2000), Give our young people the skills to make a better future in press release Belfast: CCEA.
[54]BICKMORE, Student conflict resolution.
[55]*Ibid.*

6: Peer Mediation Skills and the Northern Ireland Peace Process

[1] See http//cain.ulst.ac.uk
[2]Source: http://explorers.whyte.com/forum.htm
[3]Source: http://cain.ulst.ac.uk/issues/politics/election/rf1996.htm
[4]See reference to interviews later in Chapter 6.
[5]BRITISH GOVERNMENT, (15 March 1996), Ground Rules for Substantive All-Party Negotiations (London: House of Commons).
[6]WAHRHAFTIG, P. and GASCHO, S. (Jan. 1999), Mo Mowlam finds 10 Peacemaking Lessons from the Good Friday Negotiations, in *Conflict Resolution Notes*, 16, 3, Pittsburgh, Conflict Resolution Center International Inc., p. 25.
[7]*Ibid.*, p. 25.
[8]BLISS, T., ROBINSON, G. and MAINES, B. (1995), *Coming Round to Circle Time*, produced by Lee Cox, for Hummingbird Cameo Films. Bristol: Lucky Duck Publishing.

7: How to respond to resistance

[1]FARRELL, S. (2000), Education for Mutual Understanding, in J. McNiff, G. McNamara and D. Leonard, *Action-research in Ireland*. September books, p. 245.
[2]HICKS D. (1988), *Education for Peace*, London: Routledge.
[3]STEWART, *Conflict Resolution*.
[4]ANDBERG, K. (2–4 March 2000), Presentation at International Seminar on Conflict Resolution in Schools, The Netherlands: Soesterberg.
[5]DAVIS, H. (Oct. 1985), interview by Jerry Tyrrell, San Francisco.
[6]FARRELL, TYRRELL and HARTOP, Six of the best p. 26.
[7]MAURER, R. (1996), *Beyond the Wall of Resistance*, Austin, TX: Bard Books.
[8]FULLAN, M. (1999), *Change Forces: The Sequel*, London & Philadelphia: Falmer Press, p. 4a.
[9]FARRELL and TYRRELL, *Peer Mediation* p. 50.
[10]BIRD, J. (30 Nov. 1996) Bully Free Zone workshop at Mediation UK conference, London: Friends House.
[11]FARRELL and TYRRELL, *Peer Mediation*, p. 76.

[12]BLOMART, J., TIMMERMANS, J., and CAFFIEUX, C. (2–4 March 2000), To become one's own mediator (mimeograph), Presentation at International Seminar on Conflict Resolution in Schools, The Netherlands: Soesterberg. p. 16.
[13]DARBY, J. (1995), *What's Wrong with Conflict?* University of Ulster: Centre for the Study of Conflict.
[14]BICKMORE, Student conflict resolution.
[15]FULLAN, *Change Forces,* p. 22.
[16]FELL, G. (1992), *You're Only a Dinner Lady*, video and training package. Yorkshire: SALVE (Strategies for a Less Violent Environment).
[17]PRINCIPAL, SCHOOL A (Oct. 1999), Talk at INSET, School H.
[18]PRINCIPAL, SCHOOL H (2000), Moving towards Peer Mediation, in *EMU Promoting School Project Biennial Review, 1998–2000*, University of Ulster.
[19]HARGREAVES, A., and FULLAN, M. (1998), *What's Worth Fighting For Out There?*, Toronto: Elementary School Teachers' Federation; New York: Teachers' College Press; Buckingham: Open University Press.
HEIFTEZ, R. (1994), *Leadership without Easy Answers*, Cambridge, Mass: Harvard University Press.
[20]FULLAN, *Change Forces*, p. 23.
[21]*Ibid.*, p. 10
[22]GALBRAITH, J. (1996), *The Good Society*, Boston: Houghton Mifflin, p. 17. quoted in Fullan, *Change Forces,* p. 11.
[23]Respondent in J. Tyrrell's survey of UK peer mediation agencies.

8: How to create a self-sustaining programme in schools

[1]FARRELL and TYRRELL, *Peer Mediation*
[2]ROSENBERG, L. (2000), letter to J. Tyrrell.
[3]BJERSTEDT, Interview with Tom Roderick.
[4]POLLARD, A. (1997), *Reflective Teaching in the Primary School: A Handbook for the Classroom*, (3rd Edition). London: Cassell Education.
[5]FARRELL, TYRRELL and HARTOP, Six of the best.
[6]*Ibid.*
[7]LANTIERI, Waging peace.

9: If peer mediation is the answer, what is the question?

[1]FARRELL, S. (1998), Questioning answers and answering questions, in *EMU Promoting School Project 1997–8 Annual Review*, University of Ulster: EMU Promoting School Project, p. 38.
[2]FARRELL, S. (1999), *The Future of Peer Mediation – Transcript of a Panel Discussion at the Mediation UK Conference, Sheffield, England,*

June 1998, EMU Promoting School Project, p. 19.

[3]McGEADY, L. (2000), People costs in an attempted culture change: paper given at Action-research, Reflective Practice and Organisational Change Conference, Dublin City University, 10 June 2000.

[4]BICKMORE, Student conflict resolution.

[5]BITEL, M. (9 Sept. 2000), Talk on evaluation and monitoring, at Peer Mediation Network Meeting, London: Friends House.

[6]WEISSGLASS, J. (1991), Teachers have feelings: What can we do about it? in *The Journal of Self Development.*

[7]*Ibid.*

[8]McNIFF, J. (1988), *Action-Research: Principles and Practice*, London: MacMillan Education Ltd. p. 1

[9]McNIFF, J. and NEILL, J. (27–8 Aug. 1998), Education for mutual understanding through action-research. A summary document presented at the British Educational Research Association Annual Conference, Belfast: Queen's University.

[10]DUNN, S. (1996), Introduction, *The Emu Promoting School Project Annual Report 1995/6.* University of Ulster: The Emu Promoting School Project, p. 1.

[11]HARTOP, B. quoted in P. McGill (1996) Playground Peace Process, *Times Educational Supplement*, 26 July 1996.

[12]LAMPEN, J. (1995), Training the trainers, preparing for the schools, Peer Mediation Project, in *Peer Mediation in Primary Schools*, University of Ulster: Centre for the Study of Conflict, p. 28.

[13]McNIFF and NEILL, Education for mutual understanding.

[14]LAMPEN, Training the trainers, p. 36.

[15]*Ibid.*, p. 30.

[16]McNIFF and NEILL, Education for mutual understanding, p. 10.

[17]FARRELL and TYRRELL, *Peer Mediation* p. 83.

[18]*Ibid.*, p. 83

[19]*Ibid.*, p. 83

[20]*Ibid.*, p. 79.

[21]*Ibid.*, p. 81

[22]BICKMORE, Teaching conflict pp. 233–259.

[23]FARRELL, S. (10/11 Sept. 1997), Training the trainer course. Dungannon teachers' centre (unpublished).

[24]FARRELL, Training the trainer.

[25]McNIFF, *Action-Research*, p. 38.

[26]FARRELL, TYRRELL and HARTOP, Six of the best p. 23.

[27]*Ibid.*, p. 23.

[28]*Ibid.*, p. 23.

[29]JONES, T. S., and KMITTA, D. (2000), Report from the USDE/CREnet(CRE) Research and Evaluation Symposium, in *The Fourth R*, 91, (May/Jun/July 2000), Washington DC: Conflict Resolution Education Network (CREnet).

[30]KMITTA, D. (1994), Mediation is great . . . but does it work? in *The Fourth R*, 49, (Feb/Mar 1994), NAME (The National Association for Mediation in Education).

[31]LAM, J. A. (1989) *School Mediation Programme Evaluation Kit*, NAME. (National Association for Mediation in Education).

[32]LAM, J. A. (1989), *The Impact of Conflict Resolution Programs on Schools: A Review and Synthesis of the Evidence*, 2nd Edition, NAME (National Association for Mediation in Education).

[33]BARNES, P. *et al* (1996) *Recommended Standards for School-Based Peer Mediation Programs, 1996*, National Institute for Dispute Resolution.

[34]JONES and KMITTA, Research and evaluation symposium.

[35]*Ibid.*

[36]*Ibid.*

[37]*Ibid.*

[38]*Ibid.*

[39]JONES, T. S. (2000), email to Jerry Tyrrell.

[40]CURTIS, B. (2000), Flyer for Peer Mediation Network Meeting, London, Sept 2000.

[41]BITEL, M. (2000), The rough guide to monitoring and evaluating peer mediation programmes in schools, Presentation given at joint QSRF & Mediation UK seminar, (9 Sept. 2000), London: Friends House.

[42]FETTERMAN, D. M., KAFTARIAN, S. J. and ANDERSMAN, A. (1996) *Empowerment Evaluation: Knowledge and Tools for Self-Assessment and Accountability*, Thousand Oaks, Ca: Sage, pp. 4–5.

[43]ROSENBERG, M. (1965), *Society and the Adolescent Self-Image*, Princeton, NJ: Princeton University Press; http:www.atkinson.yorku.ca/~psyctest/rosenbrg.htm

[44]Further details about this survey will be available from Mediation UK.

[45]WEBNE-BEHRMAN, H. M. (1993), Restructuring education: Mediation as framework for the peaceable classroom and the democratic school, in *The Fourth R*, NAME (The National Association of Mediation in Education), 46. (Aug/Sept. 1993).

[46]McNIFF, *Action-Research*, p. 121.

[47]DAVIS, Interview.

[48]DADDS, M. (1995), *Passionate Enquiry and School Development: A Story about Teacher Action-Research*, The Falmer Press, p. 117.

[49]WOODHEAD, C. quoted by B. Passmore (1999) Learn from each other, says Chief Inspector, in *Times Educational Supplement*, (26 Feb 1999).

[50]WOODHEAD, Learn from each other.

[51]TYRRELL, J., HARTOP, B. and FARRELL, S. (Apr. 1999), Schools: Lessons from the Agreement, *Fordham International Law Journal*, 22, 4.

[52]DEUTSCH, M. (1993) Educating for a peaceful world, in *American Psychologist*.

[53]WEBNE-BEHRMAN, Restructuring education.

[54]*Ibid.*

[55]McNIFF, *Action-Research*, p. 131.

[56]*Ibid.*, p. 121.

[57]*Ibid.*, p. 125.

[58]*Ibid.*, p. 121.

[59]TYRRELL, HARTOP and FARRELL, *EMU – The Games Book.*
[60]WEISSGLASS Teachers have feelings.
[61]TYRRELL, J. (1991), Strategies for overcoming resistance from teachers to the National Coalition Building Institute's prejudice reduction workshop model, in the context of experiential Education for Mutual Understanding programmes in Northern Ireland. MA dissertation, University of Ulster.
[62]FARRELL, S. (1996), School E, Workshop with Principal, Teaching Staff and Ancillary Staff. (Unpublished report).

10: Is peer mediation always the answer?

[1]CREMIN, School mediation works.
[2]BARUCH BUSH, R. A. and FOLGER, J. P. (1994), *The Promise of Mediation: Responding to Conflict through Empowerment and Recognition*, Ca: Jossey-Bass Publishers.
[3]WEBNE-BEHRMAN (1993), Restructuring education, p. 10.
[4]BICKMORE, Teaching conflict, pp. 233–259.
[5]CREMIN, School mediation works.
[6]BARUCH BUSH and FOLGER, *The Promise of Mediation*, p. 24.
[7]CCEA, *Proposals for Changes.*
[8]YATES, S. (aged 11) quoted in Rosenberg, L. (2000).
[9]BICKMORE, Student conflict resolution.
[10]LEITCH, R. and KILPATRICK, R. (1999), *Inside the Gates: Schools and the Troubles – A Research Report into How Schools Support Children in Relation to the Political Conflict in Northern Ireland*, Save the Children Fund, p. 34.
[11]*Ibid.*
[12]COHEN, R. (1995), *Students Resolving Conflict*, Good Year Books.
[13]LEITCH, R. and KILPATRICK, R., *Inside the Gates.*
[14]*Ibid.*, p. 13.
[15]*Ibid.*, p. 9.
[16]*Ibid.*, p. 33.
[17]*Ibid.*, p. 33.
[18]*Ibid.*, p. 34.
[19]*Ibid.*, pp. 45–46.
[20]*Ibid.*, p. 49.
[21]*Ibid.*, p. 50.
[22]*Ibid.*, p. 50.
[23]TOBIN, J. (2000), Research and effectiveness of methods of peer mediation and peace education at International Seminar on Conflict Resolution in Schools, 2–4 Mar. 2000. The Netherlands: Soesterberg.
[24]NZIMANDE, B. and THUSI, S. (1998) Children of war: the impact of political violence on schooling in KwaZulu Natal, *Democratic Governance of Public Schooling in South Africa: A Record of Research and Advocacy*, The Education Policy Unit, Natal.

[25]TYRRELL, J. (2000), Safe schools – violence prevention and conflict resolution, in *Community Safety Matters*, 3 (Spring 2000), Belfast: Community Safety Centre, p. 2.
[26]DOVEY, V. Towards peaceable school communities, at International Seminar on Conflict Resolution in Schools, 2–4 Mar 2000. The Netherlands: Soesterberg.
[27]DOVEY, Towards peaceable school communities.
[28]BATELAAN, P. (2000), Presentation at International Seminar on Conflict Resolution in Schools, 2–4 Mar 2000, The Netherlands: Soesterberg.
[29]BICKMORE, Teaching conflict.
[30]LAMPEN, D. and LAMPEN, J. (1997), *'What Ifs?' in Peer Mediation*, The Hope Project, p. 5.
[31]BICKMORE, Student conflict resolution.
[32]*Ibid.*
[33]WEBSTER, Evaluation of peer mediation.
[34]BICKMORE, Student conflict resolution.
[35]CRICK, B. *et al* (1998), *Education for Citizenship and the Teaching of Democracy in Schools – Final Report of the Advisory Group on Citizenship*, Qualifications and Curriculum Authority.

11: The future of peer mediation?

[1]CONCHIE, J. *et al* (1998) In letter to J. Tyrrell.
[2]FARRELL, S. (1999), *The Future of Peer Mediation – Transcript of a panel discussion at the Mediation UK conference*, Sheffield, England, June 1998, EMU promoting School Project.
[3]COHEN, R. (1996) Key note speech at Peer Mediation in Schools Conference, London.
[4]HALL, R. (1996), Peer Mediation in Schools – a review and bibliography, Charles Stuart University, Bathurst, Australia (Unpublished mimeograph), p. 8.
[5]*Ibid.*, p. 9.
[6]CAMERON, J. and DUPUIS, A. (1991) 'Lessons From New Zealand's first school mediation service: Hagley High School 1987–89', *Australian Dispute Resolution Journal*, 2 (1991), 2, pp. 84–92, cited in Hall, 'Peer Mediation'.
[7]HALL, 'Peer Mediation', p. 8.
[8]McNIFF, J. and NEILL, J. (1998), Education for Mutual Understanding through action-research. A summary document presented at the British Educational Research Association Annual Conference, 27–30 Aug1998, Queen's University, Belfast, p. 3.
[9]HALL, 'Peer Mediation', p. 31.
[10]WEBSTER, C. (2000). Evaluation of the influence of peer mediation on bullying, Research report, University of Teesside School of Social Sciences.

Bibliography

Books

BARNES, P., *et al.* (1996), *Recommended Standards for School-Based Peer Mediation Programs*, 1996, Washington: National Institute for Dispute Resolution.

BARUCH BUSH, R. A. and FOLGER, J. P. (1994), *The Promise of Mediation: Responding to Conflict through Empowerment and Recognition*, San Francisco: Jossey-Bass.

BLISS, T., ROBINSON, G. and MAINES, B. (1995), *Developing Circle Time*, Bristol: Lucky Duck Publishing.

BOWERS, S. (1984), *Ways and Means – an Approach to Problem-Solving*, Surrey: Kingston Friends Workshop Group.

BURGESS, H. and BURGESS, G. (1999), *The Encyclopedia of Conflict Resolution*, Santa Barbara, Calif. ABC-CLIO.

COHEN, R. (1999), *The School Peer Mediator's Field Guide*, Watertown, MA, USA: School Mediation Associates.

— (1995), *Students Resolving Conflict, Glenview*, Ill. USA: Goodyear, HarperCollins.

CRICK, B., *et al.*, *Education for Citizenship and the Teaching of Democracy in Schools – Final Report of the Advisory Group on Citizenship*, Qualifications and Curriculum Authority.

DADDS, M. (1995), *Passionate Enquiry and School Development: A Story about Teacher Action-Research*, London and Philadelphia, Falmer Press.

DUNCAN, Y. (1992), *The Cool Schools Peer Mediation Programme*, Aotearoa/NZ Foundation for Peace Studies.

FARRELL, S. and TYRRELL, J. (1995), *Peer Mediation in Primary Schools*, University of Ulster: Centre for the Study of Conflict.

FARRELL, S. (1999), *The Future of Peer Mediation – Transcript of a panel discussion at the Mediation UK Conference, Sheffield, June 1998*, University of Ulster: EMU Promoting School Project, Centre for the Study of Conflict.

FARRINGTON, L. (1999), *Playground Peacemakers, Key Stages 1 and 2*, Plymouth: Loxley Enterprises.

FEARN, L. (1974), *The Maligned Wolf*, San Diego, Calif: Individual Development: Creativity, Education Improvement Associated.

FERRARA, J. M. (1996), *Peer Mediation: Finding a Way to Care*, York, Maine, N. J. USA; Stenhouse Publishers.

FETTERMAN, D. M., KAFTARIAN, S. J., and ANDERSMAN, A. (1996), *Empowerment Evaluation: Knowledge and Tools for Self-Assessment and Accountability*, Thousand Oaks, Calif: Sage Publications.

FULLAN, M., (1999), *Change Forces: The Sequel*, London and Philadelphia: Falmer Press.

GALBRAITH, J. (1996), *The Good Society*, Boston: Houghton Mifflin.

GIHOOLEY, J., and SCHEUCH, N. S. (2000), *Using Peer Mediation in Classroom and Schools. Strategies for Teachers, Counsellors and Administrators*, California: Corwin Press.

HARGREAVES, A. and FULLAN, M. (1998), *What's Worth Fighting For Out There?*, Toronto Elementary School Teachers' Federation; New York, Teachers' College Press, Buckingham and Open University Press.

HARTOP, B., FARRELL, S. and TYRRELL, J. (1999), *The EMU Promoting School Project Peer Mediation Manual*, University of Ulster: Centre for the Study of Conflict.

HEIFTEZ, R. (1994), *Leadership without Easy Answers*, Cambridge, Mass., Harvard University Press.

HICKS, D. (1988), *Education for Peace*, London: Routledge.

JUDSON, S. (1976), *Manual on Nonviolence and Children*, New Society Publishers, Gabriola Island, BC, Canada.

LAM, J. A. (1989), *School Mediation Programme Evaluation Kit*, Amherst, USA: National Association for Mediation in Education.

— (1989), *The Impact of Conflict Resolution Programs on Schools: A Review and Synthesis of the Evidence*, 2nd edn, Amherst, USA: National Association for Mediation in Education.

LEIMDORFER, T. (1992), *Once upon a Conflict – a Fairytale Manual of Conflict Resolution for All Ages*, London: Quaker Peace and Service.

LEITCH, R. and KILPATRICK, R. (1999), *Inside the Gates: Schools and the Troubles – a Research Report into How Schools Support Children in relation to the Political Conflict in Northern Ireland*, Belfast: Save the Children Fund.

McNIFF, J. (1988), *Action-Research: Principles and Practice*, London: Macmillan Education.

MAURER, R. (1996), *Beyond the Wall of Resistance*, Austin, Tex: Bard Books.

MORSE, P. S. and IVERY, A. E. (1996), *Face to Face: Communication and Conflict Resolution in Schools*; Thousand Oaks, Calif: Sage Publications.

MOSLEY, J. (1996), *Quality Circle Time in the Primary School Classroom*, vol. 1, Wisbech: LDA Publishing.

POLLARD, A. (1997), *Reflective Teaching in the Primary School: A Handbook for the Classroom*, 3rd edn, London: Cassell Education.

PRUTZMAN, P. (1977), *Friendly Classroom for a Small Planet*, New York, NY: Quaker Project on Community Conflict.

ROSENBERG, M. (1965), *Society and the Adolescent Self-Image*, Princeton, NJ, Princeton University Press.
SMITH, V., MAJOR, V. and MNATZAGANIAN, N. (1999), *Peer Mediation Scheme*, Bristol: Bristol Mediation.
STACEY, H., and ROBINSON, P. (1997), *Let's Mediate*, Bristol: Lucky Duck Publishing.
STEWART, S. (1998), *Conflict Resolution – a Foundation Guide*, Winchester: Waterside Press.
TYRRELL, J., HARTOP, B. and FARRELL, S. (1999), *EMU – the Games Book*, Londonderry: Positive Ethos Trust.
WALKER, J. (1989), *Violence and Conflict Resolution in Schools*, Strasbourg: Council for Cultural Co-operation, Council of Europe.

Chapters

BICKMORE, K. (1999), 'Teaching conflict and conflict resolution in school: (extra-) curricular considerations', in *How Children Understand War and Peace*, San Francisco: Jossey-Bass.
FARRELL, S. (2000), 'Education for mutual understanding', in *Action-research in Ireland*, J. McNiff, G. McNamara and D. Leonard (eds), Dorset: September Books.
HALL, R. (1999), 'Learning conflict management through peer mediation', in A. Raviv, L. Oppenheimer and D. Dar-Tal (eds), *How Children Understand War and Peace*, San Francisco: Jossey-Bass.
NZIMANDE, B. and THUSI, S. (1998). 'Children of war: the impact of political violence on schooling in KwaZulu Natal', in *Democratic Governance of Public Schooling in South Africa: A Record of Research and Advocacy*, Natal: Education Policy Unit.
PRUETT, P. (1997), 'Multiple intelligences', in *Exploring Self-Science through Peace Education and Conflict Resolution*, New York: Edwin Mellen Press.
TYRRELL, J. (1995), 'Affirmation activities used in Ireland', in *Children Working for Peace*, Oxford: UNICEF with the Oxford Development Education Centre.

Journal articles

BJERSTEDT, A. (1991), 'Peace education: a conversation with Elise Boulding' *Peace, Environment and Education* (Spring 1991).
— (1993) 'Peace education: a conversation with Priscilla Prutzman, Children's Creative Response to Conflict, Nyack, New York', *Peace, Environment and Education*' (Spring 1993).
— (1990), 'Peace education: an interview with Tom Roderick', *Peace, Environment and Education* (Winter 1990), 1.

BICKMORE, K. (2000), 'Student conflict resolution, power "sharing" in schools and citizenship education', *Curriculum Inquiry*, Blackwell.

CAMERON, J. and DUPUIS, A. (1991), 'Lessons from New Zealand's first school mediation service: Hagley High School 1987–89', *Australian Dispute Resolution Journal*.

CHETKOW-YANOOV, B. (1994), 'Conflict-resolution skills can be taught', *Peace, Environment and Education*, 4, 18.

COLLINGE, J. (1992) 'Peace education in New Zealand', *Peace, Environment and Education*. (Winter 1992) 10.

COOKE, E. and LAWRENCE, E. (21 June 1996), 'Feeding tigers with teaspoons', *Times Educational Supplement*.

CREMIN, H. 'School mediation works', *Mediation*, 63 (Aug. 2000), Mediation UK.

DEUTSCH, M. (1993), 'Educating for a peaceful world', *American Psychologist*.

JOHNSON, D. W., JOHNSON, R., COTTEN, B. and LUISON, S. (1995), 'Using conflict managers to mediate conflicts in an inner-city elementary school', *Mediation Quarterly*, 12, 4.

JONES, T. S. and KMITTA, D., (2000) 'Report from the USDE/CREnet (CRE) research and evaluation symposium', *The Fourth R*, 91 (May/June/July 2000), Conflict Resolution Education Network (CREnet), Washington DC.

LAMPEN, D. and LAMPEN, J. (1997), ' "What if's?" in peer mediation', the Hope Project.

KMITTA, D. (1994), 'Mediation is great . . . but does it work?', *The Fourth R*, 49, (Feb./Mar. 1994), National Association for Mediation in Education.

LANTIERI, L. (1995), 'Waging peace in our schools: beginning with the children', *Peace, Environment and Education*, 6, 19.

McGILL, P. (1996), 'Playground peace process', *Times Educational Supplement*, 26 July 1996.

MARESCA, J. (1996), 'Peer mediation as an alternative to the criminal justice system', *Canada's Children – promising Approaches to Issues of Child and Youth Violence*, (Fall 1996), Child Welfare League of Canada.

MEEK, M. (1992), 'The peacekeepers', *Teaching Tolerance*, 1 (Fall 1992), 48.

PASSMORE, B. (1999) 'Learn from each other, says Chief Inspector', *Times Educational Supplement*, (26 Feb 1999).

RODERICK, T. (1990), 'An interview with Tom Roderick', *Peace, Environment and Education*, 1 (Autumn 1990) 1.

ROY, I. (1994), 'Conflict resolution education in Ontario' *The Fourth R*, 49 (Feb/March 1994), National Association for Mediation in Education.

SHAUGNESSY, M. and SIEGEL, J. (1994), 'Educating for understanding', interview with Howard Gardner, *Phi Delta Kappa*, 75 (Mar. 1994), 7

TREVASKIS, D. K. (1994), 'Mediation in schools', *ERIC Digest*, (Dec. 1994) 4, Educational Resources Information Centre.

WEISSGLASS, J. (1991), 'Teachers have feelings: what can we do about it?', *Journal of Self-Development*.

TYRRELL, J. (2000), 'Safe schools – violence prevention and conflict resolution', *Community Safety Matters*, 3 (Spring 2000), Community Safety Centre, Belfast.

TYRRELL, J., HARTOP, B. and FARRELL, S., (Apr. 1999), 'Schools: lessons from the agreement, *Fordham International Law Journal*, 22 (1999), 4.

TYRRELL, J., 'Mary Robinson prepares for her work in the UN', *Mediation*, 13 (1997) 3, Mediation UK.

WAHRHAFTIG, P. and GASCHO, S. (1999), 'Mo Mowlam finds 10 peacemaking lessons from the Good Friday negotiations', *Conflict Resolution Notes*, 16 (Jan. 1999), 3, Conflict Resolution Center International, Pittsburgh.

WEBNE-BEHRMAN, H. M. (1993) 'Restructuring education: mediation as framework for the peaceable classroom and the democratic school', *The Fourth R*, National Association of Mediation in Education, 46 (Aug./Sept. 1993).

Published reports

EMU Promoting School Project, *Annual Journal 1996/7*, Londonderry, EMU psp, 1997.

EMU Promoting School Project, *Annual Review 1997/8*, Londonderry, EMUpsp, 1998.

EMU Promoting School Project, *Biennial Review*, *1998–2000*, Londonderry, EMUpsp, 2000.

Northern Ireland Curriculum Council (NICC), *Cross-curricular Themes – Guidance Materials*, (Belfast, NICC, 1990).

Northern Ireland Council for the Curriculum, Examinations and Assessment (CCEA), *Developing the Northern Ireland Curriculum to Meet the Needs of Young People, Society and the Economy in the 21st Century*, Belfast, CCEA, 1999.

Northern Ireland Council for the Curriculum, Examinations and Assessment (CCEA) *Education for Mutual Understanding, and Cultural Heritage, Guidance Materials*, Belfast, CCEA, 1996.

Northern Ireland Council for the Curriculum, Examinations and Assessment (CCEA), *Northern Ireland Curriculum Review Phase 1 Consultation (2000): Proposals for Changes to the Northern Ireland Curriculum Framework, April–June 2000*, Belfast, CCEA, 1999

Northern Ireland Council for the Curriculum, Examinations and Assessment (CCEA), *Key Messages from the Curriculum 21 Conferences and the Curriculum Monitoring Programme 1998*, Belfast, CCEA, 1999.

Scottish Consultative Council on the Curriculum (SCCC), 'Resolving Conflict', in *Climate for Learning*, Dundee, SCCC, 1996.

Ulster Quaker Peace Education Project, *Annual Report 1993/4*, Londonderry, QPEP, 1994.

Videos, etc.

FELL, G. (1992) *You're Only a Dinner Lady*, video and training package, Strategies for a Less Violent Environment (SALVE), Yorkshire.
ROBINSON, G., BLISS, T. and MAINES, B. (1995), *Coming round to Circle Time*, video produced by Lee Cox for Hummingbird Cameo Films, Lucky Duck Publishing, Bristol.

Manuscripts

ANDBERG, K. (2000), 'The pupil as a resource in school: a guide to implementation and practising of school mediation'.
FARRELL, S. (1996), 'School E, workshop with principal, teaching staff and ancillary staff'.
FARRELL, S. (1997) 'Training the trainer course – 10/11 September 1997, Dungannon Teachers' Centre'.
FARRELL, S., TYRRELL, J. and HARTOP, B. (1999), 'Six of the best – a survey on the impact of peer mediation training in six primary schools in Northern Ireland'.
HALL, R. (1996), 'Peer mediation in schools – a review and bibliography', Charles Sturt University, Bathurst, Australia.
McNIFF, J. and NEILL, J. (1998), 'Education for mutual understanding through action-research', a summary document presented at the British Educational Research Association Annual Conference, 27–30 Aug 1998, Queen's University, Belfast.
WEBSTER, C. (2000), 'Evaluation of the influence of peer mediation on bullying', research report, University of Teesside School of Social Sciences.

Appendix 1

Questionnaire: Where did peer mediation come from?

1. When was the first peer mediation training programme implemented in your country? (*or the earliest you are aware of*)

2. Where did it take place? (*in a school, youth club, etc.*)

3. What was the age range of the young people involved? (*please give years old rather than grades*)

4. Where did the initiative for it come from? (*individual teacher, principal, external agency, education policy, etc.*)

5. Was an existing mediation agency involved in initiating the programme (*e.g. community mediation, neighbourhood mediation*)?

6a. Was the motivation for it reactive, i.e. in response to a particular violent event or increasing violence in society?

6b. If you answered no to question 6a, what was the motivation behind the programme?

7. Broadly speaking, was it the initiative of an educational institution, an external agency or both?

8. Are there any other comments you would like to make about how peer mediation got started in your country?

9. Are you aware of peer mediation programmes in other parts of the world?

10. If so can, you give me names and addresses (preferably with email addresses) of individual(s) in countries other than those listed, who might be willing to answer a similar questionnaire?

11. Can you suggest any references so that I can follow this up further myself?

12. The leading peace researcher Elise Boulding, in an interview in the Boston Research Center for the 21st Century Newsletter, 9 (Fall 1997), is quoted as saying 'Conflict resolution efforts in schools and the peer mediation movement – that's very much a women-led movement.' Is this true of Nigeria, and have you any thoughts as to why/why not?

Appendix 2

Questionnaire: Summer 2000

If you do not work in a primary school, please just answer questions 1–7.

1. When did your schools programme start?
    (If in last the three years, month and year, otherwise just year)

2. How is it funded? *Please tick box(es)*

    Local council ☐   Trusts and foundations ☐

    Business ☐   Fees from users ☐   National Lottery ☐

    Other *(please specify)*

3. What was the inspiration behind it?
    (a community mediation programme wanted to develop peer mediation in schools, the level of violence in schools, etc.).

4. Who was the inspiration behind it?
    (an individual, an existing link between school and mediation programme, teachers, community workers, etc.)

5. What were the criteria for the selection of schools to work in?

(existing relationships, parents of children at the school, the school's initiative, response to letter, visits, meeting, etc.)

6. Which schools do you work with?
   (if more than one type of school, please tick each/any type you work in)

   Primary school ☐   Middle school ☐

   Secondary school ☐

7. Why did you choose to work in the particular age range?

8. What is the unexpected learning(s) from your experience so far of working with peer mediation in primary schools?

9. If you were starting again, what would you do differently?

10. What is the key message you would like to get across to the reader of a book like *Peer Mediation: a Process for Primary Schools*?

11. Have you an anecdote that sums up the value and/or the power of peer mediation as a process for children?

12. Some research indicates that the greatest challenge to schools in embracing a whole-school approach to peer mediation is in relation to managing the necessary change in ethos. Is this your experience?

13. How do you measure the effectiveness of your programme?

14. Should peer mediation play a role in making schools more democratic? If so, how?

Appendix 3

Questionnaire: Future of Peer Mediation – Follow-up

1. In the last two years there has been a mushrooming of peer mediation projects in the UK, initiated by community mediation centres. Have you any experience of them – either directly, e.g. in a consultative capacity, or indirectly? – and if so what do you think is the contribution they have made?

2. Jo Broadwood made the point that a lot of time needs to be spent 'listening' to a school, and that in the process you may find that the school isn't actually looking for what you have to offer, after all. Have you an example of this having happened to you/your agency?

3. To what extent has your experience of trying to achieve a whole-school approach led you to reflect on the suitability of peer mediation as a starting-point?

4. One of the areas where the panel had consensus was the need to become more strategically involved in the training of teachers. What successes have you/your agency achieved in this area in the past two years, and what have been the setbacks?

5. A big issue for peer mediation universally at the moment is to do with researching its effectiveness. It was clear

that, in 1998, panel members were actively monitoring their work, through debriefing individual workshops with the teachers involved to help schools to find the questions they wanted to address. (A bit of a leading question, this) –

(a) How accurately does the following series of questions describe the process of your working with schools:

What is my concern? How am I concerned? How can I show that in action? What do I think I can do about it? What will I do about it? How can I gather evidence to show that I am influencing the situation? How can I ensure that any judgements I make are reasonably fair and accurate?

(b) To what extent do you think it is appropriate to encourage teachers to ask themselves such questions in response to conflict?

6. What are the key lessons from your experience in the field of peer mediation/conflict resolution work in primary schools? What would you do/avoid doing if you were starting from scratch?

Appendix 4

Panel discussion at Mediation UK Annual Conference June 1998: Members and Organisations

- Rachel Baily. 'STEPS', Bradford
- Jo Bird. 'Bully Free Zone', Bolton, Lancashire
- Jo Broadwood. 'Leap Confronting Conflict', London
- John Conchie. 'Youth Action', Staffordshire
- Belinda Hopkins. 'Transforming Conflict', Berkshire
- Jessica Johnston. 'Kingston Friends Mediation', Surrey
- Hilary Stacey. 'Catalyst Consultancy', Birmingham
- Christine Stockwell. 'Bristol Mediation Service', Bristol
- Ruth Musgrave. 'Newham Conflict and Change', London
- Jerry Tyrrell and Seamus Farrell. 'EMU Promoting School Project', L'derry, N Ireland.